THE
MYSTERY
of the GRAIL

THE
MYSTERY
of the GRAIL

INITIATION AND MAGIC IN
THE QUEST FOR THE SPIRIT

JULIUS EVOLA

Translated from the Italian
by Guido Stucco

Inner Traditions
Rochester, Vermont

Inner Traditions International
One Park Street
Rochester, Vermont 05767
www.InnerTraditions.com

LIBRARY OF CONGRESS CATALOGING-IN-PUBLICATION DATA

Evola, Julius, 1898–1974.
    [Mistero del Graal. English]
    The mystery of the Grail : initiation and magic in the quest for the Spirit /
Julius Evola.
        p.   cm.
    Includes bibliographical references and index.
    ISBN 978-0-89281-573-9
    1. Grail—Legends—History and criticism. I. Title.
PN57.G7E913 1996   96-26858
809'.915—dc20   CIP

Printed and bound in the United States

12

Type design and layout by Kate Mueller
This book was typeset in Minion

Contents

Part Three: The Cycle of the Grail

Part Four: The Legacy of the Grail

Foreword

by H. T. Hansen

The original version of Julius Evola's *Mystery of the Grail* formed an appendix to the first edition of his masterpiece, *Rivolta contra il mondo moderno* (1934).[1] Three years later he reworked that appendix into the present book, which first appeared as part of a series of religious and esoteric studies published by the renowned Laterza Publishers in Bari, Italy, whose list included works by Sigmund Freud, Richard Wilhelm, and C. G. Jung, among others.

The Grail book is closely related to *Revolt Against the Modern World*, where Evola discussed, within the framework of his "suprahistorical" analysis, medieval chivalry and the notion of a symbolic empire based on a sacred regality. Above all, Evola wanted to make three things clear:

1. The Grail was not a Christian but a Hyperborean mystery.
2. The Grail legend deals with an initiatory mystery.
3. The Grail is a symbolic expression of hope and of the will of specific ruling classes in the Middle Ages (namely, the Ghibellines), who wanted to reorganize and reunite the entire Western world as it was at that time into a Holy Empire, that is, one based on a transcendental, spiritual basis.

The question of whether Evola was correct in his interpretation cannot, however, be unambiguously answered. Franco Cardini, a professor of medieval

This foreword first appeared in Ansata-Verlag's *Das Mysterium des Grals* (Interlaken, Switzerland, 1978). It is translated from the German by Susan Essex.

1. *Revolt Against the Modern World*, trans. Guido Stucco (Rochester, Vt.: Inner Traditions, 1995). It is not possible to have a true understanding of Evola without knowledge of his *Revolt*, which most clearly demonstrates the principles of his worldview.

studies at the University of Florence, writes in his introduction to the fourth Italian edition (Rome, 1994) of a "peculiar tendency to oversimplify among many authors, who assume that the Grail can be explained with a single, basic theory." First—and here Evola would fully agree—it's a question of a myth, and a myth is by definition not single- but multifaceted. Second, the myth of the Grail embraces many different types of influences, above all:

1. Christian legend (at least from a later period).
2. Celtic folklore.
3. The so-called *Isis Book* (the eleventh book of Apuleius's *Metamorphosis,* which, based on ancient sources, describes the opening of the way in the Isis Mystery), as well as the *Corpus Hermeticum.*

That, at least, is the view of Henry and Renée Kahane in the *Standard Encyclopedia of Religion* (vol. 6, New York, 1987), compiled under the direction of Mircea Eliade, easily the best-known scholar of religions in this century.

The various interpretations of the Grail thus differ greatly, extending from the priestly chalice to the "manna machine" for the automatic production of nourishment, or even to the equation of the "Grail of Joy" with the vagina. The cited origins range likewise from the Western world (Burdach) to the Islamic and Persian East (Corbin). To this may also be added the works by such analytical psychologists as Emma Jung, Marie-Louise von Franz, and Robert A. Johnson.

One thing appears to be certain, however: the myth of the Grail does not deal with mere fantasies in a purely aesthetic-poetic sense. As Franco Cardini writes, "No author in the Middle Ages ever wrote a single line on the basis of his pure and bare fantasies, and it would be antihistorical to suggest such a thing."

Another point of interest, in the current debate of gender differences: It is always men who go off in search of the Grail, because women, by nature, already possess it. Thus in all versions of the legend, only women are referred to as carriers of the Grail. But as Helen Luke believes, expressing a Jungian perspective, many women today have contempt for the spiritually, psychologically, and physically nourishing Grail function of their womanhood, since they are striving for the same positions as men in areas that, until now, were purely masculine domains.[2] In so doing, these women outgrow their own essence and no longer have any counterbalance to their now overpowering masculine sides.

---

2. John Matthews, ed., *At the Table of the Grail* (London, 1984), p. 92.

In other words, they have lost their own Grail, and have to go off in search of it again, just as the men do, in order to find spiritual harmony.

What did Evola hope for when he published his book? In the epilogue to the first edition (1937) he expressed it clearly:

> To live and understand the symbol of the Grail in its purity would mean today the awakening of powers that could supply a transcendental point of reference for it, an awakening that could show itself tomorrow, after a great crisis, in the form of an "epoch that goes beyond the nations." It would also mean the release of the so-called world revolution from the false myths that poison it and that make possible its subjugation through dark, collectivistic, and irrational powers. In addition, it would mean understanding the way to a true unity that would be genuinely capable of going beyond not only the materialistic—we could also say Luciferian and Titanic—forms of power and control but also the lunar forms of the remnants of religious humility and the current neospiritualistic dissipation.

But, added Evola, he would have to leave it open whether such a development would occur. It would therefore be useless to form any kind of organization that could be influenced by this development.

In order to understand these words fully, one must keep in mind that Evola's endeavor since 1925, at the latest, was to influence the political development of Italy along the lines of a spiritual restoration of the ancient Roman Empire. Fascism, which was already in power at that time, appeared to fulfill quite a lot of prerequisites for such a revolution—indeed, Mussolini himself had no aversion to such ideas.[3]

In 1928 Evola published his first political book, *Imperialismo pagano*, which fought for exactly that—a pagan imperialism—in a considerably polemic manner. Mussolini's compact with the Catholic Church in 1929, which opposed any endeavor to extinguish the power of the Church, shattered Evola's hopes once and for all. As Piero Fenili has suggested in his series of essays "Gli errori di Julius Evola" (The errors of Julius Evola; *Ignis* [December 1991]: 146ff.), Evola, in his *Imperialismo pagano*, still thought of a restoration "in the framework of a Mediterranean tradition." His belief in the independent powers of that region appears, however, to have suffered in the following years, thanks to Mussolini's behavior and the everyday reality of fascism in Italy.

---

3. See also the somewhat detailed explanation of Evola's political activities in my introduction to Julius Evola, *Menschen inmitten von Ruinin* (Tübingen, 1991; a German translation of *Gli uomine e le rovine* [Men among ruins]).

Evola put new heart into his hopes for a union of "the two eagles," that is, the German and the Roman, through his ever-closer contact with the so-called Conservative Revolution in Germany. The model was the Middle Ages, the time of the German emperor Frederick II of Hohenstaufen, the "Astonishment of the World," who was raised in Italy (Sicily, to be exact) and thus united the German and Italian regions in his Holy Roman Empire, and who also apparently personified the best of both geographical areas. In those years Evola stood strongly under the influence of Ernst Kantorowicz's two-volume biography of the Starfen emperor, at that time the object of great enthusiasm.

Here also was the point of origin of his political motivations for writing *The Mystery of the Grail*. Just as in the Middle Ages, so now would it again be possible for Germany and Italy to build a new Holy Roman Empire, to be based on a spiritual foundation—specifically, on the mysticism of the Grail. This explains Piero Fenili's accusation that Evola tends to overglorify Germany. In an informative essay in the journal *Politica romana* (no. 2 [1995]: 41ff.), Fenili tries to prove conclusively that it was exactly this Evolian high regard of the Middle Ages that allowed so many Italian Evolians to enter the traditional circles of the Catholic Church, since that enthusiasm for the Middle Ages led inevitably to the recognition of the Church's outstanding position at that time.

The times changed, of course, and nothing could be seen of that spiritual foundation—if anything, the complete opposite was true. The changed circumstances are reflected in Evola's epilogues to his only slightly altered revisions of *The Mystery of the Grail*, which were published in 1962 and 1972. Evola, free from all old political hopes, now emphasized personal initiative and the Grail's inner meaning for the individual.

While Evola's idea of the Grail as the culmination of the imperial myth has found little reverberation in the world at large, it is undeniable that, as Gianfranco de Turris and Chiara Nejrotti emphasize in their commentary to the fourth Italian edition, the Middle Ages have come in vogue in recent years. Renewed interest began with the incredible worldwide success of J. R. R. Tolkien's *Lord of the Rings* trilogy and continued not only with Marion Zimmer Bradley's *Mists of Avalon*, which was the starting point of a whole subgenre of fantasy novels, but also with Umberto Eco's *The Name of the Rose*. Eco, however, probably wrote his novel with exactly the opposite intention of the other two authors: namely, with the intention of portraying the Middle Ages as darkly as possible, in order to allow the light of reason to shine that much brighter. It was an attempt that no doubt came up short.

To what can this fascination for the Middle Ages be attributed, beyond the presumption that people have become weary of rapidly changing technology and the uninterrupted reorientations it demands? Does the paradox apply that it is progressive to be against progress and to question the power of science, as well as that of the purely utilitarian and rational? Only a short step separates a preoccupation with the past from a secret desire for another way of life.

Added to this are new historical findings, especially from the French Annales school, that no longer leave the Middle Ages looking as gloomy as the Enlightenment had painted it. Not only were the houses colorful, but so was life. And since Protestantism and the Catholic Counterreformation were still far away, the pleasures of the senses were also allowed to have their place, as in the baths, for example. When even Marxist historians such as Jacques le Goff sing the praises of the Middle Ages, and world-renowned scholars such as Régine Pernoud write books that destroy our prejudices about the Middle Ages, one can perhaps also transfer ideas or images—correspondingly adapted, of course—into our times, or at least one can think about them. Pernoud even says that contemporary people are very similar to those of the Middle Ages in certain aspects. With this the rebirth of the Arthur cycle and the myth of the Grail, especially in England, can be explained. Here also, Evola's book cannot be completely false; on the contrary, it presents a whole series of interesting ideas, as Franco Cardini points out.

The search for alternative methods of thought goes hand in hand with the growing skepticism against a purely scientific rationalism. One such alternative is the so-called Traditional method used by Evola, who describes it as follows:

> The order of things that I . . . deal with . . . is that in which all materials having a "historical" and "scientific" value are the ones that matter the least; conversely, all the mythical, legendary, and epic elements denied historical truth and demonstrative value acquire here a superior validity and become the source for a more real and certain knowledge. . . . From the perspective of "science" what matters in a myth is whatever historical elements may be extracted from it. From the perspective that I adopt, what matters in history are all the mythological elements it has to offer.[4]

In essence, this is about an intersection of history with superhistory, whose result is myth, which thus contains something from both worlds, the historical and the transcendental, and thus makes a higher claim to truth.

A maxim by Emperor Julian the Apostate, "That which never happened is eternally true," has been echoed in the title of a lecture given by Gilbert Durand at a symposium on mythology held in Cerisy in 1985: "On the Continuity of Myth and the Mutability of History." And Plutarch, in his *De Iside,* writes: "The

---

4. *Revolt Against the Modern World,* p. xxxiv.

myth is nothing but the reflection of a higher truth, which directs human thought in a perceptible course." Likewise, for Evola, a purely rational and historical way of looking at myth clearly cannot suffice.

Even leaving "transcendence" aside, myth's higher claim to truth is asserted by Robert A. Johnson, a Jungian analyst: "[Myths] seem to develop gradually as certain motifs emerge, are elaborated, and finally are rounded out as people tell and retell stories that catch and hold their interest. Thus themes that are accurate and universal are kept alive, while those elements peculiar to single individuals or a particular era drop away. Myths, therefore, portray a collective image; they tell us about things that are true for all people."[5] Elsewhere, Johnson emphasizes the enormous importance of myths: "Mythology was sacred to primitive people; it was as though their myths contained their very souls. Their lives were cradled within their mythology, and the death of their mythology, as happened with the American Indians, meant the destruction of their lives and spirits."[6]

Similarly, Elemire Zolla sees in myth a connecting link between scientific knowledge and emotional understanding. Myth, because it is not simply aligned with intellect, can never be entirely clear, but must also correspond to a nondualist metaphysics, in other words, a philosophy that is not purely rational and discursive. Zolla sees possible resolutions in Indian philosophy, such as that of Nāgārjuna and Śaṃkara. The natural scientist Costa Beauregard (quoted by Zolla) sees it this way as well in his works on the transfer of information by disintegrated atoms, where only such nondualist metaphysics can adequately grapple with the enigma of modern physics. Zolla dreams further that, perhaps after several generations of dealing with such philosophies from a logical-positive standpoint, the incompatible data of physics might become self-evident, and with that, finally, emotions and cognition might again agree.[7]

For C. G. Jung, myths reflect subliminal psychological and spiritual processes. Spontaneous creations of the collective unconscious, they bring to the surface archetypes, spiritual patterns that possess validity always and everywhere.

To understand fully something as complex as a myth calls for a special method of discovery. For Evola, that method requires an insight that holds within itself at once a vision and a call to action. Franz Vonessen concerns himself with exactly this problem in his essay "Der Mythos vom Weltscheier" (The myth of the worldly veil; *Antaios* 4 [Stuttgart, 1963]: 2):

---

5. Robert A. Johnson, *She* (New York, 1976), p. x.
6. Robert A. Johnson, *He* (New York, 1974), p. 1.
7. Elemire Zolla, *L'amante invisibile* (The invisible lover; Venice, 1968), pp. 30ff.

For an examination of a myth to be fair, it must take seriously the myth's claim to truth. This means that the philosophical problem of mythology is first of all a problem of the critique of knowledge, first articulated clearly by Schelling: "The question here is not from which vantage point can our philosophy most easily explain a phenomenon, but just the opposite—which philosophy does the phenomenon demand in order to bring the observer to its level. Not how must the phenomenon be turned and twisted so we need not step over the bounds of our principles, but rather, where must our thoughts broaden to be in proportion with the phenomenon."

Not without reason does philosophy newly concern itself with myth.[8] As B. R. Girardet formulates in his *Mythes et mythologies politiques* (Myths and political mythologies), "The myth can be understood only if it is completely lived from the heart, but to do so makes it impossible to describe it objectively."[9]

Evola naturally had forerunners for his Traditional conception of history, above all Giambattista Vico (1688–1744), who was probably the first to attend to myths to reach the inner spiritual core of antiquity. Then, as we have seen, there is the philosopher of German idealism, Friedrich Wilhelm von Schelling (1755–1854). This method was made famous, however, by the Swiss mythologist Jakob Johann Bachofen, from whom Evola borrowed basic concepts and interpretations, even if he did disagree with some of his assessments. Evola also assisted Bachofen's breakthrough in Italy by translating and publishing an anthology of his works in Italian.

A short excerpt from Bachofen's *Versuch über die Gräbersymbolik der Alten* (Essay on the ancients' grave symbolism; Basel, 1859) should clarify his view: "The language is strung together in parts and brings to light only bit by bit that which, in order to be fully grasped, inevitably must be presented to the soul at a glance. Words make infinity finite; symbols (and myth, as well) lead the spirit over the border of the finite into the realm of the infinite, manifest world."[10] In conclusion, however, it is René Guénon, Evola's great master in the area of esoterics, from whom he learned the most about the Traditional method.

---

8. See especially Kurt Hübner, *Die Wahrheit des Mythos* (The truth of myth; Munich, 1985).

9. (Paris, 1968), p. 24, quoted in Christopher Boutin, *Politique et tradition* (Paris, 1992).

10. Cited in Walter Heinrich, *Der Sonnenweg* (The solar path; Interlaken, Switzerland: Ansata, 1985), p. 25. In the same work, Professor Heinrich, a scholar of Othmar Spann's holistic philosophy, includes an essay, "Über die traditionelle Methode" (On the Traditional method), in which he reports less on the methodology than on the important modern representatives of this method—specifically, René Guénon, Julius Evola, and Leopold Zeigler. Incidentally, Heinrich sees in Evola's Grail book a prime example of the Traditional method.

What cannot remain unmentioned here, however, is the reciprocal influence that developed between Evola and Mircea Eliade. True, Eliade's approach to myth, in recent times ever more controversial, was considerably influenced by the scholar of religions Gerardus van der Leeuw.[11] Eliade also spoke of "archetypes"—granted, with a different meaning from C. G. Jung's. Still, a certain similarity with the Traditional method is definitely ascertainable, as has been noted by Piero di Vona, a philosopher at the University of Naples.[12] Eliade kept in correspondence with Evola from 1927 until his death. They also met in person in 1936 in Romania.[13]

A great and famous opponent of the Traditional method is Umberto Eco. In his introduction to Maria Pia Pozzato's *L'idea deforme* (The deformed idea; Milan, 1989), he picks to pieces René Guénon's *Le Roi du monde* (The king of the world)—one of the sources for Evola's Grail book—calling it a classic example of the "slipping away" of meaningful statement. In the Traditional point of view, he argues, everything shows a relationship of analogy, unity, or similarity with everything else, and thus no meaningful statement can be distinguished.

In a scientific, semiotic mode of thinking, such traditional analogies naturally have no place. However, they do have the capability to move deeply. And if, as Jung says, reality is that which is effective, then myths are also reality. Here, of course, completely different definitions of reality come into play.

To search for salvation in reason alone presents at least two difficulties. First, the impulse toward reason is itself prerational. Second, since humans are not entirely rational, reason alone cannot find an explanation for the entire human. Purely rational explanations can only be partial explanations.

Apropos a political thinker such as Evola, a point of utmost importance may not be left out: the problem of the political myth. In Kurt Hoffmann's *Die Wirklichkeit des Mythos* (The reality of myth; Munich, 1965), the publisher writes in his introduction: "It is the misfortune of politics that it is primarily the false myths that have shaped history—myths of earthly redemption, the apocalyptic myth of the classless society, the myths of blood and soil and the chosen people." A whole series of philosophers, sociologists, and political scientists, not to mention scholars of religion, demand for this reason a radical demythologizing and a replacement of the myth with discursive thought.

---

11. His student Ioan P. Culianu, who unfortunately died at a very young age, proved this conclusively in his work *Mircea Eliade* (Assisi, 1978), pp. 146ff.

12. See his essay in the journal *Diorama letterario* 109 (Florence, November 1987): 8.

13. See also *Diorama letterario* 109 and 120 (November 1988): 17ff., and Les Deux etandards (September–December 1988): 45ff.

David Müller calls this tendency *mythoclasm,* by analogy with *iconoclasm:* in place of the smashing of idols, the smashing of myths.[14]

Nevertheless, as the Swiss philosopher Jeanne Hersch writes in her essay "Mythos und Politik" *(*Myth and politics):

> All politics are based on myth. . . . At the level of politics, positivism, strictly taken, is thus intolerable. . . . The political myth is therefore neither positive reality nor pure fiction; it is an effective fiction. Of course, one could retort that each plan or agenda is also a fiction that claims the effectiveness for itself. The difference, however, between agenda and myth is that the agenda plans an objective change of things and relations for the future, whereas the myth at the same time relates its purpose to the immediate present, and in so doing concerns itself with the essence of the action. It holds the ambiguity of the political, human, and timely reality together in itself. . . .
>
> One doesn't reach a clear political reality by trying to justify or reveal the political myth, as if it were a matter of simple subtraction. The "end of ideologies," of which much talk is made today, would not mean the beginning of a new time when politics would be sincere and controllable and based only on social "realities" and public spirit. The end of ideologies would bring with it the underestimation of the true nature of politics. The results would be either the blind and dull role of an unknown, ignored, and unchallenged ideology, or the disappearance of the political to the advantage of a pure technocracy, whose value and purpose would be regarded as self-evident, and which would in turn, therefore, also rule undoubted and unchallenged. In both cases the people would be marked by a tyranny so deep that freedom would leave their spirits, and the people would cease to exist."[15]

Hersch also coins two infinitely important theorems for a political culture: "One doesn't attain the political truth by turning off the myth, but by tolerating in the present the tension of conflicting myths. One then takes upon oneself the contradiction that comes out of that conflict, as well as the incompatible claim of value. From this it in no way follows that these values are false and that everything is allowed, but in fact the opposite, that they are all valid, and that everything must be attempted without the promise of consummation."

---

14. In the Jungian journal *Spring* (fall 1994): 84ff.

15. Quoted in Kurt Hoffman, *Die Wirklichkeit des Mythos,* pp. 79–91.

Even though humans are "without myths not human," we must pose questions of myths and of ourselves; reason and myth must coexist in a dynamic relationship, and in so doing reflect the human essence. Here is where demythologization also has its place.[16] As Kurt Sontheimer explains in his *Antidemokratisches Denken in der Weimarer Republik* (Antidemocratic thought in the Weimar Republic), a study of a time and place in which a strong leaning toward the mythical, religious, and metaphysical was evident, what is required is not a complete rejection of myth, but a distinct means of perceiving myth. Different problems call for different methods of perception.

A final word concerning Evola's epilogue to *The Mystery of the Grail:* It cannot be disputed that Evola had a tendency to subscribe to conspiracy theories. It is important to note that he, in this case strongly under the influence of René Guénon, doesn't accuse a specific group of people of wanting to seize world domination for themselves. His theory extends itself far more into the transcendental realm and must be seen on a virtually cosmic scale. (Besides Guénon, one can also detect the influence here of an antimodernist Catholic body of ideas, to which, above all, Joseph de Maistre—who was also a Freemason—and Donoso Cortés are related.)[17] The power that Evola held responsible for the fall of the world since antiquity could be seen, in his view, only as a spiritual, "nonhuman" power. And should individuals or groups actually play a part in it, they are to him simply unconscious tools of a much higher nature in a completely different sphere.

---

16. Cf. the writings of Karl Löwith and Ernst Topitsch.
17. Detailed references to these questions can be found in Sergio Romano, *I falsi protocolli* (Milan, 1992), and in the previously mentioned introduction to Julius Evola, *Menschen inmitten von Ruinen.*

PART ONE

Approaching the Mystery of the Grail

1

The Literary Prejudice

Anyone who wants to comprehend the essence of the chivalric romances and epics to which the cycle of the Grail belongs (together with many other analogous and related writings) must overcome a series of prejudices, the first of which is what I call the *literary* prejudice.

I am referring to the bias displayed by those who regard romances and legends merely as fantastic and poetic human works, whether of an individual or collective authorship; these people deny anything that may have a higher, symbolic value and that cannot be regarded as an arbitrary creation. It is precisely this symbolic, objective, and superindividual element, however, that constitutes the core of sagas, legends, myths, adventurous feats, and epics of the traditional world.[1] This element did not always originate from a perfectly conscious intention. Especially in the case of semicollective works, the most important and meaningful elements have often been expressed almost unconsciously by their authors, who did not realize they were obeying some external influences; these influences at a certain point employed the direct intentions or the creative spontaneity of certain personalities or groups as means to an end.

Thus, even in cases in which spontaneous, poetic, or fantastic compositions appear to be in the forefront, such elements nonetheless have the value of a contingent covering and vehicle of expression, at which only a superficial reader may stop. Some authors intended simply to engage in artistic compositions

---

1. In order to understand the specific meaning that I have given to the expression "traditional world," I refer my readers to two other works of mine, *Revolt Against the Modern World*, trans. Guido Stucco (Rochester, Vt.: Inner Traditions, 1995), and *The Mask and True Face of Contemporary Spirituality*. The same meaning has been given to it by R. Guénon and his group.

and were indeed successful at that, so much so that their productions are enjoyed by those who know about and care for the aesthetic perspective only. This does not mean that these people, in their "artistic productions" and in their spontaneity, have not also done something else; they have either preserved and transmitted or activated a higher content, which a trained eye will always be able to recognize. Some authors would undoubtedly be shocked if they were clearly shown that this is indeed what has happened in their works.

In the legendary traditional compositions, however, the authors usually were not aware of engaging in something that goes beyond mere art and fantasy, even though they almost always had only a confused sensation of the scope of the themes that they put at the center of their creations. A concept from the domain of individual psychology has been extended to the domain of sagas and of legends, namely, that of a peripheral consciousness and, beneath it, an area of subtler, deeper, and more important influences. From a psychoanalytic perspective, dreams are among those states in which such influences, which have been repressed or excluded from waking consciousness, take direct control of the power of imagination, translating themselves into symbolic images. Ordinary consciousness experiences these images without understanding their real content. The more these images or phantasms appear to be extravagant or incoherent, the more we must suspect the existence of a latent, intelligent, and meaningful content.

This is what should be thought in many cases about sagas, legends, adventures, myths, and even fairy tales. And so it often happens that the most fantastic, strange, improbable and incoherent aspect, which is less likely to have an aesthetic or historical value and therefore is usually set aside, eventually offers the best way to understand the central element that bestows upon such compositions its true sense and at times even its higher historical meaning. According to a saying in a particular tradition, which later on I will show to be related to that of the Grail: "Where I have spoken more clearly and openly about our science, there I have spoken obscurely and mysteriously." The Roman emperor Julian wrote: "When myths on sacred subjects are incongruous in thought, by that very fact they cry aloud, as it were, and summon us not to believe them literally, but to study and track down their hidden meaning."[2]

This, then, is the first prejudice that needs to be overcome. This prejudice influences the interpretation of the medieval romances and especially the literature of the Love's Lieges (Fedeli D'Amore). In this type of literature, owing to the preponderance of the artistic and poetic element, which was used as a cov-

---

2. Julian, *Against the Cynic Heracleios*, 217c.

ering, many people have regarded as iconoclast any attempt to set forth an extraliterary exegesis, namely, any attempt to penetrate the mystery found within this poetic literature. Such an attempt is related not only to the influences that have generated the Grail cycle but also to certain organizations that have acted in history "behind the scenes."

2

The Ethnological Prejudice

A second prejudice that has to be overcome is the ethnological one. This prejudice essentially concerns an order of researches that have begun to unearth many hidden roots of the cycle of legends to which the Grail belongs. These studies have not been able to recognize in these legends anything other than fragments of folklore and of ancient, primitive, popular beliefs. It is important to make a clarification in regard to this subject, because the presence of such elements in the Grail tradition is real. Moreover, they constitute the guiding thread that reconnects the historical aspect, which is relative to the presence and to the effectiveness of a particular tradition, to the suprahistorical and initiatory aspect of the legend of the Grail.

First of all, it is necessary to extend to the collective dimension the relativity of the "creative" aspect that I have previously discussed in relation to individual productions, since most people see in folklore a spontaneous popular production, or a fantastic collective product, that is mixed with superstitions and needs to be considered for all practical purposes as an oddity. Influenced by such a prejudice, the so-called ethnological schools, just like the psychoanalytical trends devoted to the study of the "collective unconscious," have engaged in various researches that always amount to a systematic, contaminating reduction of what is higher and superior to what is lower and inferior.

At this point I must dispute the very notion of "primitiveness" that is attributed today to some popular traditions. Far from being "primitive" (i.e., primordial), in most cases such traditions are nothing but degenerated residues that must be reconnected to very ancient cycles of civilization. Thus I concur with René Guénon's assessment that so-called folklore, in almost every instance, contains traditional elements in the true sense of the word, although at times they are deformed, diminished, or fragmentary. These elements have a real, symbolic value and thus, far from originating in people's minds, do not even have a human origin; the only popular thing is merely the fact that they have "survived," considering that these elements belong to traditional forms that by now have disappeared.

These extinct traditional forms sometimes are to be traced to such a distant past that it would be impossible to determine it, a past that is therefore confined to the obscure domain of prehistory. In this regard, people act as some sort of more or less unconscious collective memory, the content of which is derived from some other source.[1]

Likewise, I agree with Guénon's explanation concerning the peculiar fact that people in these cases are the bearers of many elements belonging to a higher plane, such as the initiatory one, and therefore to a plane that is in essence "unpopular":

> When a traditional form is about to become extinct, its last representatives can willingly entrust to that collective memory what would otherwise be lost. This, in other words, is the only way to salvage what can still be salvaged. At the same time, the natural lack of understanding of the masses is a sufficient guarantee that what had an esoteric character may not be lost, but that it rather may continue to exist as a sort of witness of the past to those who in a later epoch will be able to comprehend it.[2]

This last observation is especially true in the case of the elements of the allegedly "pagan," Nordic-Western folklore that are present in the legends of the Grail and King Arthur. These elements, once properly integrated (i.e., brought back to their original symbolic meaning through traditional and even intertraditional references), will convey the true meaning that certain romances and epics incorporated. These romances were highly regarded in the medieval knightly world and also had a relationship with the Ghibelline ideal of the *imperium* and with various secret traditions and groups that inherited, in various forms, the spiritual legacy of this ideal.

Thus we can clearly see the difference between this perspective and the above-mentioned psychoanalytical theories concerning the subconscious or collective unconscious, in which the latter has become a sort of grab bag

---

1. R. Guénon, "Le Saint Grail," *Le Voile d'Isis* (1934): 47–48.
2. Ibid.

containing all kinds of things, all of which are considered, more or less, in terms of "life," "atavism," and the "irrational." What such theories regard uniformly as the "unconscious" should rather be considered the superconsciousness. It is simply ridiculous to regard myths and symbols as manifestations or archetypes of "life," considering that their nature is essentially metaphysical and that they have nothing to do with "life," unless we are talking about their empty shells. It is pointless to remark, as C. G. Jung and Richard Wilhelm have done,[3] that any positive consideration must be limited to the study of the manifestations of the "unconscious," understood as pure experiences, without any reference to transcendent elements.

The truth is that when there are no firm reference points, there is no hope of orienting oneself through various experiences, of understanding and evaluating them, especially when experience as a whole is abusively identified with some of its particular modalities, which at times are even affected by pathological factors. This has been abundantly demonstrated by the outcome of all the various psychoanalytical interpretations. These attempts fail to reach the plane of the spirit. Moreover, even when they do not lead to a subnormal world of neuropaths and hysterics by producing such aberrations as those found in Sigmund Freud's *Totem and Taboo,* they nevertheless produce (as in the case of Jung's theory of "archetypes") confused perceptions that are greatly influenced by the new superstitious cult of what is "vital" and "irrational," thereby proving not so much to lack assumptions as to have mistaken ones.

---

3. Jung's and Wilhelm's introduction to *The Secret of the Golden Flower,* trans. R. Wilhelm (New York: Harcourt, 1962).

3

Concerning the
Traditional Method

What still needs to be overcome is the tendency to derive the fundamental themes of the Grail and of the imperial myth solely from a particular historical movement, by supposing an external, casual, and empirical transmission. According to a widespread opinion, the Grail is essentially a Christian legend. Some have instead hypothesized a Celtic-pagan origin;[1] others favor an Indo-Chinese origin;[2] still others argue for a Syrian origin;[3] and some have made references to alchemy.[4] On another plane, not only has the Grail been associated with the doctrines of the Cathars and the ancient Persians, but some have even attempted to identify characters and historical locations described in the legend (France, according to some, Iran, according to others).

No matter how legitimate these comparisons may be, what is significant is the spirit in which they are drawn. The characteristic feature of the method that I call "traditional" (in opposition to the profane, empirical, and critical-intellectual method of modern research), consists in emphasizing the universal character of a symbol or teaching, and in relating it to corresponding symbols found in other traditions, thus establishing the presence of something that is both superior and antecedent to each of these formulations, which are

1. A. Nutt, *Studies on the Legend of the Holy Grail* (London, 1888). Also, J. Marx, *La Legende arthurienne et le Graal* (Paris, 1952).

2. L. von Schroeder, *Die Wurzel der Sage vom heiligen Gral* (Vienna, 1910).

3. L. E. Iselin, *Der morgenlandische Ursprung der Grallegende* (Halle, 1909).

4. R. Palgen, *Der Stein der Weisen* (Breslau, 1922).

different from and yet equivalent to each other. Since any one tradition may have given to a common meaning a more complete, typical, and transparent expression than have the others, seeking to establish correspondences is consequently one of the most fruitful ways to understand and integrate what in other cases is found in a more obscure or fragmentary form.

Although this is the method I intend to follow, it is not the one favored by most modern scholars. First of all, these scholars establish not true correspondences but opaque derivations. In other words, they investigate the empirical and always uncertain circumstance of the material transmission of certain ideas or legends from one people to another, or from one literature to another, thus ignoring that wherever we find at work influences characteristic of a plane deeper than that of a merely individual conscience, a correspondence and a transmission may take place also through nonordinary ways, that is, without specific temporal and spatial conditions and without external historical contacts. Second and foremost, every comparison in such modern research ends up becoming a shifting rather than a widening of perspective. For instance, when a scholar discovers the correspondence of some themes of the legend of the Grail with other themes found, say, in the Persian tradition, this is regarded by him as a "research into the original sources"; the end result is that he will proudly announce to the world, "The Grail is a Persian symbol!" The new reference does not help him to clarify one tradition through another or to understand one tradition through the universal, metaphysical, and suprahistorical element that may be more visible in a corresponding symbol formulated in another tradition. In other words, this amounts to a random shift of perspective in a two-dimensional model. It is not research into that vantage point that, more than others, may help to lead one from the two superficial dimensions to the third dimension, namely, depth, which may act as a conduit or as an ordering center for all the other data.

At this point I wish to make a further clarification concerning attempts to interpret the Grail in terms of historical figures and situations, considering that such attempts have also been made in other legends that have important connections with the Grail (e.g., those of King Arthur and Prester John).

Generally speaking, in these attempts we detect the so-called euhemeristic tendency, which has been taken up by modern scholars because of their irresistible impulse to reduce the superior to the inferior whenever possible. According to modern scholars, the figures found in myths and legends are merely abstract sublimations of historical figures, which have eventually replaced the latter and become myths and fantastic tales. On the contrary, the opposite is true: there are realities of a superior, archetypal order, which are shadowed in various ways by symbols and myths. It may happen that in the course of history, certain structures or personalities will embody these realities. When this happens, history and superhistory intersect and integrate each other; human fantasy may then instinctively attribute the traits of myth to those characters and structures because reality has somehow become symbolic and symbol has become reality. In these cases, the euhemeristic interpretation totally subverts the true relationships. Here myth constitutes the primary element and should be regarded as the starting point, while the historical figure or datum is only one of the various contingent and conditioned expressions of this superior order of things.

Elsewhere I have indicated the true sense of the apparently absurd and arbitrary relationships that certain legends have established between different historical figures. These relationships were established even though these figures, while lacking any historical common factor in space and time, were obscurely perceived to be equivalent manifestations of a single principle or function. The reason behind some genealogies, which are apparently not any less extravagant, is also analogous: a legendary lineage expresses figuratively a spiritual continuity, which may be real even without a biological continuity in space and time. The genealogies of the kings of the Grail, Lohengrin, Arthur, Prester John, Helias, and others should be regarded essentially in this fashion. Moreover, it is precisely such ideal situations, which proceed from the above-mentioned interaction between history and superhistory, that give us the fundamental key to understand the genesis and the meaning of the legend of the Grail and of those elements in it that lead back not only to the suprahistorical idea of the Empire but also to one of its particular manifestations in the Western medieval world.

4

The Historical Context of the Mystery of the Grail

When we isolate the texts that make up the Grail cycle, we find that they repeat a few essential themes, which are expressed through the symbolism of knightly figures and deeds. What we are dealing with, then, are essentially the themes of a mysterious *center;* of a *quest* and a spiritual *test;* of a regal *succession* or *restoration,* which sometimes assumes the character of a healing or avenging action. Percival, Gawain, Galahad, Ogier, Lancelot, and Peredur are essentially various names portraying the same human type; likewise, King Arthur, Joseph of Arimathea, Prester John, and the Fisher King are equivalent figures and variations on another theme. Also equivalent are images of various mysterious castles, islands, kingdoms, and inaccessible and adventurous lands, which in the narratives are described in a series that, on the one hand, creates a strange, surrealistic atmosphere but, on the other, often ends up becoming monotonous.

I have already mentioned that all this has or is susceptible of having the character of a "mystery" in the initiatory sense of the word. But in the specific form in which all this is expressed in the Grail cycle, we must recognize the point at which a suprahistorical reality imposed itself on history, closely associating the symbols of that mystery to the confused yet lively sensation that its effective realization required to solve the spiritual and temporal crisis of an entire epoch, namely, the medieval ecumenical-imperial age.

The Grail cycle originated from this very specific situation. The evocation of primordial and suprahistorical motifs intersected the ascent of a historical tradition at a point of equilibrium, around which a subject of varied nature and origin precipitated and was crystallized, unified by its susceptibility to the expression of a common motif. Thus we must start from the idea of a fundamental, inner unity of the various texts, and of the various figures, symbols, and adventures proper to them, and proceed to discover the latent capability of a text to integrate and continue another, until a thorough exposition of some fundamental themes is achieved. To bring back such motifs to their universal, intertraditional meaning and to an overall metaphysics of history would be a repetition of what I have tried to do in another work of mine;[1] here I must limit myself to articulating the reference points that are most crucial to our comprehension of the simultaneously historical and suprahistorical meaning of the mystery of the Grail.

---

1. See my *Revolt Against the Modern World.*

PART TWO

Principles and Prior Events

5

The Olympian Cycle

According to the way of thinking I have espoused, that which was manifested in various people as an authentic tradition is not something relative, determined by external or merely historical events. Rather, it always points to elements of a knowledge that is unique in its essence. These elements always have the character of constants.

Traditional teaching, though in various forms, had always and everywhere upheld the belief in the existence of a primordial race that embodied a transcendent spirituality; for that reason, this race was often regarded as divine or "like the gods." I have defined its structure as *Olympian;* by this term I mean to signify an innate superiority or a nature that is essentially supernature. A force from above is found in this race as a presence, predestining it to command, to the royal function; it shows it to be the race of "those who are" and "those who can," and sometimes to be a *solar* race.

Belief in a Golden Age, which is found in many traditions, is a distant memory of that race. Later peoples also formulated a suprahistorical view of that race's function and seat, or place of origin; this occurred because at one point, that which had been manifest became hidden. Owing to a progressive involution of mankind, which was likewise recorded in several traditions, the function exercised by this race became gradually invisible, and that direct contact between historical and suprahistorical elements was interrupted. This is the meaning, for instance, of Hesiod's teachings, according to which the beings of the primordial age never died but rather took an invisible form to guide mortal beings.[1] Thus, a shift occurred from the theme of the Golden Age to a

---

1. Hesiod, *Opera et dies* [Works and Days], trans. T. A. Sinclair (New York: Orno Press, 1979), 112–125.

metaphysical kingdom, to which all the dominators "from above" are related in a mysterious, objective, and ontological way; this is the case both with the real heirs of the primordial tradition and with those who reproduced more or less perfectly and consciously the primordial type of *regnum* in a given land and civilization. This is how the traditional notion of an invisible "King of Kings," or "Universal Ruler," or "King of the World," came to be associated with specific symbols, some of which derive directly from analogies, while others are mythologized memories of the land or lands where the primordial Olympian cycle unfolded.

These are first and foremost symbols of *centrality:* the center, the pole, the region in the middle of the earth, the central stone or the foundation, the magnet. Then, symbols of *stability:* the island surrounded by the waters, the rock, the unshakable stone. Finally, symbols of *inviolability* and *inaccessibility;* the invisible or not-to-be-found castle or land, a wild mountain peak, a subterranean region. Moreover, the "Land of Light," the "Land of the Living," the "Holy Land." Yet again, all the variations of the *golden symbolism,* which, on the one hand, includes all the notions of solarity, light, regality, immortality, and incorruptibility while, on the other hand, it has always had some relationship with the primordial tradition and with the age characterized by gold. Other symbols point to "life" in the higher sense of the word (e.g., the "perennial food," the "Tree of Life"), to a transcendent knowledge, to an invincible power; everything appears variously mixed in the fantastic, symbolic, or poetic representations that in the various traditions have foreshadowed this constant theme of the invisible *regnum* and of the Supreme Center of the world, in itself or in its emanations and reproductions.[2]

---

2. On this subject matter see René Guénon's *Le Roi du monde* (Paris, 1927) to which I will often refer in the course of this book.

6

On the "Hero" and the "Woman"

As everybody knows, the doctrine of the Golden Age is part of the doctrine of the four ages, which testifies to the progressive spiritual involution unfolding in the course of history since very ancient times. All of these ages also have a morphological meaning and express a typical and universal form of civilization. Following the Golden Age, we encounter the *Silver Age*, which corresponds to a priestly and feminine rather than regal and virile type of spirituality: I have called it *lunar* spirituality, since the symbols of gold and silver have traditionally been in the same relationship as that between sun and moon. In this context, such correspondence is particularly revealing: the moon is the feminine star that, unlike the sun, no longer has in itself the principle of its own light. Hence the shift to a spirituality conditioned by mediation, namely, an extrovert spirituality characterized by an attitude of submission, of abandonment, of loving or ecstatic rapture. Here we find the root of the "religious" phenomenon, from its theistic-devotional forms to its mystical ones.

Any insurgence of a wild and materialized virility against such spiritual forms characterizes the *Bronze Age*. This age is characterized by the degradation of the warriors' caste and by its revolt against him who represents the spirit, insofar as he is no longer the Olympian leader but only a priest. The Bronze Age is also marked by the unleashing of the principle proper to the warriors' caste, namely, pride, violence, war. The corresponding myth is the Titanic or Luciferian revolt, or the Promethean attempt to steal the Olympian fire. The age of "giants," or of the Wolf, or of the "elemental beings," is an equivalent figuration found in various traditions and in their fragments preserved in legends and epics of various peoples.

The last age is the *Iron Age*, or, according to the corresponding Hindu term, the Dark Age (Kali Yuga). This age includes every deconsecrated civilization, every civilization that knows and extols only what is human and earthly. Against these forms of decadence there emerged the idea of a possible cycle of restoration, which Hesiod called the *heroic cycle* or *age of heroes*. Here we must employ the term *heroic* in a special, technical sense distinct from the usual meaning. According to Hesiod, the "generation of heroes" was created by Zeus, that is to say, by the Olympian principle, with the possibility of reattaining the primordial state and thus to give life to a new "golden" cycle.[1]

But in order to realize this, which is only a possibility and no longer a state of affairs, it is first necessary to overcome both the "lunar" spirituality and the materialized virility, namely, both the priest and the mere warrior or the Titan. These archetypes are found in the "heroic" figures of almost every tradition. In the Hellenic-Achaean tradition, for instance, Heracles is described as a heroic prototype precisely in these terms; his perennial nemesis is Hera, the supreme goddess of the lunar-pantheistic cult. Heracles earns Olympian immortality after allying himself to Zeus, who is the Olympian principle, against the "giants"; according to one of the myths of this cycle, it is through Heracles that the "titanic" element (symbolized by Prometheus) is freed and reconciled with the Olympian element.

While, on the one hand, the Titan represents one who does not accept the human condition and who wants to steal the divine fire, on the other hand, only a small difference separates the hero from the Titan. Thus Pindar exhorted people not to "yearn to become like gods"; also, in the Hebrew mythology, the symbol of Adam's curse acted as an analogous warning and indicated a fundamental danger. The titanic type—or, in another respect, the warrior type—is, after all, the prime matter of which heroes are made. But in order to implement a positive solution to the dilemma, that is, to attain an Olympian transformation as the reintegration of the primordial state, it is necessary to fulfill a double condition.

First of all, it is necessary to show the proof and the confirmation of the virile qualification; thus in the epic and knightly symbolism we find a series of adventures, feats, and fights. This qualification should not become a limitation, a hubris, a closure of the "I," and it should not paralyze the capability of opening oneself up to a transcendent force, in function of which alone can the fire really become light and free itself. Second, such liberation should not signify a

---

1. Hesiod, *Opera et dies*, 156–73.

cessation of the inner tension; thus a further test consists in adequately re-affirming the virile quality on the supersensible plane. The consequence of this is the Olympian transformation or the achievement of that dignity which in initiatory traditions has always been designated as "regal." This is the decisive point that differentiates the heroic experience from every mystical evasion and from every pantheistic confusion; among the various symbols that may refer to this point is the symbolism of the *woman*.

In the Indo-Aryan tradition, every god—that is, every transcendent power—is joined with a bride, and the term *śakti*, "bride," also means "power." In the West, Wisdom (Sophia) and sometimes even the Holy Spirit were repre-sented as a royal woman, while in Greek mythology, Hebe, the perennial Olympian youth, was given in marriage to Heracles as a wife. In Egyptian fig-urations, divine women offer to the kings a lotus, which is a symbol of a rebirth and the "key of life." Like the Iranian *fravashi*, the Nordic Valkyrie are a figu-ration of transcendental parts of warriors, the forces of their destinies and vic-tories. The Roman tradition knew of a Venus Victrix who was credited with generating an imperial stock (Venus Genitrix); the Celtic tradition mentioned supernatural women who take warriors to mysterious islands to make them immortal with their love. Eve, according to an etymology of the name, means "Life," or "the Living One." Thus, without proceeding further with similar ex-amples, which I have discussed elsewhere, I wish to emphasize that a very wide-spread symbolism has seen in the woman a vivifying and transfiguring power, through which it is possible to overcome the human condition.

What is the foundation of the feminine representation of this power? Since every symbolism is based on specific relationships of analogy, it is necessary to begin with the possible relationships between man and woman. These rela-tionships can be either normal or abnormal. They are abnormal when the woman dominates the man. Because the symbolism of the woman connected to this second case does not concern the issue I am discussing here, I will not dwell on it. I will only say that these are instances of gynecocratic (matriarchal) views that must be regarded as residues of the cycle of the "lunar" civilization, in which we find a reflection of the theme of man's dependency and passivity toward the spirit conceived under a feminine guise (Cosmic Mother or *magna mater*, Mother of Life, etc.); this is a characteristic theme of that cycle.

However, the more general idea of the woman as the dispenser of the *sacrum* and as a vivifying principle, or as the bearer of a life that liberates, animates, and transforms mere being,[2] does not necessarily fall in this category; rather, such an idea may be (and indeed often was) considered a part of a spirituality

---

2. See my *Eros and the Mysteries of Love* (Rochester, Vt.: Inner Traditions, 1983).

that I have characterized as "heroic." In this instance, it is necessary to refer to the normal relations between man and woman as the basis of the analogy and of the symbolism; hence the fundamental concept of a situation in which the virile principle retains its own nature. The spirit, vis-à-vis the masculine, is the "woman": the virile principle is active, the spirit passive. Even before the power that transfigures it and vivifies the hero, the virile principle retains the character that man has as the lord of his woman. In passing, we must note that this is exactly the opposite of the bridal symbolism prevalent in religious and especially in the Christian mysticism, in which the soul is attributed a feminine role, namely, that of the "bride."

Having said that, and remembering what has been said about the "signs" of the center, we find mixed symbols: the Woman of the Island; the Woman of the Tree; the Woman of the Fountain; the Woman or Queen of the Castle; the Queen of the Solar Land; the Woman hidden in the Stone; and so forth. More particularly, as the widow the woman expresses a period of silence, that is, a period in which the tradition, the power, or the strength is no longer possessed, has lost her "man," and awaits a new lord or hero.[3] Analogous is the meaning of the imprisoned virgin who waits to be freed and married to a preordained knight. On this basis, everything that in epic legends and in many chivalric romances is described in terms of adventures and heroic struggles undertaken in the name of a woman is almost always susceptible to interpretation as a symbol of the tests of the virile quality, tests that are assigned as a premise for a transcendent integration of the human personality. And if in this type of literature we also find women who are seductive and who represent a potential danger for the hero, this should not be understood solely in a primitive and direct manner, that is, in terms of a mere carnal seduction. Rather, this should be understood on a higher plane as a reference to the danger that a heroic adventure can lead to a titanic fall. In this case, the woman represents the seductiveness of transcendent power and knowledge when its possession means Promethean usurpation and the sin of prevaricating pride. Another, opposite aspect may be related with what someone has called "the death which comes from a woman," referring to the loss of the deeper principle of virility.

---

3. Hence the obvious meaning of the expression "Widow's Son," which has been preserved even in Western Freemasonry from the Iranian tradition and from Manichaeism.

7

The Hyperborean Theme

Another fundamental traditional teaching, which I have discussed elsewhere with corresponding documentation,[1] is the location of the center or primordial seat of the Olympian civilization of the Golden Age in a Boreal or Nordic-Boreal region that became uninhabitable. A tradition of Hyperborean origins, in its original Olympian form or in its new emergences of a heroic type, is at the basis of founding or civilizing deeds performed by races that spread into the Eurasian continent during the period from the end of the glacial age through the Neolithic Era. Some of these races must have come directly from the North; others seem to have had as their country of origin a Western-Atlantic land in which some kind of replica of the Northern center had been established. This is the reason why various concordant symbols and memories refer to a land that sometimes is Northern-Arctic and other times Western.

Among the many designations of the Hyperborean center that came to be applied also to the Atlantic center was Thule, or "White Island," or "Island of Splendor" (the Hindu Śveta-dvīpa; the Hellenic Leuké island;[2] the "original seed of the Arian race" or Ariyana Vaego in ancient Iran); and "Land of the Sun," or "Land of Apollo," that is, Avalon. Concordant memories in all Indo-European traditions talk about the disappearance of such a seat (which later on was mythologized) following an ice age or a flood. This is the real, historical

---

1. *Revolt Against the Modern World*, Chapters 24–26.
2. Especially in the tradition referred to by Diodorus Siculus (Bibliotheca Historica II, 47), the Λευκη Νῆσος, or White Island, is identified with the land of the Hyperboreans; it was situated in the ocean, before the land of the Celts; it is also indicated as Apollo's island.

counterpart of the various allusions to something that, beginning with a given period, has allegedly been lost or become hidden and untraceable. This too is the reason why the "Island" or "Land of the Living" (the term "living" here referring to the members of the original divine race), which is the land to which the well-known symbols of the Supreme Center of the world allude, was often confused with the "region of the dead" (the term "dead" here referring to the extinct race). Thus, for instance, according to a Celtic doctrine, mankind's primordial ancestor was the god of the dead (Dispater) who dwells in a faraway region beyond the ocean, in those "faraway islands" whence, according to the Druids' teachings, some of the prehistoric inhabitants of Gaul came directly.[3] Moreover, according to a classical tradition, after having been the lord of this earth, the king of the Golden Age, Kronos-Saturn, was dethroned and castrated (that is, deprived of the power to beget, to give life to a new stock); he still lives, though asleep, in a region located in the Far North, close to the Arctic Sea, which was also called the Cronid Sea.[4]

This generated various confusions, but essentially it is always the same transposition in superhistory, under the species of a latent or invisible reality or center, of ideas referring to the Hyperborean theme. For my purposes, I will need to discuss briefly the form that these memories assumed in the Celtic and especially in the Irish cycle: the traditions concerning Avalon, the Tuatha dé Danaan, and the kingdom of Arthur. The scope of these traditions is more than local and historical; often, even the geographical data appearing in them have a merely symbolic meaning, as is often the case in these instances.

---

3. The Irish name "Land Beneath the Waves" (Tir fa Tonn), applied to an image of this region, incorporates a memory of its sinking and submersion.
4. Here it is the land of Thule, which, according to Strabo (ca. 63 B.C.E.–after 21 C.E.) was located at six days of navigation from the coast of Britannia, close to the frozen sea. In regard to the heroes of the primordial age, there is an interesting tradition according to which Kronos, already king of that age, often appears as king of the heroes (Hesiod, *Opera et dies,* 168–71).

8

The Tradition in Ireland

The legendary history of Ireland is based on the events of races that later invaded it and dominated it, coming from a mysterious Northern-Atlantic center, to which they sometimes returned. The *Historia britorum* often gives to this center the name Hiberia, but in truth such a term is only an imaginative rendering of the Irish names Magh-Mo, Tragh-Mor, or Magh-Mell, designating the "Land of the Dead," namely, the primordial Northern-Atlantic center. There are many stories surrounding such races: they were in perennial conflict with the Fomors, giants or dark and monstrous beings who, in the Christianized elements of the saga, were significantly assimilated to the antediluvian giants or to savage beings descending from Shem and from Cain. These Fomors are the equivalent of the "elemental natures" or giants who were the mortal foes of the Aesir, the "divine heroes" in the Nordic tradition of the Edda. The Fomors represent the powers of a cycle of a Bronze Age, the obscure telluric forces that were associated with the depth of the waters (in the Ulster cycle), just as the telluric Poseidon previously was. In other words, they correspond to the forces of the original cycle that became materialized and degenerated in a titanic sense. This latter aspect can be derived from Celtic traditions, considering that the king of the Fomors, Tethra, was sometimes believed to be born in the mysterious land beyond the ocean, and that the unconquerable tower of Conaan (another Fomor king), which was located in the "Glass Island in the middle of the sea," is, after all, an obvious symbol of the primordial center.

In any event, the Fomors, in their essential aspect as an obscure and telluric race, are defeated by a first nucleus of civilizers who came to Ireland from the

Atlantic region and from the race of Partholan. Eventually this race became extinct and was followed by a second people of the same origins, the race of Neimheidh. That name, which derives from a Celtic root meaning "heavenly," but also "ancient," "venerable," and "sacred," allows us to conceive this new cycle as the creation of the representatives of the primordial tradition still in a pure, Olympian state.

A symbolic episode during the age of Neimheidh recalls a counterpart in the Edda. In the Edda, the Aesir, or "divine heroes," turn to the elemental beings to make them rebuild the fortress of the central region, Midgard's Asgard. As a reward for such a job, the giants want the divine woman Freya, and also the moon and the sun. After they are refused (the Aesir having thwarted this usurpation of the forces from above, brought about by their employment of elemental powers) a struggle ensues, which culminates in the fatal "twilight of the gods." Likewise, in the Irish cycle, Neimheidh employs the Fomors to build a fortress, but then, fearing that they may occupy it, he exterminates them. This is to no avail, since the descendants of Neimheidh end up being subjected to the Fomors, who inhabit the Tor-Inis, a fortress in an island located northwest of Ireland. In this place, during an attempted rebellion, Neimheidh's descendants are massacred, just as in the saga of the Edda the struggle against elemental forces ends at first in a defeat of the Aesir. In both cases, we most likely have the figuration of the advent of a "titanic" cycle on the ruins of a civilization that is directly derived from the primordial one.

At this point of the unfolding of the Irish legend, an attempt at heroic restoration occurs. It is the cycle of the Tuatha dé Danaan, a name that means "the people of the goddess Anu or Dana." This race, on the one hand, is believed to have come to Ireland from "heaven"—hence, according to the *Leabhar na h-uidhre* (Book of the dun cow), "their wisdom and sublimity of their knowledge." On the other hand, they are believed to have acquired a supernatural knowledge in the Hyperborean region.[1] These two versions do not contradict each other, but rather shed light on each other, owing both to the more-than-human character of the primordial center, and to the fact that, according to the legend, the race of the Tuatha derived from surviving members of the Neimheidh race. These survivors allegedly traveled to the Hyperborean or Western-Atlantic land in order to acquire supernatural knowledge, which explains a relationship with certain mystical objects, more on which later.

Since the race of Neimheidh was the "heavenly" and "ancient" race that was swept away by a titanic cycle, the overall meaning is probably that this was a reintegrating contact with the original spiritual center (a center that is both

---

1. *Battle of the Magh-Tured*, 1–3.

heavenly and, in the geographic transposition of the memory, Hyperborean or Western-Atlantic). This contact reanimates and bestows a heroic form to the new stock, the Tuatha dé Danaan, who eventually defeat the Fomors and similar races (the Firbolgs) and conquer Ireland.[2] The leader of the Tuatha, Ogme, is a "solar" figure (Grian Ainech), endowed with traits similar to those of the Doric Heracles. Ogme eventually captures the sword of the king of the Fomors.

However, the rule of the Tuatha also ended. The *Leabhar gabhála* (Book of invasions) mentions the advent in Ireland of a new race, that of the "sons of Mileadh," whose physiognomy is not clear. In this race the warrior element predominates—it seems that Mileadh has the same root as *miles* (soldier)—yet it is not distinct from residues of the highest tradition proper to the previous cycle of the Tuatha. Thus even in the civilization of Mileadh we find the symbolism of the "central seat." The constitution of this people is feudal, with a supreme regality established in Tara, in the "Land of the Middle" (Meadhon), which already had been a sacred center of the Tuatha. Their king used to be consecrated by the "stone of destiny" *(lia-fail),* more on which later. This too belonged to the tradition of the Tuatha. As for the Tuatha themselves, according to some texts they allegedly left the country, assuming an invisible form as the inhabitants of marvelous "subterranean" palaces or of mountainous caves inaccessible to mortal men, among whom they appear only in exceptional cases. According to other texts, they returned to their original home in Avalon.[3]

According to what has been said, the two versions are equivalent, since they are two different figurations of the primordial center that became hidden ("subterranean") and inaccessible. In Celtic traditions, images of the Atlantic "island" of Avalon continued to be applied to it. Such an island was mainly conceived, in later times, as a place inhabited by women who attract heroes there to make them immortal. The name Avalon was explained on the basis of the Cymric term *afal,* which means "apple," or "Island of Apples."[4] This is

---

2. To this we may relate the tradition referred by Plutarch, according to whom in the Boreal land Heracles' stock (the heroic cycle) allegedly mixed with that of Kronos (primordial cycle), bringing about a civilization "similar to the Hellenic one" (the Olympian-heroic civilization of which Heracles was the symbol): "Thus Heracles is attributed the highest honor, and after him, Kronos" (*De facie in orbe lunae,* 26).

3. C. Squire, *The Mythology of Ancient Britain and Ireland* (London, 1909). The tradition of the Tuatha continues somewhat in the heroic cycle of the Ulster, who were regarded as their descendants, with a solar character analogous to that of Greek heroes.

4. From the woman of the faraway island Condla receives an apple that, no matter how much one eats of it, always grows back and reawakens in him an invincible nostalgia. This is the theme of the cornucopia, which will appear also in the Grail, together with the nostalgia that the latter induces in those who have once seen it.

naturally reminiscent of the island of the Hesperides, "beyond the ocean," with the symbolic golden apples that Heracles captured in yet another of the labors that won him Olympian immortality. The supernatural women of the island of Avalon apparently possess the gift of health: in the legend of Tir na Nog they declare that in their land "there is no death nor dissolution of the body," and that in it the hero Oisin will be crowned "King of Eternal Youth."[5]

At the same time, Avalon, the "White Island,"[6] has also the value of a "polar" and "solar" island. Avalon, according to another possible etymology, is none other than the island of Apollo, the Greek god who was called by the Celts Ablun or Belen; thus this island represents the solar land and the Hyperborean region, since Apollo had also been considered a solar king of the Golden Age and of the Hyperborean region.[7] The frequent confusion of this island with the "Glass Island" must be due to a general symbolism of glass walls and even of walls of air, signifying an invisible defense surrounding some places, blocking their entrance, and also, according to yet another symbol, of a fiery revolving wall around this island. These are variations on the theme of inviolability, which was always attributed to the Supreme Center.

The text known as the *Battle of Magh-Tured* (sections 3–6) relates that the Tuatha brought with them from the Northern-Atlantic seat four objects that were strictly related to the teaching they received there: a stone, a spear, a sword, and a bowl. The stone is the "fatidic stone" or "royal stone," so called because, acting as a sort of oracle, it allows one to recognize the legitimate king among various pretenders to the throne. The spear is the spear of Lug, the god of thunder, of which it is said that "never was a battle lost by him who brandished it." The sword is the invincible and inexorable sword of Nuadu. Finally, the bowl of Dagde is able to magically satiate with its contents any number of warriors. These objects of the Tuatha will reappear in corresponding objects of the Grail cycle, just as the Grail's seat will be shown to be in close relation to the very island of Avalon, or "White Island."

In the traditions gathered in the *Annals of the Four Teachers* we find very visibly the theme of the struggle and of victory as a test. An ever-recurring formula

---

5. The term *avallach* means apple, the apple that bestows immortality.

6. The names Albion, referring to England, and Albania, referring to a part of it, come from an application to these lands of this ancient image of the White Island or Island of Splendor. In Hindu tradition the seat of Vishnu, the solar god who carries the Hyperborean cross or swastika, is called Śveta dvīpa.

7. One of the figurations of the land I am talking about is the so-called *ten-magh-trogaigi*, which includes the following symbols characteristic of the central seat: regal women; the silver tree with the sun at the top; the tree of victory; a fountain; a bowl containing a beverage that never runs out. All of these symbols will appear again in the knightly sagas.

is: "King *X* fell to *Y*, who became king instead." Its deepest meaning reminds us of the legend of the King of the Woods of Nemi, which I have discussed in my *Revolt Against the Modern World*. In this legend, to defeat and kill a given person appears to introduce one directly to the regal and priestly function held by that person, and also to the quality of becoming the bridegroom of the "divine woman."[8] Medieval chivalric romance is filled with variations on this theme: the test of arms introduces, often almost automatically, the possession of a woman, who goes from one hero to another. On the basis of the so-called love right, according to the ethics of this literature, it was regarded almost as a natural thing for a knight to desire his own lord's wife, provided he believed to be and could prove to be better than he in the test of arms.[9] The peculiar character that all this presents, if taken literally, and its scarce correspondence with the effective customs of the time, should already induce us to suppose a hidden content as the true meaning of such adventures.[10] In these adventures, moreover, one finds distant echoes of the theme of the selection of that virile quality which is most fit to qualify one to obtain possession of the "woman."

According to the *Historia regum britanniae*, Britain was originally inhabited by giants. The main one among them was called Goemagot. Brute, conceived as one of the descendants of the Trojans who founded Rome, exterminated these giants and established the Britannic tradition. Goemagot visibly corresponds to Gog and Magog; this is indeed a significant biblical echo. Gog and Magog were demonic populations that will play an important role in the imperial myth. They correspond to the Fomors, to the "elemental beings" or *rinthursi*, to whom the "divine heroes" of the Edda (i.e., the Aesir) block the path with a wall, thus preventing them from occupying the "Seat of the Center," the Midgard, which is a particular representation of the primordial center. In a certain sense they represent the demonic character of the world of the masses.

The *Annals of the Four Teachers* mentions several revolts against the sacred dynasty of the Tuatha dé Danaan and against the later warrior dynasty of the sons of Mileadh. These insurrections were sparked by the race of the Fir-Domhnain or "race of the abyss," a telluric race associated with degenerated residues of previous inhabitants of Ireland, such as the Firbolgs. Finally, we find mention of a "plebeian race" *(aithe-ach-tuatha)*, which during a feast day

---

8. *Revolt Against the Modern World,* trans. Guido Stucco (Rochester, Vt.: Inner Traditions, 1995), chapter 2.

9. In *Le Chevalier de la charrette,* Arthur's wife will be taken away by an armed knight who challenges Arthur, provided he can win the duel.

10. Note the peculiar character of the knightly law (if taken literally) according to which the winner automatically inherited the vanquished's lady or "regal woman" and had to possess her, more as a duty than as a right.

massacres the nobility and induces the Four Lords to rebel against the supreme lord of the Seat of the Center. As a punishment for such violence the land is stricken by a widespread sterility, accompanied by all sorts of plagues: the kingdom will remain in this state of desolation until the son of the last king, who had been defeated and killed, will return to his father's land. In the Eastern saga of Alexander, the devastation and the sterility of "all the waters, so severe that it left no potable water," are referred to the time of the advent of the people of Gog and Magog. This is the same condition that affects the kingdom of the Grail, which became the *gaste Terre*, the land ravaged because of the Dolorous Stroke, a condition that will last until the arrival of the avenging and restoring hero. This body of ancient traditions and Celtic pre-Christian symbols presents the principal themes that will be embodied again in the Grail cycle. The next link in the chain is the legend of King Arthur.

9

The Arthurian Cycle

In all the forms of this legend, the historical reality of Arthur (who allegedly was the *dux bellorum* of the Nordic Cimres as they struggled against the Anglo-Saxons between the fifth and sixth century C.E.), is secondary compared to the aspect according to which we are led to see in his kingdom an image of the central regal function strictly connected to the Hyperborean tradition, to the point that it gained a value as this function in itself, with symbolic and suprahistorical characters. Thus the relation between Arthur's kingdom and England becomes accidental; in medieval literature this kingdom had instead a supranational meaning, and it embraced the best chivalry. The suggestiveness that it exercised on the heroic medieval Christianity was so great that (a) the latter came to see in Arthur its symbolic leader and (b) the ambition of every knight was to become a member of the mysterious Order of King Arthur, which is in itself a particularly significant fact.

The name Arthur is susceptible to various interpretations, the most reliable of which attributes to it the Celtic words *arthos* (bear) and *viros* (man). Nennius had already explained: *Arthur latine sonat ursum horribilem.*[1] This meaning of a dreadful virile force is connected with a symbolism of Hyperborean origin and at the same time points to the idea of a central or "polar" function. In fact, the bear is one of the sacred symbols of the ancient Nordic cult and simultaneously, in astronomic symbolism, corresponds to the "polar" constellation Ursa Major. Moreover, in the corpus of traditional texts, symbols and names eventually establish a relation between this constellation

---

1. S. Singer, *Die Arthur Sage* (Bern-Leipzig, 1926), 17.

(with the symbolism of the pole or of the center referred to it) and Thule, a name designating the Hyperborean "White Island," the traditional center.[2] Thus the polar, the Hyperborean, and the regal elements converge in the figure of Arthur. The unilaterally virile and warrior aspect that could be supposed in Arthur as an *ursus horribilis* is also modified in the legend by Arthur's being always accompanied, as some kind of complement or counterpart, by Myrddhin or Merlin, who holds a spiritual knowledge and power. This Merlin seems less a distinct person and more the personification of the transcendent and spiritual side of Arthur himself.[3]

The strict connection between the warrior and the spiritual principles already characterizes the chivalry of King Arthur's court as well as the meaning of the most typical adventures attributed to its members. The Knights of the Round Table, that is, of King Arthur, are not mere warriors:

> And when they are chosen to be of the fellowship of the Round Table, they think themselves more blessed and more in worship than if they got half the world; and ye have seen that they have lost their fathers and mothers, and all their kin, and their wives and their children, for to be of the Fellowship.[4]

The Grail itself may represent the transcendent element by which this knighthood aspired to be complemented: this will be clearly seen in the versions of the legend in which Arthur's kingdom is confused with the Grail's. At this point it may be worth recalling the episode concerning the stones of Stonehenge, which still exist and are a source of interest and bewilderment, since it is a mystery how these gigantic blocks could have been cut and carried so long ago to the place where they have been found; these stones appear to be the remains of a great solar temple dating back to the Megalithic or to the Neolithic. Merlin, by ordering his warriors to go fetch such huge stones from faraway peaks, says: "Go to work, brave warriors, and learn, by rolling forward these stones, whether physical strength surpasses the spirit or whether the spirit surpasses physical strength." The warriors prove unable to do this, but Merlin is able to accomplish this task laughingly and effortlessly. That the warrior virtue had, in the Arthurian cycle, a spiritual reference point can be seen from this exhortation in the same text, the *Historia regum britanniae:* "Fight on for

---

2. R. Guénon, *Le Roi du monde,* chapter 10.

3. After all, the name Bear *(Bjorn)* was applied in Nordic traditions to Thor, who is one of the heavenly heroes or Aesir, struggling against elemental beings; in the *Ynglingasaga,* the bear and the wolf are forms taken by Odin, the supreme chief of Valhalla and of Midgard, or "Central Seat."

4. *Le Morte D'Arthur,* ed. Janet Cowen (New York: Penguin Books, 1986 reprint), 14.2.

your own land, and even welcome death, if necessary; for death is a victory and the liberation of the soul." This is exactly the ancient view of the *mors triumphalis*, which is a main feature of the ethics of heroic traditions.

According to the legend, Arthur demonstrated his innate right to be the legitimate king of all of England by passing the so-called test of the sword, namely, by successfully taking a sword out of a great quadrangular stone on the altar of the temple, obviously a variation of the "stone of kings" that belonged to the ancient tradition of the Tuatha dé Danaan.[5] Here we find a double, convergent symbolism. On the one hand, we have the general symbolism of the "foundation stone," which hints at the polar idea; thus the allegory and the myth allegedly refer to a virile power (i.e., the sword) that needs to be drawn from that principle. On the other hand, to take the sword out of the stone may also signify the freeing of a certain power from matter, since the stone often represents this meaning.

This also agrees with another episode in the legend, that in which Arthur, led by Merlin, seizes the sword Caliburn or Excalibur, which is held by a mysterious arm hovering over the waters.[6] But this weapon, forged in Avalon, is related to the Supreme Center; its being held above the water symbolizes a force detached from the conditions of the material, passional, and contingent life, to which a fundamental aspect of the symbolism of water always referred. Such a life must be overcome, not only by those who yearn to receive a regal mandate from the "center" and become leaders of men in a higher sense, but also by every knight who wants to be worthy of belonging to the followers of Arthur and ultimately to find the Grail again.

Among the themes proper to the ancient Britannic tradition, I will mention again the institution of the Round Table and the symbolism of King Arthur's seat. Concerning the latter, we often find the recurrence of the famous symbols of the inaccessible land: according to Andrea Cappellano, Arthur's is a kingdom separated from the human world by a large river, and it can be accessed only by crossing a dangerous bridge. This kingdom is defended by giants; in it there is a castle that is constantly revolving. In this castle, which is called "regal castle" (Caer Rigor) or "rich men's castle" (Caer Golud), there is a supernatural vessel that, according to the tradition of *The Spoiling of Annwn*, was taken by King Arthur from a king of the "other world." This vessel—which, like the Grail in the castle of the "rich" king, is a facsimile of the vessel Dagde, one of the symbols proper to the Hyperborean tradition of the Tuatha dé Danaan—"satiates"

---

5. Siegfried, in the Nordic-German saga, successfully completes a similar test: he takes out of a tree a sword stuck in it, which is something no one else had been able to do.

6. *Le Morte D'Arthur,* 1.25.

everybody, heals all wounds, and protects from the erosion of time, all the while denying its gifts to cowards and oath breakers.

Such a seat, as a revolving castle (Caer Sidi), is one and the same with the "rotating island" that in the ancient Celtic saga is often the equivalent of the Glass Island and, in general, of Avalon; here we definitely find an allusion to the polar land that spins around its axis and carries along the world in its rotating motion. This is a visible reminder of the image of the Universal Ruler *(cakravartin)*, an expression that literally means "the spinner of the wheel," in reference to him who, as an immobile center, moves the wheel of the *regnum* and of the ordered universe.

These ideas can also be found in the symbolism of the Round Table, which was instituted by Arthur, under Merlin's advice, to characterize the knightly order of which he was the supreme leader. According to Sir Thomas Malory's text, the Round Table was built as an image of the world; in it the entire universe, the earthly and the heavenly, is believed to find shelter.[7] In other texts, a reference is made to the course of the stars and to the rotation of the heavens in relation to an unmovable center. From this it can be clearly seen that the knights who sit at the Round Table are also the representatives of the ordering central power.

In different versions these knights of the Round Table, or at least the best among them, are twelve in number; this points to a visible correspondence with the twelve peers who in the *Roman de Brut* "divide the earth in twelve parts, each one taking one part as his estate, and calling himself its king.'" Twelve is a solar number that always appeared, in various forms, wherever the establishment of a traditional center was either accomplished or attempted: for instance, the twelve thrones of Midgard; the twelve supreme Olympian gods; the twelve stumps of the Delphic center; the twelve Roman lictors; the twelve residents of Avallonia; and the twelve counts/paladins of Charlemagne. Moreover, in the cycle of the Grail and of King Arthur, such symbolism was connected with a further theme, that of the Siege Perilous, a seat at the Round Table purposely left vacant and reserved for an awaited and predestined knight, superior to everybody else, who sometimes is portrayed as the thirteenth knight and who clearly corresponds to the same supreme function of a center, of a leader or pole for the twelve, and who is the image or representative of the *cakravartin* or Universal Ruler.[8]

---

7. *Le Morte D'Arthur*, 14.2.
8. At this point one may be induced to think of Christ and of his twelve disciples; truthfully, there are several references of this sort in the Christianized parts of the legend. However, this symbolism is supratraditional and much earlier than Christianity; the Christian figuration is merely a particular adaptation of it within a religious context.

Naturally, when the theme of the Siege Perilous appears, one must think about a state of involution of Arthur's kingdom or of decadence of his representatives, such that it necessitates a restoration. Ideally, this is the point at which the Knights of the Round Table go in search of the Grail and at which, in the corresponding literature, the adventures of the Grail and those of the knights of King Arthur are inextricably connected. Generally speaking, the kingdom of Arthur is identified with that of Locris or Logres, an ancient designation of England, like "Albania," or "White Island," which was regarded as the seat of the Grail. The knights of Arthur go in search of the Grail in order to restore the kingdom to its ancient splendor and to destroy the magic spells that, according to the *Mabinogion,* have stricken the land. The Grail is the symbol of that which has been lost and must be found again. A person must ensure that the Grail manifests again its virtues; often this person is also the knight who will sit at the Siege Perilous.

In relation to all this, the figure of King Arthur appears to be split in two. On the one hand, there is a suprahistorical King Arthur who symbolizes a function; on the other hand, there is a King Arthur who, as a historical representative of this function, is at the center of events that have a fatal outcome and that can be connected to the ancient tales concerning the destruction and the disappearance of the Tuatha dé Danaan and their descendants. At this point, without anticipating anything substantial, I will briefly refer to the epilogue of the ancient legend of Arthur, in which we find the recurrence of the symbolism of the woman.

Two characters attempt to steal Arthur's woman, Quennuwar (that is, Guinevere, a name that means "white spirit," confirming her symbolic character). The first of these characters is Maelvas, who takes her to his own town, Glastonbury, identified with the oceanic Glass City and with Avalon *(Glastonia, id est, urbs vitrea—etiam insula Avalloniae celebriter nominatur).* Consequently, the Glass Island is besieged; eventually a reconciliation is achieved. At this point a Christian element sneaks into the legend, since in this circumstance Arthur allegedly gives away the island as an estate to a Church representative, granting him immunity. In reality, this points again to an attempt, on the part of the Christian tradition, to replace the Celtic-Hyperborean tradition by appropriating all of its main themes. Glastonbury was one of the main centers of the spread of Christianity in England; to gain more prestige, it attempted to absorb in a Christianized form the previous Nordic-Celtic traditions, until it eventually claimed for itself the role of ancient Avalon. According to the main text on the subject, the *De antiquitate glastoniensis ecclesiae,* Glastonia, or Glastonbury, was originally called *ygnis gutrin, ygnis* in Breton meaning *insula* and *gutrin* meaning *vitrea;* with the arrival of the English people, it became *Glastiburi* (from *Glas* = *vitrum* and *buria* = *civitas*), or Glastiberia.[9] The story of Arthur's donation of the island to the Church is some kind of excuse for a "traditional succession" fabricated by Christian missionaries. Nor did the forgery end there: in reference to the above-mentioned tragic epilogue of the ancient legend, it was claimed that Arthur died and that his sepulcher was located in Glastonbury. Thus the ancient center was retained, this time with the new meaning of the center of missionary Christianity.

Second, while Arthur is attempting to realize his legendary world empire and to conquer even Rome in order to be crowned emperor therein, his nephew Modred, who remained at home, usurps the throne and takes possession of Arthur's woman, Guinevere. In the war that ensues the traitor is killed, but the best knights of the Round Table also die. Arthur himself is mortally wounded; he is taken to Avalon, that the health-restoring techniques of the women inhabiting that land (especially Morgande's) may heal him and allow him to resume his function.[10] But Arthur's wounds (especially the one produced by a poisoned spear, according to some writers) open up again every year while his faithful subjects at home vainly await his return. There is a tradition, however, according to which one day Arthur will return from Avalon to resume his reign: this is why the Britons, since then, never wanted to appoint another king.[11] In other forms of the legend—for instance, in the *Otia imperialia* by Gervasius of Tilbury—Arthur is portrayed lying in bed in a wonderful palace located on top of a mountain. According to another version, which is tendentiously Christian, Arthur has "died" and his body has been buried in that abbey of Glastonbury, which, as we have seen, was portrayed as Avalon itself.

All this may be referred to a crisis and to an interregnum that will be followed by the quest of the Grail. In the meantime we have identified another

---

9. Glastonbury was itself in prehistoric times a center of the primordial tradition, as is suggested by the presence of vestiges of some kind of huge star temple, defined by the track on the ground of gigantic effigies representing the constellations and arranged in a circle.

10. In *Le Morte D'Arthur* (21.7) we read: "Yet some men say in many parts of England that King Arthur is not dead, but had by the will of our Lord Jesu into another place; and men say that he shall come again, and he shall win by the holy cross. I will not say that it shall be so, but rather I will say, here in this world he changed his life. But many men say that there is written upon his tomb the verse 'Hic iacet Arthurus, Rex quondam Rexque futurus.'" In the same text, the wounded Arthur wants his sword returned to that mysterious arm holding it above the waters; this has the visible meaning of a restitution of his mandate.

11. There is a further interference with the previously mentioned motifs (more on which later), namely, that version of the saga according to which Arthur will return from Avalon at the time of a decisive battle against the Britons' enemies; this battle is supposed to be the "last battle" (see Natrovissus, "Le mythe arthurien et la legend de Merlin," *Ogam,* issues 6, 10, 13 [1950]).

fundamental theme in the Grail cycle: the wounded king who waits to be healed in an inaccessible and mysterious seat, so that he may "return" once again. We should recall, likewise, the other preexistent theme in the Celtic saga, namely, the kingdom stricken by devastation and by barrenness owing to the plebeian revolt or to the king's wound caused by a spear or a flaming sword.

10

The Imperial Saga and the Universal Ruler

When considered from the above-mentioned perspective, Arthur's saga appears to be one of the many forms of the general myth of the Emperor or invisible Universal Ruler and of his manifestations. It is a theme that dates back to the most ancient times and that bears a certain relation to the doctrine of the "cyclical manifestations" or *avatars,* namely, the manifestation, occurring at special times and in various forms, of a single principle, which during intermediate periods exists in an unmanifested state.[1] Thus every time a king displayed the traits of an incarnation of such a principle, the idea arose in the legend that he has not died but has withdrawn to an inaccessible seat whence one day he will manifest himself, or that he is asleep and will awaken one day. And just as the suprahistorical element in these cases overlaps the historical element, by turning a real figure into a symbolic one, likewise the opposite occurs; that is, the names of these real figures sometimes survive, yet designate something that transcends them.

The image of a regality in a state of sleep or apparent death, however, is akin to that of an altered, wounded, paralyzed regality, in regard not to its intangible principle but to its external and historical representatives. Hence the theme of the wounded, mutilated, or weakened king who continues to live in the inaccessible center, in which time and death are suspended.

---

1. Alain of Lille significantly compared Arthur's disappearance with those of Elijah and Enoch, prophets who never died and who will return one day.

Without repeating what I have discussed elsewhere, in order to give a general and universalized idea of the context being discussed I will mention some typical forms in which this symbolism was expressed in ancient times.

In the Hindu tradition we encounter the theme of Mahākāśyapa, who sleeps in a mountain but will awaken at the sound of shells at the time of the new manifestation of the principle that previously manifested itself in the form of Buddha. Such a period is also that of the coming of a Universal Ruler *(cakravartin)* by the name of Śaṃkha. Since *śaṃkha* means "shell," this verbal assimilation expresses the idea of the awakening from sleep of the new manifestation of the King of the World and of the same primordial tradition that the above-mentioned legend conceives to be enclosed (during the intermediate periods of crisis) in a shell. An analogous Iranian tradition refers to the hero Kereshaspa, who, having been wounded by an arrow while he was immersed in a state of slumber (here we find again the same symbolism), survives in a lethargic state through the centuries, being nurtured by the fravashi (like the wounded Arthur, who is tended by women expert in healing techniques); he will come back to life at the time of Saoshyant's advent and will fight on his side. Saoshyant is the lord of a future, triumphal kingdom of the God of Light and the slayer of the Arhimanic dark forces: the Jewish notion of a Messiah and the Christian notion of God's Kingdom, which many people believe to have greatly influenced the medieval imperial myth, are nothing but an echo of this ancient and pre-Christian Aryo-Iranian concept.

I must refer here as well to the doctrine of Kalki-avatāra in relation to the story of Paraśu-Rāma, one of the typical figurations of the heroic representative of the primordial Olympian-Hyperborean tradition. When the forefathers of the Aryan colonizers of India were still inhabiting a northern seat, this figure allegedly slew with his battle-axe some rebellious warriors and even his own mother guilty of some crime: these are symbols of the double overcoming that I previously (at the end of chapter 7) declared to characterize the "heroic" spirit—namely, the overcoming of a degraded virility and of a spirituality that shifted to a feminine-maternal tutelage according to an involution and a process of degradation (especially when we consider that its action occurred in a period between the Silver or Lunar Age (the so-called Tretā Yuga) and the Bronze or Titanic Age (the so-called Dvāpara Yuga).

Paraśu-Rāma never died, but withdrew to a mountain named Mahendra to live as an ascetic.[2] When the right time comes, in conformity with the cyclical laws, a new manifestation from above will occur (Kalki-avatāra) in the form of a sacred king who will triumph over the Dark Age. Kalki is symbolically

---

2. *Mahābhārata*, 1.2, 3.116–17, 12.49, 14.29.

thought to be born in Śambhala, one of the names that in the Hindu and Tibetan traditions designated the sacred Hyperborean center.[3] His spiritual teacher is Paraśu-Rāma, and after being initiated into the sacred sciences he receives the regal investiture. From Śiva he receives a white winged horse (which in the legend is so important that it came to be identified with Kalki himself), an omniscient parrot,[4] and a bright sword. Recall that Arthur is believed to return one day on a white horse and that this symbol also plays a famous part in the *Revelation of Saint John the Divine;* recall also Excalibur, the lost sword that Arthur will one day yield again and that from time to time emerges from the bottom of a lake.

Led by the parrot, Kalki wins the favors of the woman; he marries Padmā or Padmāvati, a king's daughter whom no man could ever have, since every time someone fell in love with her he was transformed by divine will into a woman—a symbol with a profound meaning. Kalki and his warriors cross on foot a wide sea, which magically turns into stone as they walk over it. Finally he reaches his birthplace, Śambhala, which he finds so transformed and wonderful as to mistake it for the dwelling place of Indra, the king of the gods and the god of the heroes. Śambhala is a symbol of the new manifestation of the forces of the primordial center; in it we find again the representatives of the solar and lunar dynasties, the kings Maru and Deva, who thanks to the power of their ascetic practices remained alive in the Himalayas through the ages of the world, up to the most recent Dark Age. Here the Himalayas are conceived as the region in which the primordial age lasts forever. Finally a last battle takes place, which is Kalki's struggle against the Dark Age, personified by the goddess Kālī and by the two chiefs of the demons, Koka and Vikoka;[5] this struggle is very

---

3. The theme of the symbolic birth of the restorator of the Hyperborean center is also found in the Iranian tradition and is sometimes applied to Zarathustra himself, who according to some was born in the Hyperborean region (Ariyana Vaego) or developed his religion there (see *Bundaesh, Vendidad,* 23/19). Concerning the birth place of Paraśu-Rāma, if Śambhala is a historical city near Delhi, it is also certain that it is always designated as the "Northern City," not only in India but in Tibet as well; in any event, in cases like these, every localization is merely symbolic.

4. In the knightly medieval allegories, the parrot symbolizes knighthood and fights against the clergy for the right over the woman.

5. Koka and Vikoka are visibly the equivalent of Gog and Magog. Kālī's mount is a donkey, an animal traditionally associated with demonic and antisolar forces and to the so-called children of the powerless revolt (see my *Revolt Against the Modern World,* 285–86). Moreover, the town named Vishasana, ruled by Kālī, in which the goddess seeks shelter from Kalki and which will eventually be put to the torch, is a gynecocratic center, ruled by women; this expresses the relation between the daemonism of the masses and the usurpation realized by a feminine form of spirituality.

hard, since these demons can resurrect each other and return to fight as soon as they hit the ground. In the end, however, Kalki will prevail.[6]

Further on, I will discuss in greater detail the symbolic elements found in this story, in case the reader has not understood their full meaning. Here I have simply wished to introduce some references in order to contextualize from an intertraditional perspective the imperial myth of the new manifestations of the *regnum* and to prevent the expressions that this myth had during the Middle Ages from being read separately from each other, especially in a unilateral dependence on Christian beliefs. After all, many people thought that the Roman world, in its imperial and pagan phase, signified the beginning of a new Golden Age, the king of which, Kronos, was believed to be living in a state of slumber in the Hyperborean region. During Augustus's reign, the Sibylline prophecies announced the advent of a "solar" king, a *rex a coelo* or *ex sole missus,* to which Horace seems to refer when he invokes the advent of Apollo, the Hyperborean god of the Golden Age. Virgil too seems to refer to this *rex* when he proclaims the imminent advent of a new Golden Age, of Apollo, and of heroes.[7] Thus Augustus conceived his symbolic "filiation" from Apollo; the phoenix, which is found in the figurations of Hadrian and of Antoninus, is in strict relation to this idea of a resurrection of the primordial age through the Roman Empire. The foreboding of Rome's connection with the suprahistorical and metaphysical principle of the *imperium* may, after all, be considered the basis of the very theory of Rome's persistence and *aeternitas,* provided one is aware of the previously mentioned process of transposition of that which is proper to this principle to one of its specific embodiments in history.

During the Byzantine age, the imperial myth received from Methodius a formulation that revived, in relation to the legend of Alexander the Great, some of the themes already considered. Here again, we find the theme of a king believed to have died, who awakens from his sleep to create a new Rome; after a short reign, the people of Gog and Magog, to whom Alexander had blocked the path, rise up again, and the "last battle" takes place.[8]

---

6. In the *Viṣṇu Purāṇa* (4.3) Kalki plays the same role of slayer of degenerated and desecrated warriors *(Mlecchas)* which was previously Paraśu-Rāma's.

7. *Eclogues,* 4.5–10

8. A New Testament apochryphal text, *The Apocalypse of Peter,* mentions a "son of the lion" (the lion symbolizing the empire), who will push back and defeat all the kings of the earth, having been empowered to do so by God himself; he is portrayed as "one who has awakened from slumber." Even during this period we notice a surfacing of the Hyperborean memory, considering that Lactantius (*Institutiones,* 6.16.3) claims that the mighty prince who will restore justice after Rome's fall will come from the "faraway lands of the North."

This same idea will be revived and amply developed during the Ghibelline Middle Ages. The awaited, hidden emperor, who never died and who withdrew to an invisible or inaccessible center, is here transformed into one of the major representatives of the Holy Roman Empire: Charlemagne, Frederick I, or Frederick II. The complementary theme of a devastated or sterile kingdom awaiting renewal finds its equivalent in the theme of the *Dry Tree*. The Dry Tree, associated with the seat of the Universal Ruler, will blossom again at the time of a new imperial manifestation and of the victory against the forces of the Dark Age that are represented, in conformity to the new biblical and Christian religion, by the people of Gog and Magog, who will launch their attack at the time of the advent of the Antichrist.

This Christian reading of these ancient symbols, however, does not preclude the image of Frederick II or of Arthur asleep on a mountain, or of the latter's knights leading a charge from the top of that mountain, from being associated with ancient pagan-Nordic views, namely, with Valhalla, the mountain dwelling of Odin, leader of the "divine heroes," or with the host of the souls of slain warriors, handpicked by women (the Valkyrie). This host can be described both as the *Wildes Heer* and as the mystical army that, led in battle by Odin, will fight the last battle against the "elemental beings."

This legend appears with countless variations during the golden age of Western chivalry and Ghibellinism. In the prophetic excitement caused by the coming of a "third Frederick," the legend finds a proper conclusion in the enigmatic formula of the emperor who is both alive and not alive: *Oculus eius morte claudet abscondita supervivetque, sonabit et in populis: vivit, non vivit, uno ex pullis pullisque pullorum superstite.* [His eye shuts and loses sight with death, but it survives and will sing among the people. He lives and does not live, one with the sprouting branches and yet standing apart from the new shoots.] "He lives and does not live": the Sibylline formula encompasses the mystery of medieval civilization at its twilight. The wounded king, the king asleep, the king who has died though he appears to be alive and who is alive though he appears to be dead, are equivalent or convergent themes that we will find again in the Grail cycle. These themes acquire a particular power of suggestion and liveliness at the final moment of the West's supreme effort to reconstruct itself according to a great civilization that was spiritually virile and traditionally imperial.

11

Frederick, Prester John, and the Tree of the Empire

An old Italian romance relates that "Prester John, a very noble Indian lord" sent an embassy to Emperor Frederick (presumably Frederick II), acknowledging him to be "the mirror of the world," in order to learn for himself if this Frederick was "wise in words and deeds." Thus three stones were sent by Prester John to Frederick; at the same time, the emperor was asked what he thought was the best thing in the whole wide world. "The emperor," the tale continues, "accepted the stones and did not inquire about their value"; as for the question, he answered that the "measure" was the best thing in the world. From this, Prester John deduced that "the emperor was wise in words but not in deeds because he did not inquire about the most excellent powers of the stones." He thought that with the passing of time these stones "would have lost their value, since the emperor did not know what their value was," and proceeded to have them returned. This happened essentially through one of them, endowed with the magic power of invisibility and said to "be worthier than your whole empire."

According to another legend, preserved by Oswald der Schreiber, Frederick II received from Prester John a fireproof garment made of salamander's skin, the water of perennial youth, and a ring with three stones, which gave its carrier the power to breathe underwater, to be invulnerable, and to become invisible. Prester John's stone was particularly mentioned in German writings of the fourteenth century, together with an allusion to the power that made one invisible.

These legends are very significant, especially if we consider that the kingdom of Prester John is only one among the several medieval figurations of the Supreme Center.[1] This center was supposed to be located in a mysterious and wonderful region in Central Asia, Mongolia, India, or even Ethiopia, the latter name having a vague and various meaning. When considering the attributes conferred on this kingdom, however, there are no doubts concerning its symbolic character. Prester John's gifts to Emperor Frederick constitute a sort of mandate of a superior character, which was offered to the German representative of the Holy Roman Empire that he might establish a real contact with the principle of the Universal Ruler. The water of perennial youth visibly has the meaning of immortality. The incombustible garment is connected to the power of the phoenix to remain unscathed and renew itself in fire. Invisibility is a potent symbol of the power to contact the invisible and supersensible dimension, and to be able to be transferred to it. The power of breathing underwater corresponds to the ability of not sinking or drowning and of walking on water (this reminds us of the Kalki-avatāra's crossing of the sea, of Arthur's sword held above the water, and so on); it signifies the ability to participate in a principle that is superior to the current of the world and to the stream of becoming. In other words, these are qualifications and powers of a strictly initiatory type.

Having said that, the Italian legend seems to suggest that Frederick was somewhat inadequate to receive this mandate. Frederick's limitation is a virtue of the chivalry and mere temporal government; the "measure" is the best thing in the world.[2] He does not inquire about the symbols of the powers offered to him by Prester John. Because of this unawareness of the highest mandate, his function, with the passing of time, was destined to decay, and thus his mandate was revoked by Prester John. This is a new version of the formula "he lives and yet does not live," referring to the emperor whose life is only apparent, or to the lethargic king; this time the version is intimately associated with a fundamental theme in the Grail cycle, namely, with the fault of not asking a question that would have had a restoring power.

I would like to add some details to the image of Prester John. The *Tractatus pulcherrimus* referred to him as "king of kings" *rex regum*. He combined spiritual authority with regal power and could say about himself: *Johannes presbyter, divina gratia Dominus dominatium omnium, quae sub caelo sunt ab ortu solis usque ad paradisum terrestrem.* [Prester John, by divine grace Lord of all the

---

1. R. Guénon, *Le Roi du monde,* chapter 2.
2. It is the same virtue that allegedly characterized the fundamental style of the Aryan or Indo-European races, according to some scholars who merely analyze their ethical-naturalistic aspect.

lords that exist under the sky from the east all the way to the earthly paradise (i.e., the Far West).][3] Yet essentially, "Prester John" is only a title and a name, which designates not a given individual but rather a function. Thus in Wolfram von Eschenbach and in the *Titurel* we find "Prester John" as a title; the Grail, as we will see, indicates from time to time the person who must become Prester John. Moreover, in the legend, "Prester John" designates one who keeps in check the people of Gog and Magog, who exercises a visible and invisible dominion (figuratively, dominion over both natural and invisible beings), and who defends the access of his kingdom with "lions" and "giants." In this kingdom is also found the "fountain of youth." This reign is often confused with the seat of the three magi, namely, with the city of Seuva, which was built on orders of the magi themselves on the Mount of Victory (Vaus or Victorialis).[4]

Moreover, here we find again the "polar" symbolism of the "revolving castle" in the image of the heavens and that of the place where there are stones of light and stones "that restore sight to the blind" and cause people to become invisible.[5] More particularly, Prester John owns a stone that has the power to resuscitate the phoenix or, in other versions, the eagle; this symbolism does not go unnoticed, since the eagle has always represented, and particularly at the

---

3. The dignity of a sacred king is often accompanied by biblical reminiscenses, by presenting Prester John as the son or nephew of King David, and sometimes as King David himself: *Davis regis Indorum, qui presbyter Johanne a vulgo appellature—De rege Davis filio regis Johannis.* [David, king of the Hindus, who is called by the people "Prester John"—the King (Prester John) descends from the son of King David.] We shall learn that David was closely related with the sword of the Grail's heroes and with the tests they have to undergo.

4. The Christian legend of the three magi is an attempt to claim for Christianity a traditional character in the superior sense that I give to the term, following Guénon's lead. One of the magi presented Jesus with gold and hailed him as king; the second presented him with incense and hailed him as priest; the third presented him with myrrh, namely, the balsam of immortality, and hailed him as prophet. By doing this the magi allegedly gave the acknowledgment due to a presumed representative of the three powers at the primordial undivided state. This acknowledgment is easily found in the characters who appear at the birthplace of Kalki to honor him.

5. In the text of Johannes With De Hese we read: *Et ibi est speciale palacium presbiteri Johannes et doctorum, ubi tenentur concilia. Et illud potest volvi ad motum rotae, et est testudinatum ad modum coeli, et sunt ibidem multi lapides preciosi, lucentes in nocte, ac si esset clara dies. Ibi sunt lapilli qui vocantur midriosi, quos frequenter ad partes nostras deportare solent Aquilae, per quos reinvenescunt et lumen recuperant. Si quis illum in digito portaverit, ei lumen non deficit, etsi si imminuitum restituitur et cum plus inspicitur, magis lumen aenitur. Legitimo carmine consacrato hominem reddit indivisibilem.* [There is a special palace in which Prester John and other wise men hold council. That palace can spin like a wheel and has an arched roof like the heavens; in it there are many precious stones that shine in the night as if they were bright days. These little stones, called "midriosi," eagles often take back to our lands, and through them the light is restored. If someone wears one of these little stones on his finger, for him the light does not fail. Even if it is weakened, it is restored, and the more the stone is inspected the greater the light shines forth.]

time of these legends, the imperial function, which in its "eternal" aspect was connected in ancient Rome to the symbol of the phoenix. According to some, the Persian king Xerxes, Alexander the Great, the Roman emperors, and finally Ogier of Denmark and Guerrinus all visited the kingdom of Prester John.[6] This is but a legendary figuration of the obscure sensation of contacts that the great historical dominators and the legendary heroes of the past are believed to have had with the Supreme Center, the place in which is found the stone that has the power of resurrecting the Eagle.

According to the legend, Alexander, as the crowning accomplishment of his conquests, after heading toward India on the path once traveled by Heracles and Dionysus, asked the deity the supreme pledge of victory. He reached not only the fountain of youth but also the two trees (symbolizing the masculine and feminine principles) of the sun and the moon, which announce him his destiny and his imperium.[7] In the legends of this cycle we find several mentions of the "Tree of the Center," of the "Solar Tree," of the tree that confers victory and the Empire, and of the "Tree of Seth."

On the basis of the vague and mysterious tales of many travelers, during the Middle Ages the image of the faraway magnificent empire of the Great Khan, emperor of the Tartars, contributed to the revival of the image of the King of the World—so much so that it was often confused with the kingdom of Prester John. Thus, especially in relation to the saga of the Great Khan, the motif of a mysterious tree was developed; he who could find it or hang his shield on it was granted victory and universal dominion. Here is a very characteristic text of Johannes von Hildesheim:

> Et in ipsa civitate in templi Tartarorum est arbora arida, de qua plurima narratur in universo mundo . . . ab antiquo in omnibus partibus Orientis, fuit consuetudinis, et est, quod si quis rex vel dominus vel populus tam potens efficitur, quod scutum vel clipeum suum potentur in illam arborem pendet tunc illi regi vel domino in omnibus et per omnia obediunt et intendunt.

> [In this civilization, in the temple of the Tartars, there is a dry tree, about which many things are said throughout the whole world. Since ancient

---

6. Kings such as Rumania's Manuel were taken by Prester John to live an immortal life in his palace.

7. This legend of Alexander, which develops some elements of Callistenes' and Julius Valerio's narratives, corresponds somewhat to another saga of the twelfth century, according to which Alexander, upon reaching the place "where the souls of the just await the day of the resurrection of the body," namely, earthly paradise, obtains a stone that is the facsimile of Frederick II's and Prester John's. Of this stone it is said: "If you learn to discern its nature and power, you will be free of every mundane ambition."

times, in every part of the East there was, and still is, this tradition: if someone wishes to become king or lord, he hangs his leather or metal shield on
this tree's branches until he is obeyed and acknowledged as such.]

This tree became a point of convergence of various meanings through verbal assonances. It is not the above-mentioned symbol of the Dry Tree; "Dry
Tree" in this context is one of the interpretations of the expression *arbre solque*,
which was translated as "solar tree" *(arbor solis)*, "solitary tree" *(arbre seul)* and
as "Seth's tree" *(arbor Seth)*. Marco Polo, talking about the Great Khan's country, wrote: "et il y a un grandisme plain ou est l'Arbre Solque, que nous ap-
pelons l'Arbre Sec." Moreover, *solque*, which has an Arab root, may signify
"wide, high, lasting"; an English manuscript says that this was not the Dry Tree,
but Seth's Tree, since Seth grew it out of a sprout taken from the Tree of
Knowledge, that is, from the central tree of the Garden of Eden.

The tree that bestows on him who finds it power and universal rule evokes
a tradition concerning the "primordial state" (alluded to by the Garden of
Eden). Moreover, both the pair of solar and lunar trees and the double aspect
of a tree of knowledge and tree of victory refer back to the synthesis of the two
powers that is inherent in that very state. This synthesis predates the ensuing
separation or the feminization of the spiritual dimension and the materialization of the virile dimension. The connection of the tree of the Empire with the
tree in the middle of the earthly paradise, as it emerges in these legends, is quite
natural, considering the above-mentioned relation that occurs between every
true manifestation of the Empire and the primordial state. The "dryness" of the
tree refers to a period of decadence that must be overcome. Such a meaning is
clear, for instance, in the legend according to which the tree will blossom again
at the encounter between Prester John and Emperor Frederick.

The image of Prester John's kingdom historically served as the foundation
of the obscure idea of an integration of the forces hidden behind the symbols
of chivalry, the Empire, and the Crusades. In a materialistic transposition, this
powerful and mysterious Oriental prince, who was not a Christian but a friend
of Christians, was invoked to help the Christian endeavor in the Holy Land
during its most difficult time, in order to grant a victorious end to the holy war.
After these hopes were disappointed; after the help in the form of a rescue,
naively conceived in military terms, failed to materialize; and after people failed
to recognize what was hidden behind the symbol of Prester John and of his
"help," his legend lived on as an element of various myths, such as the saga of
Ogier.

In Danish tradition, Ogier or Holger is a facsimile of the Ghibelline emperor
who never died: he is a national hero taken into the depths of a mountain or

locked in the cellars of Kronburg's castle, to appear again whenever his land will need a savior. It is in the cycle of Charlemagne that Ogier's saga displays the features most interesting to this book, since it significantly brings together the various themes that I have individuated so far. Ogier of Denmark appears as one of Charlemagne's twelve knights, who, after having been in conflict with that emperor, ends up assuming the traits both of a savior of the Christian world at a time of extreme danger and of a world conqueror. He extends his power over the entire East and, like Alexander, travels to the kingdom of Prester John, where he sees the two trees, the solar and the lunar; these two trees, we may recall, correspond respectively to the tree of the universal power of the Great Khan's legend and to the tree of the center associated with the primordial or "paradisiac" state.[8] Interestingly enough, here Prester John's kingdom is identified with Avalon, that is, with the center of the Hyperborean tradition;[9] moreover, a strict connection is established between the "balsam" of the two trees and Ogier's assuming the form of he "who always lives" and "who will return one day." In this regard, in Otto von Diemeringen's German translation of the travels of John Mandeville, we read: "Man saget auch in den selben Landen das Oggier by den selben boumen were und sich spyset mit dem balsam und do vo lebt er so lang, und meinen er lebe noch und solle har wider zu inen komen" [It is also said in those lands that Ogier was at those same trees and took the balsam, which caused him to live so long. They believe he is still alive and will return to them again].

After his conquest of the East, Ogier finally reaches Avalon, where he becomes the lover of the supernatural woman Morgan, who is Arthur's sister. Here he lives secluded from the world in a state of perennial youth. Christendom, however, finding itself in dire straits, needs him again. The archangel Michael visits Morgan, and by divine order Ogier appears again in the world and achieves victory. At this point a new characteristic theme appears, which will be found again in the Grail saga, especially in reference to the son of the Grail's king, namely, Lohengrin: the hero who has been sent forth from the Supreme Center must not reveal his name nor the place from which he comes. The function that he embodies and that is truly acting in him must

---

8. The two trees may be related with the solar and the lunar dynasties, the representatives of which, according to the legend of Kalki-avatāra, never died, but are awaiting Kalki's coming in order to manifest themselves again; this event is also found in another form in the medieval sagas, in the symbol of the blossoming of the Dry Tree.

9. This same relation is also found, indirectly and more obscurely, in the Italian and French sagas of Guerrino or Guérin, considering that in these sagas the kingdom of Prester John is regarded as a solar center of Apollo's cult (the hero finds in it Apollo's priests); Apollo, as we may recall, is the Hyperborean god of light.

remain unknown, nor should it be confused with his own person or even attributed to him. Since he disobeys this law and reveals where he "has been," the law of time overtakes Ogier again; he suddenly ages and is about to die. At the last minute Morgan appears again and takes him back to Avalon, where he will be confined until for the seventh time Christendom will need him again.[10]

If we take all of this in consideration, it is very significant that in Wolfram von Eschenbach, Prester John is thought of as a descendant of the Grail dynasty; that in the *Titurel*, Percival himself assumes the function of Prester John; and that it is in the latter's country that the Grail eventually ends up in order to indicate time after time who must absolve the function of Prester John. In the German version of Ogier's saga, Prester John and the Great Khan are presented as two companions of Ogier's, who create two powerful dynasties. These are various figurations of the inner unity of the same theme, variously expressed in the cycle of various legends that focus on this or that symbolic figure.

---

10. The number seven plays an important part in every tradition with reference to cyclical developments.

12

Dante: The Greyhound and the *Dux*

To conclude this series of comparisons, I will remark that Dante's view of the "Greyhound" and of the *Dux* should be referred to a similar order of ideas.

From an external point of view we cannot exclude that Dante chose the name "Greyhound" on the basis of the phonetic similarity between *cane* [Italian for "dog"] and Khan, the latter being the honorific title of the great leader of the Mongol Empire. As I have already indicated, at that time such an empire was sometimes confused with Prester John's, Alexander's, Ogier's—that is, with obscure representations of the Center of the World. At that time the Great Khan of the Tartars had not yet become the terror of Europe, but according to the descriptions of Marco Polo, of Haithon, of Mandeville, of Johannes de Plano Carpini, and so forth, he was conceived as the powerful emperor of a mysterious, faraway, and huge empire, or as a wise and happy monarch, a friend of Christianity though a "pagan" himself. The verbal assimilation that leads from "Khan" to "Greyhound" is found as early as the German translation of Mandeville's text: "Heisset der grosse hundt, den man gewonlich nennt Can ... der Can ist der oberst und machtigst Keiser den die sunne ubersccheinet" [The great dog is normally called Khan ... the Khan is the greatest and most powerful emperor on whom the sun shines]. Boccaccio himself, though he rejected it, mentioned an interpretation of Dante's *veltro* [Italian for "greyhound"] in relation to the Great Khan. After all, in the ancient German language, *huno* meant "lord," "dominator," and this word appears in names of ancient German families, such as Huniger.

This is not totally preposterous, and it is not as odd as it may first appear to be if we refer to what has been discussed to show that "the Great Khan" was a mere expression designating a function that was not contingent upon any particular person or historical kingdom. In Dante, this function is evoked; in him it becomes a symbol and simultaneously a political faith and a hope. This will take us very close to what was the spirit animating and generating the Grail cycle.

It is not necessary here to examine the symbolism of the *Divine Comedy* according to the various interpretations to which this work is susceptible. I will limit myself to pointing out that, generally speaking, Dante's otherworldly journey may be understood as the dramatized outline of a progressive purification and initiation. Moreover, such an adventure, as in the case of the Grail, has a close relationship with the Empire. We may recall that Dante got lost in a wild and dark forest, "the defile of which no living person had ever passed before."[1] His references to "a stretch of desert" and to the "death he is struggling with, by that river over which the sea is powerless,"[2] to his ascent of the "delightful mountain," and to "the top of the hill that I lost hope of reaching"[3] remind us of analogous situations incurred by the knights in search of the Grail. These knights have to cross powerful rivers and face mortal dangers in the "wild land" in order finally to climb the wild mountain Montsalvatsche, where the Castle of Joy is located.

In Dante's Beatrice, and especially in the general symbolism of the Love's Lieges (an organization to which Dante belonged), we find again the theme of the supernatural woman; and in love, which motivates her to help Dante from heaven, we can detect a similarity with the theme of predestination or election. This kind of otherworldly help is very much needed if the knights are to find the Grail and successfully undergo a series of adventures and symbolic duels; incidentally, the latter express the same process of purification that in Dante's work took the form of a journey through hell and purgatory. Also, Dante's purification process was less informed by the spirit of a heroic tradition than by the spirit of a theological-contemplative tradition.

Going back to the initial episode, the direct ascent to the mountain was barred to Dante by a lion and a she-wolf, who have a visible correspondence in the symbols of a harlot "secure, like a city set on a hill," and of the giant embracing her, mentioned in the second part of the poem. The most current

---

1. *The Divine Comedy,* trans. C. H. Sisson (Oxford: Oxford University Press, 1980), *Inferno,* 1. 26–27.
2. Ibid., 1.29, 107–8.
3. Ibid., 1.77, 54.

interpretation, according to which the she-wolf or the whore represents the Catholic Church, while the lion or the giant represents the House of France, seems to me to be the correct one; however, I think that those who from the historical and contingent reference (concerning the destruction of the Order of the Knights Templar) ascend to the corresponding principles go too far. The lion and the giant would then appear as the representations of the principle of a degraded, secular, and prevaricating royalty or of the unrestrained warrior principle, while the wolf and the whore allegedly are references to the corresponding involution or degradation of the principle of spiritual authority. Concerning this second point, however, Dante's view is limited by his Christian faith. When he accuses the Church (more or less like Luther, a few centuries later) he blames her for her corruption, namely, for her being mundane and for fostering political intrigues; he doesn't accuse her with the assumption that even if the Church had remained the pure and incorrupted representative of Christ's original teaching she would still have been an obstacle, since Christianity's essence would have amounted to a lunar spirituality (ascetic-contemplative at best), unfit to be the supreme reference point for an integral traditional restoration.

In any event, Dante predicts the advent of one who will put an end to the double usurpation; this figure is the Greyhound,[4] who, according to the previously mentioned convergence of symbols, is the same as the *Dux*, or "God's messenger," who "shall kill the whore together with the giant who shares her."[5] The general symbol is that of an avenger and of a restorating agent; it is the image of the Universal Ruler mentioned in Dante's *De monarchia,* and of a "restitution" based on the destruction of the two parallel principles of decadence, which is definitely reminiscent of the deeds of Paraśu-Rāma (see chapter 11): this is true regardless of the historical persons in whom Dante, following his hopes as a militant Ghibelline, thought he recognized that figure. To this we must add references pointing to other symbols that we have encountered in the legends of the Great Khan, of Prester John, of the Ogier, and of Alexander, and in the imperial cycle in general, especially the Dry Tree, its new blossoming, and the eagle.

In Dante the tree assumes the double meaning of Tree of Knowledge and "earthly paradise" (owing to its reference to Adam) and of Tree of the Empire (owing to its reference to the eagle); altogether it symbolizes the Empire, which justifies itself as a function of the primordial tradition. Dante's tree is first of all

---

4. Ibid., *Inferno* 1.101–5.
5. Ibid., *Purgatory* 33.43–45. In reference to the Greyhound, the defeat of the lion is secondary to the defeat of the she-wolf.

the *Arbre Sec* or *Durre Baum* of the imperial cycle; a "defoliated tree" and a "widowed bough." It is said that "whoever robs the tree or snaps off pieces offends against God by a blasphemous act; it was created holy for his use."[6] Concerning the development of Dante's view, leaving aside the elements that have a historical and contingent reference (the symbols of the various phases of the Church and of her relations with the Empire), note that Dante has the vision of the Flowering Tree immediately after enjoying the vision of the uncovered face of the supernatural woman, whom he significantly compares to the "splendor of the live eternal light."[7]

Moreover, while the vision of the Flowering Tree leads to the prophecy of the coming of the *Dux*, that is, of a new avenging manifestation of the Universal Ruler, at the same time the image of the primordial state, or of the earthly paradise, emerges, and it is said: "For a little while you shall dwell in these woods; and with me shall eternally be a citizen of that Rome of which Christ himself is a Roman."[8] This is, in other words, the effective participation in the metaphysical *regnum*, for which the Roman symbol is evoked, so that it may be superimposed over Christianity itself (the "Romanness" of Christ).

Finally, this vision is followed by Dante's regeneration through the water of remembering. This change opens to him the heavenly path, a path that leads toward purely metaphysical states of existence, a development to which the symbolism of blossoming (already applied to the "defoliated tree") is applied: "I came back from that most sacred of streams made afresh, as new trees are renewed with their new foliage, and so was I clear and ready to go up to the stars."[9]

In Dante, the spiritual itinerary represented by the symbolism of the *Divine Comedy* ends up having a contemplative outlet, in conformity to Dante's dualism, according to which the Empire, with its inherent *vita activa* and in its very spirituality, represents a mere preparation for the *vita contemplativa*. Something like this will be seen in some forms of the Grail cycle, namely, in its latest versions, which, like the Italian legend of Guerrino, conclude with the main character's withdrawal to ascetic life. Yet in the Grail cycle, this appears in some kind of pessimistic conclusion, the main forms of which witness a different spirit, a higher tension, a more unconditioned attitude, which is a sign of the influence of a more original tradition than that by which Dante's thought was influenced.

Having gathered almost all the necessary references, let us proceed to consider the mystery of the Grail.

---

6. Ibid., *Purgatory* 32.38, 50, 33.58–60.
7. Ibid., 33.133–40.
8. Ibid., 32.100–103.
9. Ibid., 33.142–45.

PART THREE

The Cycle of
the Grail

13

The Sources of the Grail

It has been correctly pointed out that from a historical point of view the most characteristic texts concerning the Grail suggest the existence of a hidden current that briefly surfaced at one particular point in time and then disappeared, almost as if in response to an obstacle or to a specific danger.[1] In fact, these texts crop up during a short time frame; apparently, none of them predates the last quarter of the twelfth century and none is later than the first quarter of the thirteenth century. This period also corresponds to the apogee of the medieval tradition, to the golden era of the Ghibelline movement, of knighthood, of the Crusades, and of the Knights Templar, and also of the synthesis attempted by Thomism, on the foundation of a pre-Christian and non-Christian legacy that was also assumed by the Arab civilization (alongside an analogous blooming of a knightly and mystical spirit), namely, Aristotelianism.

The sudden popularity of the Grail romances was followed by a similarly strange oblivion. During the early years of the thirteenth century, almost as if obeying a password, Europe ceased writing about the Grail. A new revival occurred after a sensible interval, during the fourteenth and fifteenth centuries, in altered and often stereotypical forms, which underwent a rapid decadence. The period of syncope of the first tradition of the Grail coincides with that of the greatest effort on the part of the Church to repress trends that she considered "heretical." The revival occurred some time after the destruction of the Order of the Knights Templar, which was followed, especially in Italy and in France and partially in England, by the organization in a more secret form of the

---

1. J. L. Weston, *The Quest of the Holy Grail* (London, 1913).

representatives of similar influences. These influences were not without relation to the same tradition of the Grail, and they perpetuated some of its aspects up to relatively recent times.

The main sources of the Grail legend that I will use in my exposition are given here in an approximately chronological order:

1. The cycle of Robert de Borron, which includes:
   a. *Joseph of Arimathea*
   b. *Merlin*
   c. *Perlesvax* (i.e., Percival)
2. Chrétien de Troyes's *Conte du Graal* (Story of the Grail), together with:
   a. A first continuation by Gautier de Doulens
   b. A second continuation by Manessier
   c. An interpolation by Gerbert de Monstreuil
3. The so-called *Grand Saint Graal*
4. The *Perceval li Gallois*, written in prose
5. The *Queste del Saint Graal*, which is the penultimate part of the work Lancelot, written in prose
6. Wolfram von Eschenbach's *Parzifal*, which can be associated with Albert von Scharffenberg's *Titurel* and *Wartburgkrieg*
7. Malory's *Le Morte D'Arthur*
8. Heinrich von dem Turlin's *Diu Crone*

These are the primary literary sources of the Grail legend. Let us now briefly examine the inner sources of the tradition, according to some indications supplied by these texts.

Let us note, first of all, the theme of *Avalon*. In *Perceval li Gallois* it is explicitly said that the Latin book containing the story of the Grail was found on the island of Avalon, in a "sacred house atop adventurous lands" in which "Arthur and Guinevere are buried too." In one part of Robert de Borron's text, which is one of the oldest of the cycle, Avalon is described as a country located in the Far West, to which some of the knights of Joseph of Arimathea's host (such as Petrus and Alain) travel, obeying a divine injunction. It is written that Petrus must go "where his heart tells him to," namely, to "Avalon's valleys," and remain there until the advent of one who will know how to read a divine letter and who will announce the power of the Grail. We already know that the Western Avalon is one and the same with the "White Island." According to Gautier, Joseph of Arimathea himself and the Grail travel to the "White Island," which owing to a transposition is conceived as a part of England; there, being attacked by enemies, he and his troops are "nourished" by the Grail itself, which gives to them whatever they wish. After all, according to others, Joseph of Arimathea himself is buried in the *insula Avallonis,* which is confused with Glastonbury for reasons I have already explained.[2] This island is a facsimile of the island to which many heroes of the Grail are taken; their adventures and most significant trials take place there. Moreover, this island takes up again the ancient Nordic-Celtic "polar" symbol of the primordial center whenever it is portrayed in the form of a rotating island.

In reality, it is this center that is being discussed in this context. This is the "promised land" of the Grail, conceived either as the place where the sources of the Grail are to be found, or as the land to which the Grail is taken, or as the place in which it is sought. The different travels attributed to it have a symbolic character and the meaning of a contact with forces or centers of the primordial tradition; this can be seen, for instance, in the fact that in the *Grand Saint Graal,* England, which is conceived as the Grail's "promised land," is reached by Joseph of Arimathea and his knights through supernatural means. They have to face the challenge of crossing the waters in a supernatural way; the pure and the elect will pass this test, while those who lack faith will drown. I have already discussed the meaning of this symbolism.

The tradition related by Wolfram von Eschenbach leads to Avalon: in that tradition the founder of the dynasty of the future king of the Grail is Mazadan, who is led to Feimurgan by a supernatural woman named Ter-de-la-Schoye. Through a visible exchange of names, here we recognize the Morgan of the Arthurian cycle, who lives in the Land of Joy, one of the names given to the Western Island of the Celtic tradition, which sometimes ends up being applied to the kingdom of the Grail itself. The theme of a primordial tradition connected with Avalon, which needs to be resurrected in a heroic way, plays an important part in the formulation of the legend by Robert de Borron: Percival eventually learns that the Rich Fisherman (a title that is often applied to Joseph of Arimathea himself) is his father; by divine order he "has traveled to the far Western lands, where the sun sets," and there he has been kept alive until Alain's son will perform deeds that will prove him to be the best knight in the world.

The references to Joseph of Arimathea constitute the Christian, though not the Catholic and apostolic, component of the legend. Joseph is portrayed as a pagan "noble knight" who landed in Palestine; because of his seven years of faithful service as a warrior under Pontius Pilate, he obtained from the latter

---

2. In many other tales, Joseph of Arimathea continues to remain as a sort of presence in the castle in which the adventures of the predestined heroes unfold; sometimes he assumes himself the traits of the wounded king.

Jesus' body. Joseph was then believed to have filled a cup, which, according to some texts, was the Grail itself, with the blood flowing from the Nazarene's side. Having been imprisoned "in a house like a hollow pillar in the middle of a swamp," Joseph has an apparition of the Lord, who gives him the sacred cup; the cup gives him life and light until he is finally released, according to some texts, forty years later.[3] All these events took place while Joseph was still a pagan. Then Joseph was baptized and anointed by the Lord as the first Christian bishop with an oil that is used in both a regal and a priestly consecration. In fact, later on, this oil will consecrate the entire dynasty of Britain's kings, up to Uther Pendragon, King Arthur's father. Before traveling to England (a land that acquired the meaning of "White Island") in the miraculous way previously mentioned, Joseph and his peers undergo various symbolic adventures (more on which later) in which the theme of the island appears again. In *Perceval li Gallois* we find the important reference that already prior to Jesus' death, Joseph had visited the island to which Percival himself will travel: moreover, Robert de Borron mentions the mysterious ancestors of Joseph, whom one must serve as a condition for being admitted into the order. This order allegedly existed prior to Jesus' time and to the advent of Christianity.

If one wanted to give a sui generis historical content to these aspects of the saga, it may be formulated along the following lines: some Christian elements find their way into the Nordic-Celtic area and reawaken the tradition of Avalon. According to these traditions, Britannia, which is associated with memories of the White Island, and later on with King Arthur's kingdom, is the Grail's promised land, or the place where the Grail is eminently manifested. Moreover, an English center (Glastonbury and even Salisbury), again confused with Avalon or with equivalent symbolic places, preserves the "sources" of the Grail's story. The reference according to which the Grail fed the knights who traveled to Avalon and who fell into a state of indigence may allude to a period of decadence of the visible forms of the ancient Nordic tradition. This tradition, as a Grail tradition, was destined to awaken to new life as a result of the contact with the Christian religion, which had reached northern Europe. This may be reconnected with the theme of the spells from which the Grail was supposed to liberate England and, according to some, the entire world; with the theme of Arthur's court, which had undergone a period of decadence because of the Dolorous Stroke; and also with the need on the part of the Knights of the Round Table to participate in an adventure unknown to the most ancient texts of the Nordic-Celtic tradition, namely, the quest for the Grail.

---

3. The numbers seven and forty have an esoteric character and have also been referred to inner processes of development and purification.

In its Christianized form, this quest is also unknown to the early texts of orthodox Christianity; moreover, the tradition of the Grail has ostensibly little in common with the apostolic-Roman tradition. Concerning the second point, we have already seen that the forefather of the Grail's regality, Joseph of Arimathea, receives the investiture directly from Christ. The former's dynasty, which is essentially regal, does not have a relation with the Church of Rome, but rather leads directly to the Nordic kingdom of King Arthur. In one of its ramifications, according to Wolfram von Eschenbach, that kingdom converges into the symbolic kingdom of Prester John, who is "king of kings." Concerning the first point, while the ecclesiastical literature already knew the figure of Joseph of Arimathea and his imprisonment,[4] it was silent about the Grail; nor do we find ancient Briton texts (with one exception, which seems to be a case of interpolation) in which Joseph appears as a Christian missionary to England. The chronicler Helinand, who first related the story of the Grail and mentioned the figure of Joseph of Arimathea, wrote:

> Gradalis autem vel gradale dicitur Gallice scutella lata et aliquantulum profunda in qua preciosae dapes, cum suo jure divitibus solent apponi, et dicitur nomine Graal . . . . Hanc historiam latine scriptam invenire non potui, sed tantum Gallice scripta habentur a quibusdam proceribus, nec facile, ut aiunt, tota inveniri potest.

> [Daylight, however, was called by the Galls a wide plate that holds a holy feast. At this feast you are to be served good fortune, and it is called by the name of Grail. . . .This is the history as it is written in Latin (that is, in the writings of the church). It was not discovered, but was held in all the Gallic scripts by certain princes.]

In 1260 Jakob van Maerlant declared the story of the Grail to be a fake, on the basis that up to that time the Church knew nothing about it, or better, did not want to hear about it.[5]

---

4. See *Gesta Pilati* 12, 14.

5. E. Wechssler in his *Die Sage vom heiligen Gral in ihrer Entwicklung* (Halle, 1898) wrote: "Despite its markedly religious character, the legend of the Grail was never acknowledged by the Church and the clergy. No ecclesiastical writer talks about the Grail. In the very abundant ecclesiastical literature that we have today, nowhere do we find mention of the Grail, with the exception of the chronicler Helinand. Yet the ecclesiastical authors could not but have known the wonderful story of the symbol of the faith. It is likely that they built around the legend a conspiracy of silence."

J. Marx in his *Legende arthurienne* remarks: "The Church never claimed for herself the adventure of the Grail. It seems that in it she sensed something predating her, something primordial and mysterious."

If in some texts Joseph's cup is identified with the cup used during the Last Supper, we do not find references to such an association in the Christian tradition. On the other hand, even when in later and more Christianized texts the Grail assumes an analogous function to that played by the eucharistic cup in the mystery of the Mass, Robert de Borron's aversion to talk about the nature of the Grail and the mention of secret words that no one is supposed to repeat and that were allegedly entrusted only to Joseph of Arimathea suggest that this is a different mystery from that celebrated in the Catholic rite. In any event, this rite seems to have been officiated by people other than regular clergy, with a symbolism and an esotericism totally foreign to Christianity. And when some texts identify the Grail as Jesus' cup at the Last Supper and the spear as the weapon that pierced Jesus' side at his crucifixion, those who follow the inner logic and grasp the overall picture cannot but wonder if here is something more than images of the predominant religious conscience, borrowed as instruments for the expression of a different content. The facts that such a content originates from traditions extraneous to Christianity and that it reflects a climate that can hardly be reduced to Christian religiosity can be seen rather clearly by those who consider the legends of the Grail in their entirety.

Wolfram von Eschenbach attributes the sources of his story to a certain "Kyot the Provençal," who in turn allegedly found the legends of Percival and the Grail in pagan texts he decoded thanks to his knowledge of magical characters. In very ancient times, Flegatanis, of Solomon's stock, had written the story of the Grail found in these texts on the basis of his knowledge of astrology, having read the name of the Grail in the stars. "By examining the stars he discovered deep secrets about which he talked only with shivers and great fear."

Thus the story of the Grail generally presents supernatural, secret, and initiatory characters. Robert de Borron attributes its true sources to a "great book" that he was never able to read, "in which the great mysteries of the so-called Grail are inscribed"; in the *Perceval li Gallois* it is also written: "This story must be held in high esteem and never told to people who would not understand it, since evil men will never understand a good thing when they see one." Robert de Borron adds: "The great story of the Grail was never started by a mortal man" *(unque retreite este n'avoit—la grant estoire dou Graal—par nul homme qui fust mortal)*. According to him, the metamorphoses that occur in the vision of the Grail cannot be expressed, "since the secrets of the sacrament must be revealed only to him whom God has given the grace of being worthy of it." Vauchier says that it is dangerous to talk about the Grail other than at the right time and place, and that "one cannot talk about the mystery of the Grail without trembling and changing complexion."[6] The so-called *Elucidation* that

---

6. Weston, *Holy Grail*, 8–10.

precedes the text of Chrétien de Troyes mentions a certain Master Blihis, who was in charge of a tradition that must remain secret: "Car, se Maistre Blihis ne ment, nus ne doit dire le secree."

The most recent and Christianized text of the first period, the *Grand Saint Graal*, substituted the original secret and mysterious character surrounding the Grail with a more mystical one: the book of the Grail was written by Christ himself and transmitted to the author during a vision. One can approach it only after an ascetic and purifying preparation. When reading it, apparitions are experienced, and one's spirit is taken by angels to contemplate directly the mystery of the Trinity. To open the casket that contains the Grail means to enter into direct contact with Christ himself. However, even in the case of the blinding or combustion that this text says will plague those who want to get too close to the Grail, we find the permanence of the ancient and more original meaning of a *mysterium tremendum* that has little in common with the Christian pathos.

14

The Virtues of the Grail

In the various texts, the Grail is essentially portrayed under three forms:

1. As an immaterial, self-moving object, of an indefinite and enigmatic nature ("it was not made of wood, nor of some metal, nor of stone, horn, or bone").
2. As a stone—a "heavenly stone" and a "stone of light."
3. As a cup, bowl or tray, often of gold and sometimes adorned with precious stones. Both in this form and in the previous one, we almost always find women carrying the Grail (another element totally extraneous to any Christian ritual, since no priests appear in it).

A mixed form is that of a cup carved out of a stone (sometimes of an emerald). The Grail is sometimes qualified as "holy," sometimes as "rich"; "this is the richest thing that any man hath living."[1] This text, like many others of the same period, uses the expression "Sangreal," which is susceptible to three interpretations: Holy Grail, Royal Blood, and Regal Blood.

The main virtues of the Grail may be summed up as follows:

1. Virtue of Light, that is, an enlightening virtue. The Grail radiates a supernatural light. In the words of Chrétien de Troyes: "Une si grans clartes i vint— que si pierdirent les candoiles—los clarte, com font les estoiles—quand si solau

---

1. *Le Morte D'Arthur,* 11.2.

64

lieve ou la lune." ["Such a great brightness shone forth that the light of the candles was lost in it just as that of the stars is dimmed by the rising sun or moon."] Robert de Borron describes the appearance of the Grail in the prison of Joseph of Arimathea as that of a great light, adding that "as soon as Joseph saw the bowl, he was entirely filled with the Holy Spirit." In Vaucher, the Fisher King, who carries the Grail with him at night, lights his path with it. Talking about its appearance to Joseph, the *Grand Saint Graal* says that out of it "came such a light, as if from a thousand candles" and mentions being taken beyond time: the forty-two years that Joseph spent in jail seemed to him as three days. In Gautier, Percival follows a maiden into a dark forest despite her protestations; immediately a great light appears, the maiden disappears, and a great storm breaks out. The following day Percival learns that the light came from the Grail, as it was carried about the forest by the Fisher King.

In Wolfram the Grail is a "stone of light": "The Grail is a perfect fulfillment of every desire and true paradise; it is a stone of light before which any human splendor pales." In the *Queste du Graal*, Galahad, upon seeing the Grail, shivers and says: "Now I can clearly see what a tongue could never express and the heart fail to realize. Here I see the beginning of all great deeds and the reason behind courageous feats; behold, the wonder of wonders." In *Le Morte D'Arthur* the manifestation of the Grail is accompanied by the sound of thunder and by a "ray of sun seven times brighter than the light of day"; at that time "they were all enlightened by the grace of the Holy Spirit." In that occasion the Grail appears in an enigmatic form, and "there was none might see it, nor who bare it," "and every knight had such meats and drinks as he loved best in this world."[2]

2. This corresponds to the second virtue of the Grail. Besides being light and an enlightening supernatural power, it gives nourishment and "life." In Wolfram, all the Knights Templar receive nourishment from the Grail, which is conceived as a "stone" *(lapsit exillis)*: "sie lebent von einem steine." When it is taken to the dining table, or at its magical appearance, every knight receives what he wishes for the most. In this context, mention of various physical foods that correspond to different tastes is the materialization of the superior meaning of the various effects of the same gift of "life" according to the will, the vocation, the nature, or the qualifications of those who receive it. This nourishment eventually destroys every material craving; thus in the *Perceval li Gallois*, in virtue of the fragrance emanating from the Grail, the guests even forget to eat and Gawain, during an ecstatic trance, achieves the vision of angels.

---

2. Ibid., 13.7.

In the *Grand Saint Graal* the Grail reproduces the miracle of the multiplication of the loaves of bread. In the *Queste du Graal,* in which its apparition is preceded by "a light as bright as the sun," the Grail moves around in a magical fashion; after giving to each his own food, it disappears, just as in the previously mentioned account of *Le Morte D'Arthur.* In particular, the strong and the heroes love the food supplied by the Grail; Robert de Borron gives the following etymology: "It is called Grail because the brave like it *(agree as prodes homes).*" We have already seen that Joseph of Arimathea himself, together with his knights, received not only light but also life (nourishment) from the Grail during the entire forty years of his imprisonment, which was inflicted on him by King Crudel.

3. The Grail's gift of life manifests itself even in its power of healing mortal wounds and of supernaturally renewing and prolonging life. In Manessier, as Percival and Ector fight each other, they are both mortally wounded and await their death, when at midnight, the Grail, carried by an angel with "imperial" looks, makes his appearance and heals both of them instantaneously and entirely;[3] the same episode is also found in *Le Morte D'Arthur.* In the *Queste du Graal* mention is made of a suffering knight lying in a coffin, who drags himself to the Grail and by touching it feels rejuvenated, falling out of pain into a deep sleep. In this case we have also the interference of a further motive, namely, that of the kings who, as they await a predestined avenger or restorer, are artificially kept alive by the Grail.

Wolfram, by relating that in virtue of the Grail "the phoenix is consumed and turned into ashes, but it is also transformed, appearing again in all its splendor, more beautiful than ever," clearly establishes a relationship between the Grail's gift of life and the regeneration of which the phoenix was traditionally a symbol. Wolfram says that "this stone [i.e., the Grail] infuses in man such a vigor that his flesh and bones are instantly rejuvenated." Thus the Grail not only enlightens but also renews; yet it refuses its symbolic nourishment or gift of life to those who are guilty of serious offenses, namely, to cowards and to liars.

4. The Grail induces a power of victory and domination. Those who use it *n'en court de bataille venchu.* According to Robert de Borron, all those who get a glimpse of it, besides rejoicing with eternal joy, will never be deprived of their right or defeated in battle. In the *Lorengel* the Grail appears as a "stone of victory" with which Percival pushes back Attila and his hordes of Huns at the mo-

---

3. To a careful reader, the fact that according to this text the vision occurs at midnight is not devoid of an esoteric meaning (i.e., the midnight sun).

ment in which they are about to overcome Christianity. Wolfram says about him who passes the test of the Grail: "At this point there is no one in the whole wide world who can excel you in nobility and honor. You are the lord of all creatures. Supreme power will be given unto you." The aspect of the Grail according to which it bestows the power of victory will be emphasized in relation to the "sword of the Grail." What is already foreshadowed in this text by Wolfram, however, is the highest essence of the Grail, or the relation it has with a transcendent regality, with the principle of the Universal Ruler. Moreover, we will see that the Grail itself, like an oracle, designates the knights who are called to become kings in various lands. Some have rightly compared the Grail to the object that symbolizes and embodies the heavenly power of regality according to the Iranian tradition (the *hvareno*) and that assumes the various aspects of magical stone, stone of kingship and victory, or cup: these are all aspects that are also found in the Grail.

5. If, on the one hand, the Grail has a vivifying virtue, on the other hand it has a dreadful and destroying virtue. The Grail blinds, incinerates, and may even act as a sort of vortex. Nescien recognizes in the Grail the object of his desires when he is still a young knight, but as soon as he opens its case, he trembles and loses his sight and control over his own body. The *Queste du Graal* adds that Mordrain, with a similar act, had attempted to contemplate what no tongue can express. His attempt unleashes a supernatural wind that blinds him; he is condemned to remain alive until the arrival of the hero who will realize the mystery of the Grail and heal him. The theme is not new. Dante himself, while contemplating the empyrean, loses his sight, even though he gains it back and improved at a later time.[4] The deeds of the Persian hero Rostan aim at restoring the sight and the freedom of a king whose Promethean inclination is evident by the latter's attempt to reach heaven with the help of eagles.

Other examples may be easily adduced. According to Gerbert's story, Mordrain, who has built an altar for the Grail, finds its access barred by an angel with a fiery sword (in an analogous episode in the Bible, the entrance to the primordial location is guarded by an angel; compare also the wall of fire that in some texts surrounds the island, etc.). The angel, as a punishment for his attempt, tells him that he will not be able to die and that his wounds will remain open until the coming of the knight who "will ask the proper question." In the *Diu Crone,* to pursue the Grail is said to be a "mortally dangerous thing." And yet, in *Le Morte D'Arthur,* it is to the same close view of the Grail that

---

4. *Divine Comedy, Paradise,* 30.

caused Mordrain's and Nescien's downfall that Gawain aspires; he leaves in quest of adventures, vowing not to return until he finds the Grail.[5]

Moreover, the dangerous nature of the Grail can be seen in relation to the theme of the Siege Perilous and to the test it constitutes for those who want to assume the role of the "awaited hero" and supreme leader of the Knights of the Round Table. This is the "empty chair" or "thirteenth chair" or "polar seat" that I have previously discussed; every time a nonchosen or unworthy person takes this seat, either an abyss opens up underneath him or he is stricken by a thunderbolt. Thus when the disciple Moses sits at the table of Joseph of Arimathea (which is not to be confused with the Round Table), he is grabbed by seven fiery hands and destroyed "just as a fire incinerates a piece of wood."[6] Later on, the text describes this event in the following terms: half of the fire that consumes Moses is put out, but the other half will keep on burning until Galahad comes to bring the adventure of the Grail to a successful end. A variation is the "test of the vessel"; the only ones who enjoy the ecstasy of the Grail are those who, sitting at the table of Joseph of Arimathea, are not stained with any offense. On this occasion, Moses, after taking a seat analogous to the Siege Perilous, is swallowed up into an abyss that opens underneath his feet; according to a Christian explanation, this happens because of his lack of faith, he being a false disciple.

We also encounter another theme, according to which the only person who can successfully seek the Grail is the one who will sit in the golden seat represented by the supernatural woman. Six knights who have attempted to sit in it have suddenly fallen into an abyss; when Percival sits in it, a terrible thunder resounds and the earth opens up, yet he remains sitting calmly at his place. Impassible, clothed in his calm dignity and in the purity of his strength, nothing can overcome him. In Robert de Borron, after this test, another series of adventures must be undertaken by Percival and all the Knights of the Round Table; these adventures eventually lead to the definite conquest of the Grail. The *Queste du Graal* and *Le Morte D'Arthur* present the theme in an even more direct form: the dangerous seat is successfully occupied only by he who has passed the "test of the sword," which consists in drawing a sword out of a stone, thereby demonstrating himself to be the best among all knights. After this test (the meaning of which I have already explained) is successfully completed, the

---

5. *Le Morte D'Arthur,* 3.6.
6. Here we find again the traditional number seven, which reminds us of the particular effects of an awakened force (kuṇḍalinī) on seven centers of life, mentioned in esoteric teachings. See my *Yoga of Power.*

Grail appears at Arthur's court; a light brighter than the sun shines forth and the Grail magically appears, emanating its fragrance and giving to each knight his own nourishment.[7]

This dangerous aspect of the Grail should be considered as a limit case of what the Grail can do, depending on the nature of those who come in contact with it. The power of the Grail destroys all those who try to hold it without having the proper qualifications, or who attempt to usurp it by repeating the Titanic, Luciferian, or Promethean deed. A significant expression is found, in this regard, in Wolfram, when he says figuratively that to those who are guilty, the Grail is so heavy that they could not hold it up even if they all tried to at the same time. What causes the power of life to act as a destructive force (e.g., the fire that consumes Moses) is the very excess that the transcendent power constitutes for a conditioned being who is tied to his own limitations.

A variation of this meaning is found in *Le Morte D'Arthur* in the following form: When perceiving the great brightness caused by the Grail, "as if all the torches of the world were gathered in that hall," Lancelot steps forward. A voice warns him not to enter, but to run away; otherwise he will regret it. He disobeys and goes in anyway. When a fire strikes him in the face, he falls to the ground and cannot get up, having lost control of his limbs. To his peers, who think he has died, an old man says, "In God's name, he is not dead, but has more life in him than the strongest among you." Lancelot remains in this state of apparent death for twenty-four days, and then the first words he utters are: "Why have you awakened me? For I was more at ease than I am now." This experience is attributed to his having seen the Sangreal like no one else before.[8] Obviously this was an initiatory state, or a state in which the participation in the power of the Grail is made possible by the suspension of the waking consciousness and of the individual limitation relative to it. This avoids the negative, destructive, and overpowering effect that the experience of the contact has in those who are not able to shift to higher forms of consciousness or other states of being.

6. The double virtue of the Grail is somewhat related to the meaning that the dyad cup-lance has, in general, in the concordant traditions of various people, and even outside any relation with Christian symbolism. The cup corresponds to the feminine, vivifying, and enlightening aspect, and the lance to the virile, fiery, or regal (i.e., the scepter) aspect of the same principle. Or better, the former corresponds to the lunar tree and the latter to the solar tree. Again, the former corresponds to the holy wisdom and the latter to the dimension of

7. *Le Morte D'Arthur*, 13.4–6.
8. *Le Morte D'Arthur*, 17.15.

fire and denomination of the same principle. In the same context, however, we could insert the ambivalence of the lance itself, which is taken from the Irish tradition and which on the one hand inflicts the *coup douloureux* by causing a destruction, while on the other hand it has the power to heal.

This brief overview of the virtues attributed to the Grail sheds light on the subjective side of its quest. This quest is essentially an inner event. As an experience it does not amount to some mere mystical ecstasy: it is rather a primordial power that is positively evoked. Those who know how to assume it are qualified for the other tasks mentioned in the legend, which indeed constitute its central nucleus.

I wish now to discuss those episodes in which the Grail appears as a stone, and also to emphasize the particular meaning that emerges in the tradition portraying the Grail as a stone fallen from heaven and particularly as a "Luciferian" stone.

Wolfram von Eschenbach connects to the Grail the enigmatic term *lapsit exillis*. This term has been interpreted by scholars in various ways: *lapis erilis,* or "Lord's stone" (San Marte); *lapis elixir,* in reference to the alchemical elixir of regeneration (Palgen); *lapis betillis* or *betillus* (Hagen), which may be a reference to *baitulos,* the stone fallen from the sky according to Greek mythology; *lapis ex coelis* or *de coelis,* a "heavenly stone" (Martin); and finally, *lapis exiliis,* or "stone of the exile." In reality, no matter how accurate these conjectural interpretations are from a purely etymological point of view, the Grail is susceptible to all of these meanings, according to its various aspects.

The Grail is first of all a *lapis ex coelis* because, according to Wolfram, it was originally brought down to earth by a host of angels. In this tradition, also referred to in the *Titurel* by Albrecht von Scharffenberg, the Grail appears as a stone, a jasper or silica, and is connected to the symbol of the phoenix. According to Wolfram, these were the angels who were condemned to descend to earth for having remained neutral when Lucifer rebelled against God. The Grail was guarded by them and did not lose its qualities; later on it was entrusted to a stock of knights, who were appointed from above. This tradition was modified in the *Wartburgkrieg* in the following way: a stone fell off Lucifer's crown when the latter was stricken by the archangel Michael. This is the stone of the elect, which fell from heaven to earth, which Percival found again, and which was previously picked up by Titurel, who is the founder of the Grail dynasty; thus the Grail allegedly is this Luciferian stone.[9]

---

9. In some manuscripts of this text the stone was found by Percival, while in others it *is* Percival himself: an interesting identification indeed.

According to others, the stone that fell to earth was an emerald that adorned Lucifer's forehead. It was cut into the shape of a bowl by a faithful angel, and thus the Grail was born. It was given to Adam before he was expelled from the Garden of Eden. Seth, Adam's son, having temporarily returned to the earthly paradise, took the Grail along with him.[10] Other people transported the Grail to Montsegur, a fortress in the Pyrenees, which Lucifer's armies besieged in order to get the Grail back and put it into their leader's crown, out of which it had fallen; but the Grail was allegedly saved by knights who hid it within a mountain.

---

10. See René Guénon, *Le Roi du monde,* chapter 5. This may recall the Arab saga concerning the black stone of Kaaba, given by Gabriel to Adam; this stone, which was taken back to heaven after the flood, was subsequently returned to earth by Gabriel, that it might become the foundation stone of the Islamic tradition. After the original sin, this white, shiny stone turned black. Concerning this last interpretation, it probably needs to be rectified in the sense that the color black designates what is occult, unmanifested, as is the Supreme Center during the decline of every traditional civilization.

15

The Luciferian Stone

In these legends, no matter how free of religious overtones, we find again the connection of the Grail, conceived as a heavenly stone, with a mysterious legacy and power associated with a primordial state that was somehow preserved during a period of exile. The reference to Lucifer, beyond a Christian and theistic context, may be seen as a variation on the theme of an aborted or deviated attempt at a heroic reattainment of this state. The theme of the host of angels descending from heaven with the Grail resembles the theme of the race of the Tuatha dé Danaan, which was believed to be composed of divine beings. This race came to Ireland from heaven, carrying a supernatural stone (the stone of the legitimate kings) and other objects that, as we have noted, correspond exactly to those of the cycle of the Grail: a sword, a lance, a bowl that feeds people without ever being depleted. At the same time, the homeland of the Tuatha was that Avalon which, according to a noted tradition, is also the seat of the books of the Grail and which has often been confused, owing to obscure associations, with the place in which the Grail was eminently revealed.

There is more. In some Celtic legends, the fallen angels are identified with the Tuatha dé Danaan; in other legends mention is made of spirits who, as a punishment for their neutrality, were forced to descend on earth. They are described as the inhabitants of a Western-Atlantic region, which was visited by Saint Brendan. This region is a facsimile of Avalon, just as the journey is a Christianized image of the journey undertaken by various Celtic heroes to reach the "Island," the original homeland and inviolable center of the Tuatha. Thus we have a curious interference of motifs that finds an expression, for instance, in the *Leabhar na h-uidhre*, in that it is written that the Tuatha are "gods who begat wise men. It is likely that they arrived in Ireland from heaven, which explains the superiority of their science and of their knowledge."

A careful separation of themes may here differentiate that which refers to authentically Luciferian elements (to which we may correctly apply the idea of a "fall" and of life on earth as a punishment) from that which (through a tendentiously deformed representation) refers to earthly custodians of the power from above and of the tradition symbolized by the Grail as a persistent, unaltered, secret presence of that which was proper to the primordial and divine state. The neutrality of the Grail's angels (mentioned in Wolfram) is reminiscent of a state ideally prior to that differentiation of spirituality which the Luciferian theme characterizes. And if Wolfram later on presents a different version, making Trevrizent say that the neutral angels did not return to heaven (unlike the Tuatha, who returned to Avalon) but were responsible for their eternal downfall and that "those who want to be rewarded by God should not become an enemy of these fallen angels," we must remember how Christianity deformed prior traditions, substituting their original meaning with totally different interpretations.

Generally speaking, owing to its prevalently "lunar" view of the sacred, Christianity has often stigmatized as Luciferian and diabolical not only that which is truly such, but also any attempt at heroic reintegration and any spirituality that does not foster a relationship of devotion and of creaturely dependence on the divine, theistically conceived. Thus we often come across mixtures of motifs analogous to that of the Tuatha dé Danaan in certain Siriac-Hebrew literature, in which the fallen angels eventually become one and the same with "those who are awake" (the ἐγρηγοροι).[1] Tertullian did not hesitate to attribute to the fallen angels the body of magico-hermetic doctrines,[2] namely, those doctrines that helped Flegetanis penetrate the original texts of the Grail and that *Le Morte D'Arthur* attributed to Solomon, conceived as a forefather of the heroes of the Grail, in the same terms as Tertullian's: "This Solomon was wise and knew all the virtues of stones and trees, and so he knew the course of the stars and many other diverse things."[3] When Innocent III accused the Knights Templar of "following doctrines of demons" *(utentes doctrinis daemonorum)*, he no doubt had in mind the anti-Christolatric mysteries of the Knights Templar; this pope instinctively proceeded to the same assimilation,

---

1. Julius Evola, *The Hermetic Tradition*, trans. E. E. Rehmus (Rochester, Vt.: Inner Traditions, 1995), 2–12.

2. *De cultu feminarum*, 1.2b.

3. *Le Morte D'Arthur*, 17.5.

through which the primordial "divine race" was represented as the guilty or Luciferian race of the fallen angels.

I believe I have already supplied sufficiently precise reference points to help the readers orient themselves before similar distortions and establish both the limit that separates the Luciferian spirit from that which is not and the Christian perspective from the point of view of a higher spirituality. Thus it will be easy to distinguish the individual elements that we encounter in the Grail cycle, which were mixed with many interpolations and deformations. Having showed that the titanic element is indeed the prime matter out of which the hero is made, it is understandable that Wolfram bestows upon Percival some Luciferian traits, though he makes him successfully complete his adventure, so much so that in the end Percival assumes the luminous form of a restorator and of a king of the Grail. In fact, Percival accuses God of having betrayed him, of not being faithful to him, and of having failed to assist him in the conquest of the Grail. He rebels and in his anger he says:

> I used to serve a being called God before I was ridiculed and covered with shame. . . . I was His humble servant because I believed He would grant me His favor: but from now on I will refuse to serve Him. If He persecutes me with His hatred, I will resign myself to that too. Friend [he says to Gawain], when the time for you to fight has come, may the thought of a woman [rather than of God] protect you.

Animated by such indignation and pride, Percival, after failing in his first visit to the castle, fulfills his adventures. And thus, being separated from God, avoiding churches and performing "wild" knightly deeds *(wilden Aventure; wilden, ferren Ritterschaft)* he eventually triumphs, achieving the glory of the king of the Grail. Trevrizent will tell him, "Rarely was a greater miracle seen: by showing your anger you have received from God what you desired the most." Also in Wolfram, Percival appears as the one who reaches the castle of the Grail in an exceptional way, without having been designated or called like others before him. His election occurs later on; in a way, it is the very adventures of Percival that bring his election about and almost bestow it upon him. Trevrizent says, "It never happened before that the Grail could be achieved by fighting." This trait too helps us recognize the heroic type, the one who, not by nature (as in the case of the Olympian type, to whom the legitimate king of the Grail may correspond, prior to his getting old, wounded, or falling asleep), but because of the reawakening of a deeper vocation and thanks to his action, successfully participates in what the Grail symbolizes. This character reaches such heights as to become a knight of the Grail and finally achieves the supreme dignity of the Order of the Grail.

16

The Test of Pride

In Wolfram these meanings are detailed and confirmed in relation to Gawain and Amfortas. In Wolfram, Trevrizent is the brother of the fallen king of the Grail, who withdrew to ascetic life by the Wild Fountain (Fontane la Salvatsche), trying to alleviate, through his asceticism, the sufferings of his brother and also to stem the decay of the Grail's kingdom. His own name may be translated as "recent truce," which suggests a provisional solution based on the ascetic principle as people await a true restoration. Trevrizent does not fail to remind Percival of the fate of Lucifer and his hosts after the latter decides to proceed in his adventure without the help of God. At the same time, however, Trevrizent indicates to him the true limit and the true cause of Lucifer's fall: if, on the one hand, in order to have the right to look after the Grail it is necessary to demonstrate an exceptional strength and bravery, on the other hand it is also necessary "to be free of pride." Trevrizent tells Percival, "Perhaps your youth will cause you to show a lack of the virtue of renunciation," and he reminds Percival of Amfortas's situation, "the misery tormenting him, which was the 'reward' of his pride." And because "in his quest of love he did not respect chastity, Amfortas was stricken by evil, which eventually plagued all those around him."

Wolfram has portrayed in Amfortas the type of the wounded king who awaits the hero who will heal him and to whom he will transmit the mandate of the Grail's kingship. Amfortas's fall is explained in the following way: choosing as his battle cry "*Amor*, which does not become humility," he puts himself at the service of Orgeluse de Logrois, performing brave deeds "characterized by the yearning for love." In one of these adventures, however, he ends up being wounded in his manhood by a poisoned lance (*mit einem geluppeten sper—*

wart er ze tjostieren wunt) thrust by a pagan knight who was certain of being able to conquer the Grail. His opponent is eventually slain, but Amfortas's wound remains and his strength disappears. He can no longer adequately function as the king of the Grail, and therefore the whole kingdom falls into a deep state of prostration and desolation.

Behind the erotic symbolism of this episode it is relatively easy to recognize the allusion to a Luciferian deviation, that is, to an affirmation or action guided not by a transfiguring orientation but by craving and pride. Ordinary chastity is not the Grail's law; in Wolfram, the Grail's kings are allowed to have a woman, designated by the Grail itself. In other texts the Grail's knights accept the sexual favors of the woman of the castle, and some even go as far as raping her;[1] yet these men are not allowed to devote themselves to or marry that woman who is a symbol of pride, whose name is Orgeluse ("the Proud One"). This already amounts to wounding and poisoning heroic virility, sentencing it to a restless and unextinguishable love, which somehow has the same meaning as Prometheus' punishment.[2]

Such is the meaning of Amfortas's wound, which is synonymous with his own downfall. Thus one can understand why Trevrizent mentions Amfortas immediately after warning Percival by reminding him of Lucifer's fall.

Interestingly enough, Wolfram also mentions another knight who undertakes the same adventure as Amfortas's, though with a different outcome, namely, Gawain. Gawain listened to Percival's advice to entrust himself to a woman rather than to God. In Oblilote he finds a woman who "will protect him in every difficult adventure," or one "who will be his escort and follower," or "a roof that will protect him during storms and times of calamities." This woman says:

---

1. J. Marx (*Legende arthurienne,* 211–13) noticed that originally, the first and foremost virtue of the hero of the Grail was not chastity at all; on the contrary, his romantic adventures have sometimes a sexual outcome and are characterized by their fleetingness and lack of commitment. Only later on, as a result of the influence exercised by Robert de Borron's version, will the Grail's knight become the chaste virgin; this moralizing version will be popularized by Wagner. Likewise, the women of these sagas give themselves freely, after requesting from the men who want them to pass this or that test; they reproduce the Aphroditic and unsteady type of many Celtic figures. Arthur's woman herself has an ambiguous behavior, since she does not seem very unhappy about having been abducted. And so we may conclude that chastity and Platonic love are not at the forefront.

2. For the meaning of Prometheus's punishment, see my *Revolt Against the Modern World,* 225. The reader will also notice that it is not very clear why Amfortas's battle cry does not become humility, unless "love" has a coded and initiatory meaning in reference to the Italian and Provençal Love's Lieges.

My love will give you peace and successfully protect you from all dangers, even though you will valiantly defend yourself. I am in you, and my fate is strictly connected with yours; I want to be close to you during combat. If you firmly believe in me, luck and valor will never desert you.[3]

Having defined in these terms the union with his woman and her occult efficiency, Gawain undertakes the adventure of the "Castle of the Maiden" or Schastel Marveil. This adventure had been indicated by Kundry, the Grail's messenger, as the one that the Knights of the Round Table must undertake because Percival, though he reached the castle of the Grail, did not successfully accomplish his restoring mission. In Wolfram this is declared to be the most daring of all his adventures, and in *Le Morte D'Arthur* it is declared "a great folly."[4] In Wolfram this adventure unfolds in the dream of the lady who had already been Amfortas's ruin, namely, Orgeluse. Gawain succeeds in his adventure without getting himself killed. We shall learn the details further on; here we only need to note that in this adventure Gawain must prove to be ready to undertake all kinds of tasks, humiliations, jokes, and disavowals. It is, all things considered, a real test of pride, and of the ascetic faculty to struggle and to overcome any hubris, thus exhibiting a subtle inner self-control.

This self-control may well be demonstrated in the allegory of Gawain's walking through the "estroite Voie" with which the adventure begins, that is, through a dangerous path, which in the *Diu Crone* is made of steel, as wide as a hand and laid over a dark and deep river; this is the only access to the "rotating castle" and one that another knight, Kay, did not dare to attempt (generally speaking, this is the symbol of a tough path, equally distant from Prometheism and from a nonvirile sacrality).

Gawain succeeds and makes Orgeluse his bride, instead of ending up like Amfortas. It is also a significant symbol that Gawain reaches Orgeluse's kingdom just when he finally finds the man who had previously "wounded" a knight whom he found in the arms of a woman: in other words, the same path is traveled again, the same cause is sought after, but the deed is successful.

In relation to this, we notice the double aspect that, in conformity with what I have already discussed, the theme of the "woman" assumes. On the one hand, here we find the distinction between an earthly knighthood, which is inspired by a woman, and a heavenly knighthood, the object of which is the Grail. This can be seen, for instance, in the *Queste du Graal,* in which the knights about to

---

3. To this Gawain replies, "It will look as if I am fighting, but the truth is that it will be you fighting in me."

4. *Le Morte D'Arthur,* 13.15.

leave in search of the Grail wish to take their women along but are prevented from doing so by an anchorite who declares that "the earthly knighthood must be transformed into a spiritual knighthood."

More interesting yet, the texts of the Grail mention frequently and openly Lucifer's temptation by a woman:[5] this is rather odd, prescinding from the interpretation I have suggested, since Lucifer's action traditionally has never had anything to do with a sexual temptation.

At the same time, the Grail cycle develops in multiple forms the notorious theme of kingdoms obtained by a woman who is seduced after successfully completing various heroic tests. It is through this way, for instance, that not only Percival's father, Gamuret, becomes king twice, but Percival himself achieves this dignity through Condwiramur, the invocation of which is assimilated by Wolfram to that of the Grail itself. Gerbert de Mostreuil attributes Percival's initial lack of success with his having abandoned his "woman" (here named Blancheflor). The Grail itself appears in strict relation with women. Regal virgins and crowned women always carry it and sometimes even embody some attributes of the Grail.[6] Percival's stepbrother, the "pagan" knight Feirefis, who "ardently yearned for the reward that women can give," devoting himself for this reason to every heroic and dangerous deed and concentrating his mind on the "woman," gains so much strength as almost to defeat Percival himself; he even becomes the bridegroom of the lady carrying the Grail (Repanse de Schoye). In this way, having been "baptized," he obtains the vision of the Grail and participates in the transcendent regal function, becoming the forefather of the dynasty of the Prester Johns. Antikonie's "kiss" has a peculiar power: once given to a knight, "it inflamed him to such a degree that he was ready to tear down entire forests with which to make countless spears." But Antikonie is also she who "makes a knight promise to go loyally and without hesitations to conquer the Grail for her."

It is especially in Heinrich von dem Turlin that one can see the connection and almost the identification of the theme of the woman as "supernatural woman" (Vrowe Saelde) with the theme of the Grail. Frau Saelde's palace—made of gold and precious gems, and of such a blinding brightness that at first Gawain believes the entire land is ablaze and containing an equivalent symbol to that of the Revolving Island—is a facsimile of the Grail's castle. The quest of the residence of Frau Saelde has many traits in common with the quest of the

---

5. *Le Morte D'Arthur*, 14.9–10. Here the temptation is related to "the one who was the mightiest angel in heaven and who lost his inheritance."

6. Of Repanse de Schoye it is said: "Her countenance irradiated such a brightness that everyone thought he was seeing the sun at dawn."

Grail and is conditioned by analogous trials (e.g., defeating a wizard and a lion that spits fire); in other words, it appears as a phase preparing for the true winning of the Grail.

The text offers some significant symbols, beginning with the test of the glove. This is a glove that, once worn by the "pure," makes the right side of their bodies invisible, while in the "impure" it points out the part of the body that has sinned. Those who pass the test receive from Frau Saelde the second glove and obtain from her assistance and protection during the quest for the Grail. Though it is not mentioned explicitly, it is alluded that the second glove produces invisibility of the other half of the body of the elect, that is, total invisibility. This symbolism may be interpreted in the following fashion: since the virtue of invisibility corresponds to the power of stepping into the invisible dimension, of assuming a state that is not tied to a physical form, the woman (in relation to Saelde's second glove) here acts in the sense of integrating that which may be derived from the "purity" of the knights who undertook this test (here only Arthur and Gawain pass the test).

In another episode of the same story, Gawain reaches the residence of Saelde and obtains from her the wish of "health and victory for all time" for himself and of "eternity" for Arthur's kingdom, to which he belongs. Shortly after this virtual chrismation, Gawain must face a test that corresponds, in its effects, to that of Wolfram's Gawain, namely, the test of steadfastness, of inner self-control: he must go ahead, impassibly, without responding to provocations, challenges to duels, cries of distress, or knightly deeds concerning a rightful revenge. If Gawain had failed in this test willed by Frau Saelde, the text says, "the court would have been dissolved": this is analogous to the effect caused by Amfortas's fall. The same symbol appears in another form, when Gawain, asked to choose between the possession of a regal woman (and thus of her kingdom) and eternal youth, does not hesitate to choose the latter, namely, a supernatural life. This adventure precedes a test that is the exact copy of that which Wolfram's Gawain performs in the Castle of the Maiden and which ends with the possession of Orgeluse.[7]

In summary, the meaning of all this, esoterically speaking, is that the woman (i.e., the vivifying force, the power, the transcendent knowledge) represents a danger only when she is yearned after; only as such does she substantiate the

---

7. In the symbolism of the German minnesinger literature Saelde is identified with Felicia and her son is named Heil. She personifies felicitas in the Roman sense of the word. *Saelde* means *Gluck,* the quality of one who happily reaches his goal; this quality in turn generates Heil, namely, "health," "salvation," in reference to Saelde as a divine woman. The symbolism could not be more transparent, and thus I believe it to be a precise confirmation of my interpretation.

Luciferian temptation and cause the wound in Amfortas's "virility," which degrades and paralizes him. She is the woman who, in Kalki's myth, never marries anyone but the restoring hero, since all other men, as soon as they lust after her, are transformed from men into women, or in other words, like Amfortas, they lose their spiritual virility. When considered as a craving, or as an uncontrolled desire, the heroic *eros* is a danger. In this context chastity signifies control, limit, antititanic purity, overcoming of pride, and immaterial unshakability, rather than a moralistic and sexuophobic precept. There is a significant saying of Trevrizent to Percival: "There is only one thing that the Grail and its secret virtues will never tolerate in you: countless desires."

The "triumphal peace" corresponds to the Olympian state that is regained by the hero: "By fighting on you have pacified your soul." Asceticism of power; the overcoming of both the wild, virile element and of desire;[8] and purity in victory: only when these characteristics are present does the unshakable, sidereal, and purified virile nucleus develop in a human being. This nucleus makes one fit to assume the Grail, to enjoy the full view of it without being blinded, destroyed, or incinerated on the spot.

This is all I have to say concerning the most essential meaning of these parts of the Grail's legend. After having determined it, it may be worthwhile to allude briefly to yet another possible interpretation of what happened to Amfortas, an episode under which the theme of the woman, in a more concrete sense, may fall.

The possibility of admitting in even a subordinate manner such an interpretation depends on the supposition that the authors of the medieval romances had some knowledge of sexual magic and that they alluded to it in their symbolism. It is not easy to answer such a question definitively. In any event, the following are the main reference points.

According to secret traditions, man possesses the principle of an eminently virile force that, once freed from matter, is believed to manifest itself as a magical and commanding power. Such force is paralyzed by sexuality, unless sexuality is given a particular orientation. The woman acts in a lethal way on this force when she awakens desire in the initiate, drawing him into a sexual intercourse aimed at procreation; and since the power of magical and supermaterial virility is that which allows one to "cross over the river of death," one can rightly speak of a "slow death which woman imparts." Thus we can see a new aspect of the symbolism of a man who paradoxically turns into a woman as

---

8. See *Le Morte D'Arthur*, 10.4, in which this double overcoming is expressed through the allegory of Sir Tristan, conceived as a knight of the Round Table; this knight, with the assistance of Morgan le Fay, the supernatural woman, smites both Sir Sagramor le Desirous and Sir Dodinas le Savage.

soon as he desires a woman, and especially at the time when he engages in sexual intercourse. Beyond any moralism, whenever this happens to an initiate under the aegis of desire or abandonment, it amounts to a devitalization, to a wound or lesion of his magical virility.[9] With due reservations, a similar view could also apply to a further, subordinate interpretation of Amfortas's motif, who is wounded and weakened, in particular reference to the fact that such a poisoned wound is usually referred to the genitals. Moreover, in the field of sexual magic, the woman is endowed with an essential and dangerous force.

9. Concerning these views see my *Eros and the Mysteries of Love: The Metaphysics of Sex* (Rochester, Vt.: Inner Traditions, 1991).

17

The Thunderbolt
and the Lance

At this point I will focus on the Grail itself.

It has been noted that the Grail, as a stone fallen from Lucifer's crown, resembles in a specific and significative way the frontal stone *(urna)* that in
Hindu symbolism and especially in Buddhism often represents the place of the
"third eye," or "Śiva's eye."[1] This is an eye that is endowed with both a transcendent or "cyclical" vision (known in Buddhism as *bodhi,* or spiritual enlightenment) and a fulgurating power. This latter aspect is in direct relation
with what I have previously discussed, considering that it is with this eye that
Śiva incinerated the god of love Kāma, when the latter attempted to awaken in
him desire for his consort Śakti. Moreover, in some esoteric traditions of yoga,
the frontal eye corresponds to the so-called center of command *(ājñā-cakra),*
which is the highest seat of "transcendent virility," namely, that virility in which
Śiva's symbolic phallus manifests itself in the form of *itara,* to which it is attributed the power to cross the "stream of becoming" or to go beyond death.[2]

After all, according to its generic aspect of stone fallen from the sky, the
Luciferian stone recalls the fulgurating power through the symbolism of the
so-called stones of thunderbolt, or meteorites, mentioned in many traditions,
in which they often represent the thunderbolt itself. Here René Guénon has
shown the possibility of referring to the symbolism of the ancient stone battle-
axe that breaks and shatters; this axe too has symbolized the thunderbolt in

---

1. R. Guénon, *Le Roi du monde,* chapter 5.
2. A. Avalon, *The Serpent Power* (London, 1924).

traditions that almost always are reconnected with the primordial Hyperborean tradition and with its heroic or Olympian representatives (in any event, anti-titanic).[3] Thus the axe refers not only to Śiva, who incinerated the Hindu Eros, but also to Paraśu-Rāma; it corresponds to Mijolnir, Thor's war hammer, and is the symbolic weapon with which these two gods strike and defeat telluric, titanic, or wild beings. Thus the battle-axe is synonymous of that thunderbolt with which the Hellenic Olympian god exterminates the Titans, and especially of the vajra of Indra, the heavenly and warrior god of the primordial Indo-Aryan hosts.

This last reference is particularly interesting, inasmuch as the *vajra* includes three meanings: scepter, thunderbolt, and adamantine stone. The first meaning recalls the meanings expressed in the symbolism of the lance. A Celtic saga that has a strict relation with that of the Grail, is the saga of Peronnik. Its main motifs are a golden bowl and a diamond lance that must be taken from a castle inhabited by a giant. The bowl has the same beneficial qualities as those of the Grail: "It instantaneously provides all the food and riches one desires; when drinking from it, one is healed from all sickness and the dead come back to life." The adamantine lance presents the "dreadful" characters of the Luciferian stone, of the *vajra*, the force-scepter-thunderbolt; it is an inexorable lance, the *lance sans merci;* bright as a flame, *elle tue et brise tout ce qu'elle touche*, but as such it is also a pledge of victory. As soon as the hero Peronnik touches these objects, the earth shakes, an awful thunder resounds, the palace disappears, and Peronnik finds himself in the forest with the lance and the bowl, which he brings to the king of Britain.[4] This phenomenology parallels that of the Grail and the Siege Perilous.

Cyclical view, transcendent virility, power of command, axe-thunderbolt, thunderbolt-scepter—all of these, in the context of myths, are associated with the mysterious stone out of which the Grail came. This stone adorned Lucifer's crown, which he, together with his hosts, attempted to take back, in a sort of angelic revenge. Again, this mysterious stone was in Adam's possession during

3. It is interesting to find the axe or the Hyperborean double battle-axe, carried by some kind of centaur, in several drawings and symbols of ancient Scotland and Ireland. See J. Romilly Allen, *The Early Christian Monuments of Scotland* (Edinburgh, 1903), 223, 253, 297. Naturally, with the "migration of symbols," the axe came to be associated with various figures having a loose connection with the Hyperborean tradition, and sometimes real usurpations took place (e.g., in the cycle of the Pelasgic civilization).

4. J. Marx (*Legende arthurienne,* 130–35) mentions the Gai Bolga as an antecedent in the Irish tradition. The Gai Bolga was originally the lance of the god Lug; it casts thunder and has the power to poison and to destruct, which needs to be attenuated with a certain mysterious procedure, lest it should burn the one who uses it. This lance is believed to have imparted the Dolorous Stroke, which endangered the regality and well-being of the court of the Round Table; it also wounded the Grail's king as well as Gawain during a night of unsuccessful tests.

the "primordial state," in the "earthly paradise," though he too lost it. Moreover, in a sense, it is still mysteriously present here on earth as the "stone of the exile." The tradition of the earthly paradise as a seat of the Grail corresponds to the tradition that identifies them with each other. Wolfram talks of the Grail as "such an august object the like of which is not found in heaven." In the *Queste du Graal*, Galahad, contemplating the Grail in the *palais espirituel*, experiences an awesome shudder and begs God to take him out of this life and to let him into heaven, having already fully known the mystery of the Grail. In the *Perceval li Gallois*, the castle of the Grail is named Eden. In the *Diu Crone* the quest leads Gawain to a country that "may well be considered the earthly paradise." During the fifteenth century Veldenaer relates that according to ancient sources, Lohengrin, the "knight of the swan," "allegedly came from the Grail *(dat Greal)*, which earlier on was called the earthly paradise; and yet it is not paradise, but a place of sin that is reached through great adventures and out of which, through great tribulations, one can leave." Thus the Grail, in one way or another, is also reconnected with the new attainment of the primordial state, which is represented by the earthly paradise.[5]

I have already mentioned the tradition according to which Seth allegedly attained the Grail again in the earthly paradise. This is a very interesting motif, considering that Seth, in Hebrew, is a name susceptible to two opposite meanings: "ruin" and "upheaval" on the one hand, and "foundation" on the other hand. The first meaning points to the Luciferian substratum, to the wild warrior principle that is destined, through heroic reintegration, to change nature and be transformed into a foundation; hence, the second meaning of Seth as "foundation," or "pole," having an essential relation with the regal function generally conceived as an emanation of the power of the center. In this we may encounter the interpretation of Wolfram's mysterious *lapsit exillis* as *lapis beryllus*, "central stone," and as *lapis erillis*, "stone of the Lord."

In some Syriac texts, mention is made of a precious stone that is the foundation, or center of the world, hidden in the "primordial depths, near God's temple." It is put in relation with the body of the primordial man (Adam) and, interestingly enough, with an inaccessible mountain place, the access to which must not be revealed to other people; here Melchizedek, "in divine and eternal

---

5. The "knight of the swan," named Elias or Lohengrin, comes from a place that is portrayed as the earthly paradise where the Grail is located (*annales quosdam veteres volunt prodidisse, Heliam istum e paradysi terrestri loco quodam fortunatissimo, cui Graele nomen esset, navigatio tali venisse*), as Arthur's seat, and as a mountain. The theme of the swan leads back to the same swan on which Apollo came from his Hyperborean seat, namely, from the solar island, which is the same as the island of Avalon; the latter, through the theme of the knight of the swan, is connected to the Grail.

service," watches over Adam's body. In Melchizedek we find again the representation of the supreme function of the Universal Ruler, which is simultaneously regal and priestly;[6] here this representation is associated with some kind of guardian of Adam's body who originally possessed the Grail and who, after losing it, no longer lives. This is found together with the motifs of a mysterious stone and an inaccessible seat.

I have previously pointed out that a "central" meaning is inherent to the symbolism of the heavenly stones that are to be found wherever a given race either embodied or intended to embody a polar function within the cycle of a given civilization. Thus from the Irish regal stone, which I have repeatedly mentioned, we go to the *lapis niger* that was put in ancient Rome at the beginning of the "sacred path"; to the black stone of Kaaba, a traditional center of Islam; to the black stone transmitted (according to a legend) from the Universal Ruler to the Dalai Lama;[7] to the sacred stone that in the Greek hymns is the altar and the house of Zeus and the "throne at the center of the world"; and finally to the *omphalos,* the sacred stone of Delphi, the traditional center of ancient Hellas, which was conceived also as the first postdiluvian creation of the primordial race, the race of Deucalion.[8]

This sacred central stone *(omphalos)* was also called "betil," betil being a stone that, like the Grail, represents victory. We learn from Pliny: "Sotacus et alia duo genera fecit ceratniae, nigrae rubentisque, similes eas esse securibus, ex his quae nigrae sint ac rotundae sacros esse, urbes per illas expugnari et classes, baetulos (betillos) vocari, quae vero longae sint ceraunias." [Sotacus creates two other types of thundering objects, black and red. Those that are red are similar to an axe head. Those that are black are round and sacred, and it is through them that cities and fleets are defeated, and they are called baetulos (meteorite). Those that are drawn out are called ceraunias (thunderbolt).][9]

But the name βαιτύλος is identical to the Hebrew *beth-el,* which means "the house of the Lord," and suggests the famous story of Jacob, who "defeated an angel." Jacob named Bethel the region in which a sacred stone indicates the dreadful place where a ladder joins heaven and earth. "How awesome is this place! This is none other than the house of God, and this is the gate of heaven," says Jacob.[10] And yet in Jacob we can still discern the Luciferian component

---

6. R. Guénon, *Le Roi du monde,* chapter 6.
7. Ibid.
8. The reader may recall the Muslim legend according to which the stone of heaven returned to earth after the flood.
9. *Naturalis historia,* 37.135.
10. Genesis 28:17.

proper to heroic realizations: his name means "usurper".[11] Jacob struggles with the angel and forces him to bless him; he manages to see "Elohim face to face" and "to save his life" by fighting against the divine. The angel says to him: "Your name shall no more be called Jacob, but Israel, for you have striven with God and with men, and have prevailed."[12] Here we can notice a singular analogy between Jacob and Percival, who, despite scorning God, achieves his goal and asserts his election; likewise Jacob, by winning, obtains his blessing. I wish to point out an even more enigmatic correspondence: the king of the Grail, who waits to be healed, either limps or is wounded in the thigh. In Jacob's story, Jacob is wounded in the thigh by the angel and limps. When the angel "saw that he could not prevail against Jacob, he touched the hollow of his thigh; and Jacob's thigh was put out of joint as he wrestled with him."[13] Once again we find further connections that I cannot pursue or develop in this context. Therefore, I wish to make this point: the Grail-betil is connected to the primordial state as a foundation, and in relation to this, like Jacob's stone, it represents something that unites heaven and earth, essentially under the sign of a supernatural-heroic victory and of a "central" function.

Moreover, it is clear that the tradition that makes of Seth a conqueror of the Grail is related to another tradition, according to which Seth allegedly took a sprout from the plant located in the middle of the Garden of Eden. From this sprout grew the tree that appears in the legends of Prester John, Alexander, and the Great Khan in various forms, including that of the Dry Tree of the Empire. Such a tree appears in the *Grand Saint Graal,* in the *Queste du Graal* and in *Le Morte D'Arthur* (17.5–7), in relation to the so-called ship of Solomon and to the test of the sword. This is a mysterious ship on board which are a bed, a golden crown, and a sword ornamented with "strange pendants." These pendants are made with three strands of different colors (white, red, and green), which were woven by Solomon or by his wife with branches of a tree grown from a sprout of the central tree of paradise, in three phases of its development.[14] The sword is that of David, the priestly king who was often confused

---

11. Genesis 27:36.
12. Genesis 32:28.
13. Ibid., 32:25.
14. The explanation given by the texts is an example of the coatings of Christian elements: the ship represents the Church, and the three colors are those which the tree assumed at the time of Eve, of the birth of Abel, and of his death at the hands of Cain. In this last regard, we could utilize the mention of a fratricidal struggle to which the Celtic story of the Dolorous Stroke may be referred. Most likely the meaning of the three colors will become apparent to those who associate them with the ones present, for instance, in the Hermetic Tradition. In the Hermetic Tradition the three colors designate three degrees of the initiatory development and of the work of the "stone" from the

with the figure of Prester John.[15] Here is a significant detail: the scabbard of this sword is named "memory of blood," *memoire de sangc.* An inscription warns that only one knight will be able to hold this sword; he will exceed all those who preceded him and who will follow him.

The ship carrying these objects does not have a crew, since it was abandoned at sea and navigates under divine guidance. All this is clearly an equivalent of the "question that must be asked" as I will interpret it later; in other words, it apparently symbolizes the abandoned legacy of the primordial regal tradition, which awaits the chosen one who will restore it. Another equivalent symbol is Arthur's lost sword, which from time to time emerges out of the waters, flashing, awaiting the one who will wield it again. In the *Grand Saint Graal* this ship comes to get Nescien from the *isle tornoiante* (an island that constantly rotates because it is fixed to the terrestrial magnet and eludes the influence of every element); analogously, in *Le Morte D'Arthur* (17.4) the ship comes from "parts west, that men call the Isle of Turnance." And so the motifs of the ancient Hebrew tradition merge with those of the Celtic-Hyperborean tradition, since the revolving island has the polar meaning of King Arthur's court, of the Round Table, of the wheel spinning before Frau Saelde, and of Avalon or the Glass Island or the Western Island.

The Grail reveals its meaning of "central stone," and thus also of the Empire *(lapis erilis)*, in the close association it has with the various themes and legends I have previously discussed. As a way of concluding this order of comparisons, I will recall that Alexander, like Seth, allegedly came close to the primordial center here on earth, to the earthly paradise, bringing back from it a stone with the same characteristics as those of the Grail, which Seth had previously taken from the same place: the stone is as bright as the sun, bestows an eternal youth, and grants victory. It is shaped like an eye (an allusion to the frontal eye?) or like an apple (the Hesperides?) or like a sphere.[16]

Like Alexander's imperialness, however, Rome's too seems to have been enigmatically characterized by the legend with the same symbols that reemerge in the Grail cycle. As a *pignus imperii,* in order to ensure Rome's eternity, Numa allegedly received from the Olympian god a bowl forged out of a meteorite, that is, a "stone of heaven"; at the same time, it allegedly corresponded to an ancient bowl containing ambrosia, which was the nectar of the immortals. The

---

albedo to the *rubedo.* After all, red is the color of the Grail's "red knight." The theme of the fratricide probably refers to a test of arms ending in a usurpation, as I will explain in chapter 19.

15. *Le Morte D'Arthur,* 17.6.

16. In Wolfram von Eschenbach, Alexander is portrayed as the one who, more than others, since Adam, knew the virtues of magical stones like the ones found in the armor of Feirefiz, Percival's stepbrother.

bowl was guarded by the college of the Salii, who also guarded the *hasta* (lance). The Salii were twelve in number, the solar number that also appears in the Order of the Round Table and of the Grail itself. The heavenly stone, the bowl that provides supernatural nourishment, and the lance are three essential objects of the Nordic-medieval legend that can be found again as prophetic "signs" foretelling the mystery of Rome's origins and its destiny as a universal imperial center. There is an almost magical concordance of meanings among all these traditions, which are so removed from each other both in space and time.

18

The Mystery of the
Lance and of Revenge

I have previously mentioned the complementarity existing between the lance and the cup. In the traditional representations of the "double power," the scepter is often confused with the lance. Also, the symbolism of the lance, like the scepter's, often interferes with the symbolism of the "axis of the world" and thus points to the well-known polar and regal meanings. In the cycle of the Grail, the lance appears mostly with regal figures and presents a double character: it wounds and it heals. This requires some further explanation.

In the cycle, the Grail's lance is often bloodied: sometimes, rather than being drenched in blood, it produces a trickle of blood. In the *Diu Crone*, the king is fed by this blood. In later texts the blood acquires an increasingly important role, so much so as to overshadow the bowl that contains it and that originally played the most important role. In these texts, the Grail becomes *Sangreal*, with the double meaning of Christ's blood and regal blood. In the Christianized elements of the cycle, the lance of the Grail is sometimes believed to be that which pierced Jesus' side; thus the blood that flows from it is "the blood of redemption," symbolizing the regenerating principle. This, however, does not explain the fact that the lance wounds a person such as Nescien, who wanted to get too close to the Grail, only to be wounded and blinded; his sight returns and the wound heals in virtue of the blood that flows from the lance's blade, once it is pulled out of the flesh.

In the *Grand Saint Graal*, when such a phenomenon occurs, a shining angel declares that this is the beginning of the marvelous adventures that will take place in the land to which Joseph of Arimathea will travel, namely, in the North-Western region. Thanks to these adventures, "true knights will be recognized from false ones and the earthly knighthood will become the heavenly knighthood"; then the miracle of the blood flowing from the blade will occur again. Even the last king of Joseph's dynasty will be wounded in both of his thighs by the lance and will be healed only at the arrival of the one who will discover the mystery of the Grail, being qualified to do so. In this context, the blood of the lance seems to be related to the virtue of the restoring hero. But in this text one also finds mentioned that the *lanche aventureuse* can inflict a wound, in the sense of inflicting a punishment that is meant to recall Jesus' wound. All this seems to overshadow the "sacrificial" motif; in other words, what is recalled is the necessity of a "mortification," or of a "sacrifice" as a preliminary condition for the Grail's experience not to turn lethal. In other texts, however, this motif is mixed with the theme of revenge: the lance, with its blood, hints at a vengeance that the chosen one must exact, for only then, together with the fulfillment of the mystery, will peace and the end of the kingdom's crisis be ushered in.

In relation to this variation the restoration assumes the character of a reaffirmation, or of a victorious assumption of the same force or tradition that others had previously picked up only to fall or be wounded by it. In this context the Christian theme of sacrifice is modified according to a more virile sense, which should be considered the original one. In Vauchier the steel of the lance is found fixed in the body of a dead knight. The one who pulls it out must avenge him; thus, the avenger is also the restorator. In any event, from a blood of enigmatic characteristics (redemption blood, blood of sacrifice or of revenge) we go to blood conceived as regal blood; the lance, in the end, leads to the "triumphal peace." The central and solar vein of this tradition is reconfirmed again and again, shining through the labyrinths of symbols and the opacity of historical stratifications.

The theme *la pes sera pas ceste lance* is already found, together with that of revenge, in the Celtic legend of Peredur ab Evrawc, which probably influenced the Grail stories. Like Percival, the hero Peredur is cursed for not having "asked the question," which here means for not having inquired about the "extraordinarily big lance" from which three rivulets of blood trickle out. In some forms of the legend, the castle in which these objects are found is confused with a second castle, the king of which is an old and lame knight. Peredur exclaims, "By my faith, I will not sleep tranquilly until I know the story and the meaning of the lance." The explanation, which is found at the end of the tale, is that the supernatural Amazons of Kaerlayw had wounded a king (who turns out to be this old knight) and killed his son, to whom the severed head belongs. Peredur significantly turns to King Arthur and with his help exacts vengeance and exterminates the supernatural women; after this, the lame king regains his health, his kingdom, and his peace.

The women recognize in Peredur "the one who had studied martial arts under their tutelage, though they knew he was destined to kill them." A perceptive reader will understand what this is all about. Concerning the wound caused by the women, the reader may refer to what I previously said from a double interpretative perspective concerning Amfortas's wound. More in general, we have here the aspect according to which the heroic type always overcomes the woman. The Amazon, symbolically speaking, is the feminine principle that usurps the function of dominion; though the hero needs the woman and through her is able to become such, he still must destroy in her the traits according to which she proved fatal for the previous dynasty.

Moreover, the quality that makes the revenge and, in general, Peredur's mission possible is connected to the test of the sword, more on which later. In the castle of the old man, Peredur had broken his sword by striking an iron pole, proving to be able to repair it immediately; but after two times, at the third test, the sword remains shattered and the old king says: "You only have two thirds of the force; you must conquer the last third. When your sword will be whole, no one will be able to compete with you."[1] This deficiency implicitly appears as the cause owing to which Peredur does not "ask the question" and thus cannot carry out the task of revenge. These are three degrees of a test that may be characterized by the following formula: "Once stricken, I rise up again." This refers to the capability of taking up again and reaffirming in a sacrificial manner (hence, eventually, a reconnection with the Christian theme) an energy that is broken in one of its material and elementary forms.

The theme of revenge is probably related to some historical element that was absorbed by the saga, the king's wound always corresponding to some rebellion of forces or people that have usurped or are trying to usurp its function. The complete form of the legend follows this pattern: The blood that drips from the lance calls for revenge. Thus, to mend the broken sword is the first task, which leads to the question test. This is followed by the revenge, the restoration, and the glorification. Then the lance becomes a bright symbol of peace.

The fundamental themes of the ancient Celtic legend of Peredur correspond exactly to those of the legend of Percival, which in this way evokes ancient elements of a non-Christian origin and spirit. A last reference in this sense may be

---

1. There may be a correspondence between the number of such tests and the three rivulets of blood that flow from the lance.

indicated in the *Destruction of Da Dargas Hostel* and in the *Musca Ullad*, ancient Celtic legends in which mention is made of a powerful and lethal lance and of a bowl containing blood mixed with a flaming poisonous substance. As soon as the lance is immersed in this bowl its flames are extinguished. In Wolfram, Amfortas owes his wound's torment and incurability to a burning poison in which the tip of the lance was dipped. In this it is said: "God has manifested His wonderful and terrible power."[2] It is the equivalent of the poisonous and burning bleeding substance mentioned in the ancient Celtic legend. The lance, in its positive aspect of scepter, dissolves and puts out this substance, much as Heracles, as an Olympian hero, becomes the liberator of the titanic hero Prometheus. Then the darkness and the tragedy are dispelled, and the Hyperborean "memory of blood," which guarded the sword, is reawakened. The mystery of the "regal blood" is realized.

---

2. If we were to adopt the interpretation according to which these are experiences of sexual magic, the "blood mixed with an inextingushable and flaming poisonous substance" would be a very fit alllusion to describe the state of obsessive desire, in which nothing can quench the thirst of the person "wounded" by such experiences.

19

The Dolorous Stroke

Let us now examine the various forms assumed by the motif of the fallen king, besides the one previously considered in reference to Amfortas.

In the *Grand Saint Graal* and in the *Queste du Graal* the king has received wounds, from which he now suffers, when fighting against King Crudel, an enemy of Christianity. These wounds are not felt until he loses his sight for having gotten too close to the Grail. We could interpret the symbol in the sense that the failed realization of the Grail leads to the acknowledgment of an inferiority, or having been wounded without knowing it, when struggling against the representatives of traditional non-Christian forms and defeating them.

In these texts the wound is also related to the test of the sword that lies, together with the golden crown, in Solomon's ship; this sword is sometimes drawn halfway out of its scabbard, named "memory of blood" and according to *Le Morte D'Arthur* (17.6), partially made with the wood of the Tree of Life. This sword, as I have explained, awaits one who has been predestined: a sign warns that he who wants to use this sword will find it useless in time of need. Nescien wields it against a giant, but it breaks in half. After Mordrain puts it together again, Nacien is wounded by another flaming sword, wielded by an invisible hand, as a punishment for having unsheathed the sword *ax estranges renges*.[1] In the *Queste du Graal* and in *Le Morte D'Arthur*, Nacien is told that his right hand has been smitten by the sword because of his sins; in the *Grand*

---

1. In an interpolation to the text of Chrétien de Troyes, we find this interesting detail: the sword of the Grail breaks in half at Percival's first strike against Orguilleus; consequently he has to fight without this sword, but with his own, namely, with the sword of the Red Knight.

Saint Graal Nacien is healed by a priest who walks barefoot on the sea, as if to symbolize the qualification Nacien should have exhibited in order to wield the sword legitimately.[2] Pelles too unsheathes the sword halfway, but is immediately wounded in the thigh by a lance; he will not heal before the arrival of Galahad, who is the predestined one.

Besides all this, in the *Grand Saint Graal* we also find the principle of faith. Just when Nacien thinks that Solomon's ship, carrying sword and crown, is a mirage, the ship disintegrates and he is thrown into the sea. Here the theme of usurpation merges with the theme of lack of faith; in one of the versions, Joseph of Arimathea's disciple Moses, lacking faith, is swallowed up by a chasm that opens up beneath the "perilous" seat reserved for the elect one. The weapon cannot be brandished against the giant without breaking, or before the one wielding it assumes a different quality from all that may have a relation with the elemental, the wild, the titanic (the giant) and before his faith becomes unshakable.

The story of the sword is almost always related to *le coup douloureux*, the Dolorous Stroke. The following is the version found in the *Queste du Graal*. This sword was used by Labran to treacherously murder King Urban in the kingdom of Logres (an ancient name for Britannia); since that time, the kingdom of Logres has been devastated by an epidemic. Labran himself, while on Solomon's ship, drops dead at the act of sheathing the sword back into its scabbard. It is said that from then on, no one was ever able to either wield or unsheathe this sword without either being killed or wounded by it.

Further developments of this theme are found in *Le Morte D'Arthur*. The revelant character here is Sir Balin le Savage, also called The Knight with Two Swords, who was believed to be the one who imparted the Dolorous Stroke. In these texts the sword is related to Avalon and is a facsimile of Arthur's own sword: it is carried by a maiden sent by the great lady Lile of Aveilon and may be extracted only by a knight "without villainy or treachery, and without treason." Sir Balin passes this test; that is, he successfully draws the sword but refuses to return it to the woman. Thus he is told that the sword will become the cause of his perdition.

Balin later finds himself battling King Pellan: the sword breaks in half, and as he looks for another weapon, he finds the prodigious lance on top of a golden table. With it he wounds Pellan, who passes out and does not heal until "Galahad, the noble prince, will come to heal him as he follows the quest of the Sangreal." Next to the table, on a bed, lies Joseph of Arimathea, plagued by old age. This is the Dolorous Stroke that partially destroys the kingdom of Logres

---

2. *Le Morte D'Arthur*, 17.4.

and attracts some kind of nemesis. In fact, Balin ends up fighting his own brother Balan, without recognizing him, and the two knights slay each other.[3] In all this we can clearly see the representation of a wild irruption (Balin le Savage) who, next to a fallen regality (symbolized by the decrepit Joseph of Arimathea) does not act in the sense of a restoration, but rather in the sense of a usurpation, or, in other words, in the sense of a usurped force that only leads to an internecine conflict: Balin striking Pellan, of Joseph's dynasty (representing a power that more or less corresponds to that which is conferred by the sword), and Balin fighting against his own brother Balan. After these events, nobody else will own the sword, with the exception of Galahad, who will be able to take it out of a marble stone hovering above the waters, that is, out of a supernatural and immaterial stability.[4]

In Gautier, the sword belongs to a knight killed by an unknown hand. Gawain puts on his armor (which is to say, he takes on his function), picks up his sword, and carries it with him into the Grail's castle. The king of the Grail takes this sword and notices that it is broken and that the other half is stuck in the body of a knight lying in a crypt. He asks Gawain to put the two halves together, but when the latter is not successful, the king tells him that he is still not ready to undertake the task for which he has come there. As Gawain begins to "ask the question" and receives some preliminary explanations, he learns that the power of the lance has been neutralized by the Dolorous Stroke, which has impoverished Logres's kingdom. But as soon as the king begins to talk about the secret connected with the sword, Gawain falls asleep. The king, after all, had previously warned him that since he was not able to piece the sword together, such a secret could not be revealed to him. Here the theme of the broken sword assumes its most significant form: a part of it belongs to the type of a stricken hero, whose function is assumed by Gawain, while the other part refers to the dead king and, by correlation, to the task of restoring the *regnum*. To reconnect the two parts means to get at the heart of the synthesis proper to the restoration

---

3. *Le Morte D'Arthur*, 2.1, 2, 15, 16, 18.
4. *Le Morte D'Arthur*, 2.19. In the *Grand Saint Graal* we find the following version: the king of the Grail's dynasty, Lambor, was wounded by an enemy named Bruillant holding Solomon's sword. It was the first stroke that this sword imparted in Britannia. To avenge this stroke, several conflicts erupted, ravaging the land, which came to be known as *la terre gaste*. At the act of resheathing the sword (we should recall that the sheath's name is *Memoire de sangc*), Bruillant falls dead. The same text mentions Lambor's successor, King Pelleant, who also belonged to the dynasty of fisher kings; he is wounded in both thighs in battle before Rome, and as a result he comes to be known as the lame king *(li rois mehaignies)*, who will heal only at the arrival of the predestined hero Galahad. In these versions what seems to be most important is the theme of a test of arms, which concludes with the inferiority of some representative of the Grail's regality.

and to the primordial king, who rises up again thanks to the hero. But Gawain fails, at least at first. His consciousness is not able to follow the mystery of the sword; he falls asleep.

In another development of the cycle, sleep, owing to which Gawain fails in his task, becomes the cause of the wound. Alain, in his Terra Faraine, had a beautiful castle built to keep the Grail, in the middle of an overwhelming current; the castle, named Corbenic, should be identified with the Grail itself, since in Caldaic, according to the text, "Corbenic" means "most holy vessel," *saintisme vaisiaus*. This is the castle of the "perennial wake" and of the test of sleep; no one is allowed to sleep in it. When the king, Alfasem, tries to fall asleep, a fiery figure pierces both his thighs with a lance; this wound will later cause his death. Corbenic is *le palais aventureus*, and every knight who falls asleep in it is found dead the morning after.[5]

An analogous theme is found in the *Diu Crone*. Unlike his companions, though he is asked to drink, Gawain refuses; this symbolic abstinence allows him not to fall asleep like the others and thus to "ask the question," "without which everything he had done up to that point and everything that he still could have accomplished would have been useless." The meaning of this is rather obvious. Just as "sleep" is a well-known initiatory symbol, so is that of the "Awakened One" and of the "Sleepless One." In every initiatory tradition, to overcome sleep has had the meaning of participating in a transcendent lucidity, free from the contingencies of material and individual existence.

A variation on the theme of usurpation, which is somewhat connected to the theme of Amfortas, is found in the so-called *Elucidation:* the kingdom of Logres is ravaged and sterile because King Amagon and his knights raped the "women of the Fountain" and stole from them a golden cup. Since then, the court of the Fisher King, or the Grail's court, which was the wealth of the country, disappeared, and the throne remained vacant for more than a thousand years. In the end, at the time of King Arthur, Gawain learns about this and begins his quest for the Grail's court and king. In Wolfram, Klinschor too is portrayed as a man who violates women; this characteristic of his, presented in the allegorical form of adultery, is the cause of his emasculation and ensuing involvement in black magic, which is a counterfeit of true supernatural power. Klinschor owns a castle to which, with the aid of his magical arts, he draws and imprisons various women, including Arthur's mother. It is in this castle that Gawain's final test takes place, at the end of which he takes Orgeluse, the woman who previously ruined Amfortas and the Grail's realm. All this is rela-

---

5. A night of tests was already a constant motif in the ancient Irish tales. See A. Brown, *The Origin of the Grail Legend* (Cambridge, 1943), 218–25.

tively clear, provided one follows the interpretation I suggested at the end of chapter 16. One can see that the various themes of these tales form an overall pattern, at the center of which is one basic idea.

In Manessier, the sword is that with which the brother of the Grail's king was treacherously slain and which on this occasion broke in half. The person killed is the corpse that lies in the coffin in the Grail's castle. The broken sword was preserved, but with its pieces the next king of the Grail accidentally wounded himself and lost all his powers: the employment of the wounded strength, if not reintegrated, proves to be fatal too. Here the theme of revenge is at the forefront. The sword needs to be mended; the one who is capable of doing it must then avenge the slain person by reaching Partinial, who is the lord of the Red Tower. After various adventures, which have an initiatory character, Percival kills Partinial (who in this context may be the equivalent of the "giant," fighting against whom the heroes who are not qualified break David's sword); when this happens, the king of the Grail jumps out of bed, healed.

In Gerbert, the lesion or wound caused by the broken sword corresponds to a crack that still remains in the mended sword and that motivates Percival to seek new adventures in order to win the Grail. During these adventures we find again the theme of revenge, since Percival regains his health and avenges his first instructor, Gurnmeant, whom he found lying mortally wounded. Second, we find the following important episode. At Arthur's court, to which Percival returns, arrives a boat led by a swan and bearing a coffin, which nobody knows how to open. Percival opens it and finds a dead knight inside, whom he must avenge. Having resolved to do so, Percival comes across another adventure; he opens a tomb in which a live man had been buried. At first the man tries to lock Percival in the tomb, but Percival succeeds in pushing him back into it. Then Percival reaches the fatal castle, and here he mends once and for all the broken sword. The same episode is found in Gautier, where the knight pleading for help from inside the tomb succeeds in temporarily locking Percival in it and then attempts to steal his horse. In yet another of these texts, the knight in the tomb is said to be the devil himself.

The apparition of the swan is significant, since the swan is strictly related to the Hyperborean tradition and to Apollo, the Hyperborean god of the primordial or Golden Age. The coffin carried by the swan (the animal that will lead Lohengrin out of the Grail's land) evidently symbolizes a mute invocation to make something that is either dead or decayed come back to life again, namely, the ancient Hyperborean tradition (sometimes the hero is also presented as the son of a widow who dwells and rules over a solitary, desolated forest; concerning the widow, see chapter 6). And yet there is the danger that the hero may fall victim to this death or to this sleep: such is the meaning of the demonic attempt to lock Percival, the chosen one, in the same tomb where a live person was crying for help.

This meaning is integrated from what is written in the *Diu Crone,* in which the king of the Grail is said to be old and apparently ill. When Gawain, who does not fall asleep like his companions, asks the question, the king shouts with joy and gives the following explanation: he, with his men, had died a long time ago, though he looked alive and retained a semblance of life until the quest for the Grail was fulfilled. This happens thanks to Gawain, to whom the old king gives the sword, which will always make him victorious; then the king disappears with his men and with the Grail itself, in the obvious sense of inaugurating a truly living and restored kingdom. In other texts, the purpose of the question is analogous: it has the power to heal the king and, at the same time, to restore his mortality, which was retained only in an artificial manner. In Wolfram, though the wounded king is healed, he nevertheless abdicates the throne, which is assumed by Percival. This is the real sense: a transmission. An ancient and decayed dynasty is liberated from its artificial life and ends at the moment in which a new dynasty proves to be capable of assuming the regal function by wielding or mending the sword, carrying out the revenge, and restoring what had fallen. The substitution, which occurs in an irregular and arbitrary fashion, accompanied by violence and a lack of proper qualifications, or in terms of a fratricidal strife, is the meaning of the story of the Dolorous Stroke, both according to my summary of *Le Morte D'Arthur* and according to various other confused and complicated versions.

In Wolfram von Eschenbach, next to the wounded king, a magnificent old man lies on a bed. His name is Titurel, the first person to whom the "Grail's banner" was entrusted. The Grail—that is, the function of which he still remains the representative—keeps him alive, although he is "afflicted by a paralysis that cannot be cured." The fallen kings mentioned in other texts often have an unnaturally prolonged life: some are a thousand, others four hundred, others three hundred years old.[6] They cannot die before the coming of the chosen one. This is an allusion to an interregnum, in the sense of a simply formal survival of the *regnum.* It is a mandate that is retained at a latent state and carried on by wounded, paralyzed, or blinded people until the restorer arrives. When we read in the *Perceval li Gallois* that Percival's father, obeying a divine calling, traveled to the far Western countries and could not die there until the arrival of the man who deserved to be called the best knight in the world, we find once more the theme of the "Western island," of Avalon and the wounded Arthur.

Another interesting reference is provided by Wolfram, according to whom

---

6. In Albrecht's text, Titurel is five hundred years old.

the poisonous and burning wound of Amfortas gets worse, especially under the sign of Saturn, or Kronos.[7] Saturn-Kronos is the king of the primordial age, who is asleep in the Hyperborean seat; according to some myths he was castrated at the beginning of a new cycle. What has been expounded helps to explain why Amfortas's wound grows worse and opens up again under the sign of Kronos. Moreover, in the Hermetic tradition Saturn-Kronos is the deceased who must be resuscitated; the royal art of the heroes consists in freeing lead from its "leprosy," namely, from its imperfections and darkness, transforming it into gold, thus actualizing the Mystery of the Stone. Moreover, Kronos, gold, and "foundation stone" are different references to the primordial regal tradition. Wherever the sign appears again, the wound of the person who has either degenerated or usurped burns and becomes troublesome.

The theme we have already encountered, of a slain or wounded knight whom the seekers of the Grail find by his woman (sometimes, significantly enough, next to a tree),[8] refers to the motif of the hero who has failed in his task; in other words, it awakens the Grail seeker to the reasons why he failed in his mission at first. Significantly, such a woman, conceived as a relative of the seeker of the Grail, makes him aware of his own name, which he himself has ignored. In any event she offers some explanations regarding the mystery of the Grail's castle; she blames the knight for not having asked the question, and sometimes she gives instructions on how to mend the sword should it break. Since in Wolfram the woman stands by the embalmed body of the dead knight, there seems to be a further interference, namely, the mixing of the motif of the king of the Grail, whose life is only apparent, with that of the hero struck down before he was able to conclude his adventure. In Wolfram this woman is named Sigune; she even curses Percival for his indifference toward the suffering king in the Grail's castle and the meaning of the Grail itself.

A variation of the previous theme is that according to which the king is not ill and his kingdom is not devastated, and yet all this happens exclusively because the Grail has been sighted together with the lance and the sword as many as three times, without anybody asking what purpose they served. Indifference and lack of understanding have caused a "great misfortune"; this is why King Arthur's court has lost its ancient splendor and why various conflicts have erupted all over the earth. This particular version of the legend has something that recalls the tragic tone of the "twilight of the gods." When Percival arrives,

---

7. Wolfram goes on to say that his sufferings increase also under the signs of Jupiter and Mars, the representatives of Olympian regality and the warrior principle, respectively.

8. The tree is almost always an oak, which in ancient Celtic traditions played the role of Tree of the World and Tree of the Center.

the Fisher King has already died; his opponent, the king of Chastel Mortel, has seized the Grail, the lance, and the sword. Percival regains these objects and forces the enemy king to commit suicide, but he does not found a new dynasty of the Grail; rather, he retires to an ascetic life with his companions. A divine voice warns him that the Grail will never manifest itself other than in a mysterious place that will be revealed to them; Percival and his companions leave to seek this place and never return. We will see later on that this episode may also have reflected a particular historical situation.

20

The Fisher King

A rather enigmatic problem is posed by the title Fisher King or Rich Fisherman, which was bestowed on the Grail's king since Joseph of Arimathea, when the Grail's wounded king turned into another character, who at first assumed the traits of a fisherman.

In its most exoteric aspect, such a symbolism can be reduced to two sources, Christian and Celtic. The Gospel narrative of the miraculous fishing is well known; moreover, the multiplication of fishes is the equivalent of the unexhaustible food supernaturally supplied by the Grail. This seems applicable especially to the *Grand Saint Graal*, in which all those who had not been fed by the Grail were fed by a fish caught by Alain: this is why this knight was named *li riche pescheour*, a title that was passed on to the entire dynasty of the Grail. In Robert de Borron it is added that he who will call the vessel by its true name will be called "the rich fisherman," precisely in virtue of the fish caught when the mystery of the Grail began. Moreover, here there seems to be a distinction: although the effects of the Grail and of the fish are equivalent, the fish appears as a sort of complement to the Grail; it integrates the latter's efficacy in regard to a certain group of knights who were not "fed" by the former.

The Celtic tradition already knew a "fish of wisdom" (or "salmon of wisdom"), which burns one's hands but which, once eaten, bestows all kinds of knowledge. This symbolism is so transparent as not to require further elucidation. Second, the fish plays a role in the legend concerning the transmission of the primordial tradition in Ireland. The *Leabhar na h-uidhre* relates that when the primordial race of Partholan, which conquered Ireland, became extinct, a man survived, named Tuan, who by assuming at various times the form of symbolic animals, managed to preserve the memory of the first generation. At the time of the Tuatha dé Danaan he assumed the form of an eagle or a sparrow hawk; then he assumed the form of a fish, at the time the race of Milhead came to power. Once caught and eaten by a princess, Tuan was born again in a human form as her son and as a prophet. The king of the Grail as a fisherman might possibly have some relation with the obscure idea of a renewal of the legacy of the stock of Partholan, of its "memory" conceived as a mystery of "nourishment" that either equals or integrates that of the Grail.

The dynasty or tradition of the Grail was often connected to Solomon. Some Arabian legends, which became common knowledge in western Europe during the Middle Ages through their Spanish versions, introduce the theme of the fish in connection with a quest for a ring that is equivalent to the Grail as a regal stone and stone of power. The ring has a stone with the character of a "fire that fills heaven and earth," a symbol of supreme power. Solomon, having lost this ring, decays. The ring has been thrown into the sea. When Solomon is fishing, he finds it again inside a fish and thus gains back the power of a visible and invisible dominion over people, animals, and demons. This ring of King Solomon is in turn a facsimile of the stone that Alexander the Great allegedly found in a huge fish and that, like the Grail carried by the Fisher King, has luminous properties, manifesting itself as a great light in the night.[1]

The last aspect of the symbolism of the fish may be derived from the evangelical saying "I will make you fishers of men" (Matthew 4:19) and also through Peter himself, the apostle-fisherman to whom Jesus later applied the symbolism of "foundation rock" in his aspect as the founder of the Church and as the center of the new religion and the apostolic tradition. The "fisherman's ring" is one of the papal insignia. The explanation found in Chrétien de Troyes is that the king of the Grail, having been wounded, has no other possible occupation and joy besides fishing. Here the king of the Grail obviously appears as the one who, acknowledging his powerlessness, looks for the chosen one, namely, the hero, as a fisher of men. A significant detail: in the *Perceval li Gallois*, the hook with which he fishes is made of gold. Both in this text and in Wolfram, the fisherman is also he who points out to Percival the way to the Grail's castle, where he appears again, this time as a sick king. But Wolfram also says, "What he fishes when his pain abates does not suffice for his needs."

A deeper meaning of these symbols can be found through intertraditional comparisons. As Guénon rightly noted, several elements suggest that the sym-

---

1. In the French and Italian versions of Merlin's prophecies we find an analogous theme, the crown of the emperor Hadrian of Orbates, which was lost at sea; its stones were allegedly brought to Frederick by a fisherman.

bolism of the fish has a Northern and even a Hyperborean origin: "Its presence was noticed in Northern Germany and in Scandinavia [besides Scotland]; these regions are likely to be closer to its point of diffusion than central Asia, to which this symbol was taken by the great current, that is, by the primordial tradition that eventually originated the Indian and Persian traditions." Yet another fact supports this thesis: in the Hindu tradition, "the manifestation in the form of a fish (Matsya-avatāra) is regarded as the very first manifestation of Viṣṇu, which occurred at the very beginning of the present cycle and therefore is related to the beginning of the primordial tradition."[2]

As a fish swimming in the waters, Viṣṇu leads the ark that contains all the germs of the future world, and after the flood he reveals the Vedas (which, as the root *vid* suggests, indicate science par excellence), just as the wise Chaldaic god Oannes, after assuming the form of a fish, teaches mankind the primordial tradition. Thus the Celtic and Christian elements of the symbolism of the fish appear to be fragments of a wider view that sheds light on the Grail legend. The Fisher King is the fallen dominator who seeks to reactivate the primordial tradition, the Hyperborean legacy. This will be possible only at the coming of the hero who will know the Grail and who will be aware of its function and benefices, which, as we have seen, are integrated and mixed with those of the fish. Hence the other aspect of the same symbolism, namely the Fisher King as "seeker of men," of men in an eminent sense, beings who are qualified for that function.

---

2. R. Guénon, "Le poisson," *Regnabit* (December 1926): 35, 36.

21

The Seat of the Grail

We have seen that of all the places in which the tests of the Grail's knights occur, the "Island" and the "Castle" seem to be in the forefront.

The journey to such places should essentially be regarded *sub specie interioritatis,* that is, in terms of a shift of consciousness to a world that is usually precluded to human beings. The journey assumes a general and universal initiatory symbolism, besides those specific references that I have previously mentioned that refer to the tradition of Avalon and of the White Island.

Pindar said that the land of the Hyperboreans cannot be reached on foot or by ship, and that only such heroes as Heracles could find it. In the Chinese tradition, the island located at the further ends of the Northern lands can be reached only by a flight of the spirit; in the Tibetan tradition, Śambhala, the mystical Northern seat related to Kalki-avatāra, was said to "dwell in my spirit."[1] This theme occurs also in the Grail cycle. The castle of the Grail in the *Queste* is called *palais spirituel* and in the *Perceval li Gallois* it is called "castle of souls" (in the sense of spiritual beings). Mordrain reaches the rocky island, which is located in a place whence "the real crossing to Babylon, Scotland, and Ireland begins" and where his trials begin after he has been taken there by the Holy Spirit. And while Plutarch relates that the vision of Kronos in the Hyperborean seat occurs in a state of sleep,[2] it is in a state of apparent death that Lancelot, in *Le Morte D'Arthur* (17.15) has the vision of the Grail. Moreover, in the *Queste,* it is in a state of either sleep or death that Lancelot has

---

1. See my *Revolt Against the Modern World,* 201–2.
2. *De facie,* 26.

the vision of the wounded knight crawling up to the Grail to sooth his suffering. These are experiences beyond ordinary consciousness.

Sometimes the castle is described as invisible and unreachable. Only the elect can find it, either out of sheer chance or through a magical spell, since it usually vanishes from the sight of its seekers. In Wolfram the Grail itself is invisible to those who have not been baptized. "The water causes all creatures to prosper. It is thanks to this water that our eyes can see. The water cleanses the souls and make them shinier than the angels themselves." This description of the baptismal water should suffice to prove that Wolfram is not really referring to the Christian baptism, but rather to a real enlightenment, the water having here more or less the same meaning of the "divine water" or of Hermeticism's "philosophical water." In many instances the castle, after the hero has found it and visited it, suddenly disappears, and he finds himself on a deserted beach or in a forest. In other cases, the adventure of the hero ends with the discovery of the castle, even though he never gets a chance to ask the question about the Grail. The figurations of the castle surrounded by waters, or by the sea *(Queste)*, or by a raging river *(Grand Saint Graal)*, or by a lake, and in which we find the Fisher King (Wolfram), are symbols of inaccessibility and of isolation (in addition to what has already been said about the "polar" figurations).

We also find the theme of the "dangerous crossing." In the *Queste du Graal* the castle is guarded by two lions, the same animal that Gawain will defeat in the trial of Orgeluse's castle, which, again, is an initiatory experience. In Wolfram, the arrival at the castle in an extraordinary way is described as Percival's covering ground in the woods, while riding his horse, as a bird would. Here the castle is presented as "strong and mighty," with smooth walls that would make it impregnable even if it were besieged by all the world's armies. In the castle are "many splendid things that have no equal on this earth; but those who look for it unfortunately never find it, though many start this quest. In order to see it, one must arrive in it without knowing it." The place in which it is built is deserted, wild, and ghostly: It is the Montsalvatsche in the Lands of Salvatsche, and "the path leading to it is filled with ambushes." Wolfram adds: "One is not likely to ride so close to Montsalvatsche without engaging in a dangerous fight or without encountering that expiation of sins which the world calls 'death.'" The knights of the Grail, or Templars *(Templeisen)*, prevent people of all nations from approaching, with the exception of those who are indicated by an inscription that appears on the Grail itself: they commit themselves to fight to the death any invader.[3] According to the *Titurel,* in the middle

---

3. In relation to this, it can be said that the Grail's knights "live dangerously."

of the woods is a mountain that nobody can find, unless one is led there by angels. This mountain, called Montsalvatsche, is protected and well guarded. Upon it floats the Grail, held by invisible beings.

In later texts, the meaning of the mountain of the Grail, Montsalvatsche, often shifts in meaning from *mons silvaticus* to *mons salvationis,* in relation to the Land of Salvaterra and of San Salvador in Spain, where it is allegedly found. Generally speaking, various symbols always express the idea of inviolability before any profanation. Moreover, the theme of invisibility, together with other related themes, underlines the notion of inaccessibility, which is proper to anything that escapes the control the physical world, of form and the physical senses, according to a limitation that, in the case of ordinary people, is identified with death or with sleep.[4] We have already seen how the Grail's castle, upon which "the flames of the Holy Spirit" descend, is also that in which the "test of sleep" takes place. To pass this test means to go beyond the realm of waking consciousness proper to the physical individual. And yet this does not happen without a crisis and some difficult and risky action: according to a particular interpretation, this may be what the "dangerous fights" mentioned by Wolfram allude to. Those who have experience in such matters know very well that similar adventures may also end in sickness, derangement, or death.

In relation to this, it is interesting to note the image found in a text: to walk on the edge of a sword. Lancelot reaches the castle of his adventure by going over a bridge as thin as a sword's blade. It is a theme known to several traditions, especially the Iranian and Persian-Islāmic tradition, which refers to both postmortem experiences (the other world) and to those of the initiatory path: the *Kaṭha Upaniṣad* compares the ascent toward wisdom to walking on a razor's edge.

The custody of the Grail and of its seat is about the defense of a certain spiritual center. The seat of the Grail always appears as a castle or fortified regal palace, but never as a church or temple. Only in later texts is mention made of an altar or chapel of the Grail, in relation to the more Christianized version of the legend, in which it is eventually identified with the chalice used at the Last Supper. In the most ancient redactions of the legend there is nothing of this sort; the close relation of the Grail with the sword and the lance, as well as with the figure of a king or a person with regal traits, suffices to reveal the later Christian representation as extrinsic. The seat of the Grail, which must be defended "unto death," can be related neither merely to the Church and

---

4. In an English version of *Merlin,* some knights of the Round Table witness a procession of the Grail, acclaimed by a voice from above in these terms: "Honor, glory, power, and eternal joy to the destroyer of death."

Christianity, which, as I have argued, constantly ignored this cycle of myths, nor even, more generally speaking, to a religious or mystical center. It is rather an initiatory center that retains the legacy of the primordial tradition, according to the undivided unity of the two dignities, namely, the regal and the priestly.

22

Initiatory Adventures of the Grail's Knights

In Wolfram it is written: "Anyone who wants to win the Grail must clear his path toward this precious object with weapons at hand." This summarizes the spirit of the entire cycle of adventures undertaken by the Knights of the Round Table in their quest for the Grail. These are adventures of an epic and warrior character that also have a symbolic character expressing mainly spiritual deeds and not material actions, though not, in my view, to the point where such symbolism represents only a casual and irrelevant element. This clearing the path to the Grail "with weapons at hand," with all its duels, struggles, and related fights, definitely recalls a specific path of inner realization, in which the "active," warrior, or virile element plays the main role. The way that must be cleared by fighting is always that which leads from the "earthly knighthood" to the "spiritual knighthood." According to traditional expressions that I have employed elsewhere,[1] this is not a "lesser war" but is first and foremost the "greater holy war."

Overall, in such adventures or trials, we can distinguish two themes and two degrees:

1. They are destined to confirm the warrior quality, causing the predestined individual to appear as invincible and as the best knight in the world. But for this, besides strength, wisdom and a certain mysterious vocation are required.

---

1. *Revolt Against the Modern World*, 116–28.

Concerning the "vocation" element, recall that in the *Perceval li Gallois,* in Wolfram, and in Chrétien de Troyes, Percival awakens to the desire of knightly adventures that will lead him first to become a Knight of the Round Table and then to seek the Grail when, taken by the birds' chirping, he goes on to obey "his nature and his innermost desires." This is a symbol I will mention only in passing. If we compare the atmosphere to a condition that no longer belongs to the earth element, then the beings living in the atmosphere, namely, birds, have often symbolized supernatural natures, gods, or angels in many traditions, including the Christian one. Consequently, the birds' language has symbolized the "language of the gods," which is understood when one reaches a certain phase of inner awakening.

I will provide further references: in the Nordic-German saga, Siegfried understands this language after slaying the dragon. In Cesare della Riviera (1605), to understand "the occult and various chirping of the birds" is one of the gifts that the hero obtains from the Tree of Life (the birds dwelling in it are "angels," according to an evangelical symbolism).[2] Solomon, whose relation with some elements of the Grail tradition has been repeatedly pointed out (as well as other wise men, especially in Arabic traditions), was credited with being able to understand the language of the birds. Moreover, in some Celtic sagas the Tuatha dé Danaan, who had become invisible, often manifest themselves in the guise of birds, sometimes in order to lead the elect to their "underground" dwellings. It is to this supernatural element, as some kind of higher calling that corresponds to a mysterious echo (this could also be connected with the saying "No one will recognize the Grail unless he has seen it in heaven first"), that we must connect the symbol of Percival, who is awakened to the vocation of a Grail's knight by the birds' voices and not by other earthly beings, and who in this way becomes free from the bond with his mother.[3]

---

2. Cesare della Riviera, *Il mondo magico degli eroi* (1605; Bari, 1932), 169. [See also the thirteenth-century text by Farid al-Din Attar, *Mantiq ut-Tair* (The Conference of the Birds): *A Philosophical Religious Poem in Prose* (Boulder, Colo.: Shambhala, 1971)—Trans.]

3. Percival's mother—who is opposed to his heroic vocation; who hates birds for reawakening this vocation in her son; who, with the hope of keeping him from leaving, provides her son with an inadequate horse; and who eventually dies—is the symbol of a gynecocratic bond that is overcome by Percival, who, once he separates from his mother, develops the cycle of his adventures in the quest for the Grail. In Wolfram, the teaching transmitted by Gurnemanz to Percival amounts to an "overcoming of the mother." Gurnemanz, who teaches Percival everything that may contribute to "achieving earthly happiness," reproaches Percival for constantly having his mother's name on his lips. After Percival has learned from him the principles of the ethics of honor (which is carried to the extreme of saying about anyone who commits a dishonorable act, "Everything in him that is noble is irreparably lost and he goes straight to hell"), he eventually stops talking about her. This may be connected not only to the principle of the so-called men's societies but also, and more in

The hero of the Grail is naturally requested to espouse the principles of faithfulness, honor, and truth, which are characteristic of the knightly ethics; these principles must not be compromised by later achievements. Of Trevrizent it is said that he freed Percival from the latter's sins committed during a period of ascetic life "without violating the laws of chivalry." For instance, it is repeatedly stated that in King Arthur's order there is no place for cowards and for those who are disloyal. In the cycle of the Grail, to be faithful and to abhor lies is the first qualification. In Wolfram's prologue this characterizes an essential, almost metaphysical and ontological distinction among human beings, which is obviously an influence of the Nordic-Aryan component of the medieval warrior and virile world. On the one hand, there are those who know the feeling of honor and of shame, while on the other hand, there are those who are unable to experience this feeling. These two groups are like two races consisting of different substances, sharing absolutely nothing in common.

2. The virile qualities, however, even if integrated, bind one to a specific task; this is, in the various legends, the main point. In the context that is the scope of this book, these qualities are accursed whenever their presence or acquisition does not lead to "asking the question" or some other equivalent. The hero admitted to the Grail's castle has to heal again, to reaffirm or assume the *regnum*. If he remains indifferent before the mute problem, or before the wounded, paralyzed, eviscerated, degraded, or senile representative of the Grail's regality, the demonstrated or acquired *virtus* turns out to be meaningless; that is to say, it proves to be incomplete, illusory, and almost "demonic," accursed by God.[4] In other words, the initiates of the Grail must aspire to a suprapersonal mission, which is the true measure of their qualification. According to previously mentioned texts, to know the Grail and yet not ask, "What is its use?" is a proof of the hero's insufficiency. This is a matter of a committed spirituality, the ideal of which is not transcendence separated from this world.

The countless adventures of the heroes of the Grail refer to a few motifs; having understood them, readers of these romances find only their endless repetition through the most various forms. As I have said, the readers find themselves immersed in a fantastic, surreal atmosphere, and in a merging of the supernatural world with the real world; what is missing are the connections of coherence or of a true "literary" plot. The adventures are for the most part greatly disconnected; but often it is exactly their incoherence, coupled with the intervention of the supernatural dimension almost as if it were a natural fact,

general, to the previously mentioned opposition between the civilization of the mother and the heroic civilization.

4. In Wolfram, Percival is even called a diabolical instrument for not having asked the question.

that gives the sense of the events unfolding outside of time. The repetitions en-
hance the nonepisodic, typical, and symbolic character of the facts and deeds.
First of all, I have already mentioned the episode of Mordrain, who is taken
by the Holy Spirit to an island-tower in the middle of the ocean. The island is
deserted. Mordrain is exhorted to remain steady in his faith. What ensues is the
temptation of a woman, and we learn that it is Lucifer who acts in her. Then
comes the trial of a terrible storm, with thunders and flashes of lightning, followed by the apparition of some kind of phoenix (the miraculous bird of
Serpolion), which strikes and wounds Mordrain; the latter remains unconscious for seven days (initiatory sleep) until, having overcome a new demonic
temptation, thanks to an interpretation of one of his dreams he comes to know
about the dynasty predestined to generate the hero of the Grail.[5]

In similar adventures we have first of all the arrival at the revolving island
or island-tower, a facsimile of Avalon, which is presented as a deserted and dangerous place. After various trials the ship appears. This ship (like the Hyperborean coffin drawn by swans) introduces the further theme of a mandate or
task because it contains the sword and the golden crown, not without relation
to the Tree of Life and to the sacred regality (David).

An analogous theme is found in the *Queste du Graal*. Percival is thrown into
a stream by a diabolical horse riding as fast as the wind. He manages to reach
the island, where he helps a lion fighting against a snake (purification of the
"lion" strength). He resists the temptations of a woman in whom a demonic influence is at work. Then a priestly figure appears and takes him aboard a ship.
Manassier's text has this variation: while Percival rests under an oak, a diabolical horse appears, which throws him into a stream. Percival is assisted by a boat
carrying a woman, whom he mistakes for his lady, Blancheflor, but who really
is a demonic creature. The priestly boat arrives and takes Percival to a beautiful castle; there, a little later, he undertakes and successfully completes the test
of mending a broken sword (initiatory integration of being). In that text, as in
a previous adventure, as Percival approaches a bright tree, he watches the tree
turn into a chapel in which the corpse of a knight lies next to an altar. The light
is suddenly put out by a dark hand. Percival returns to the chapel to spend the
night (the equivalent of the test of sleep undergone at Corbenic) and later

---

5. In regard to recurrences of the traditional number seven, I will mention that in *Le Morte
D'Arthur* and in the *Queste du Graal* Gawain must defeat seven knights to enter the *chastiax as pu-
celles;* that in the Elucidation the Grail is sought after seven times; that in the *Grand Saint Graal*
Moses is grabbed by seven fiery hands after he fails the test of the perilous seat; that in Gerbert,
seven years must pass before Percival, whose sword breaks, is able to find again the path to the
Grail; an analogous theme is also found in *Perlesvax;* and so forth.

learns that the devil himself was present in that hand, which had already killed a great number of brave knights, all buried nearby. He is told this by a hermit, a personification of the ascetic principle, who warns him to seek not only glory but also the salvation of his soul. Percival is then thrown from his horse and thus he cannot catch up with the hermit; while he waits under an oak he finds the demonic horse and the adventures I have already mentioned ensue. Both groups of adventures are clearly two different versions of the same motif. The mortal danger of the trial of the chapel is the same that Percival faces when he mounts the demonic horse by the oak and lets it carry him.[6]

Considering the abnormally important part that the horse plays in the knightly literature, it is appropriate to recall briefly what I have previously mentioned concerning the horse as a symbol.

If the knight represents the spiritual principle of the person engaged in various trials, then the horse must necessarily represent that which "carries" such a principle, namely, the vital force, which is mastered by it in different degrees. Likewise, in the ancient classical myth related by Plato, the personality principle is represented as a charioteer; his fate depends on how he masters the two symbolic horses carrying him. In the days of old, the horse was sacred to two gods, Poseidon and Mars. Poseidon is also the telluric (the "earth shaker") and the sea god, and thus the symbol of an elemental force; this sheds some light on the relationship that in the previously mentioned adventures the horse has with the waters and with the current into which it hurls its rider. In relation to Mars, the horse expresses a warrior orientation of the vital force, which corresponds to the vehicle of the heroic adventures that are typical of knighthood.

This explains the esoteric meaning of being thrown off the horse; it represents the danger that the elemental or unrestrained force may take over. Likewise, we can now see the meaning of other episodes. The knight in the coffin, who tries to lock Percival in it, also tries to steal the latter's horse. In the "test of pride" that Gawain successfully completes, as a condition for being taken across a river on a ferry, the hero is asked to surrender the horse belonging to the knight whom he is attempting to defeat.[7] To successfully tie one's horse to the column of Mount Orguellous, which was created by Merlin and the "polar" meaning of which is rather obvious, is the test that characterizes the best knight. This test is followed by the "sacred mystery," namely, that of the

---

6. The various demonic creatures, whether horse or women, are unmasked and their plans thwarted when the hero crosses himself; this is the Christian version of the evocation of the supernatural principle.

7. At first Percival only wanted to fight. This episode alludes to tests of a superior order, for which it is necessary to go beyond the strength symbolized by the horse.

tree turned into a chapel, and then by the "test of the chapel." And so on. What I have mentioned so far should suffice to help readers orient themselves wherever, in such adventures, something singular and abnormal relative to the rides of individual knights seems to suggest the presence of a hidden meaning.

Coming back to the adventures that I have previously mentioned, the thunders, storms, and analogous phenomena found in them visibly correspond to those that occur during the trial in the Siege Perilous. The theme of the integration offered by the Grail beyond the purely "natural" or warrior unshakableness, a theme that more or less corresponds to that of the boarding of the ferry or of the mending of the sword after the first test, assumes in Robert de Borron the following form: Percival remains calm and unmoved when, after he sits in the Siege Perilous, the earth opens up and thunder booms as if the whole world were exploding. Percival, however, owing to his bravery, which was not accompanied by asking the question (hence the reproach of one of the women: "Your Lord hates you: it is a miracle that the earth does not swallow you up") must now go through a series of adventures. Only after he receives the Grail is the stone of the Round Table, which broke in half under him, completely restored.

Those who are familiar with the mysteriosophical literature will easily recognize in these adventures the allusion to typical initiatory experiences, which are expressed through more or less identical symbols in the traditions of different regions. Storms and thunders, crossings of waters, developments of the themes of the Tree and of the Island, abductions and apparent deaths are constants in initiatory tales in both the East and the West. It would be trifling to make comparisons, which could go on indefinitely. In Plutarch's and in Emperor Julian's works; in the testimonies of the Hellenic Mysteries; in the *De mysteriis;* in the *Tibetan Book of the Dead* and the *Egyptian Book of the Dead;* in the so-called *Mithraic Ritual;* in the teachings of esoteric yoga and Taoism; in the oldest kabbalistic tradition of the Merkava—in all these works even a non-specialist can discern the supratraditional mutual correspondence of various symbols. Moreover, if one does not fall under the impression that all these things amount to poetic creations or fantastic projections that should be interpreted from a psychoanalytical perspective on the basis of the "collective unconscious," then one may recognize in them the corresponding stages of the same inner journey. I could refer my reader to other works of mine that deal specifically with this subject matter,[8] since this is not the proper context to discuss *ex professo* the phenomenology and symbolism referring to the destruction of the physical "I" and to the participation in transcendent states of being.

---

8. *The Hermetic Tradition; The Yoga of Power; Introduzione alla magia.*

I presume that my reader already has some knowledge of the matter and thus will limit myself to emphasizing the elements that are easier to understand. One of the more noteworthy adventures is that of the Castle of Wonders (Chastel Marveil), of which Wolfram says: "The fights you have engaged in until now were just child's play; anguishing events are waiting for you." I have already noted that this adventure is announced by Kundry, the Grail's messenger, after she reproaches Percival for failing to ask the question with these words: "The praises people sing of you are unjustified. The Round Table has compromised its prestige by welcoming Sir Percival." The adventure of Chastel Marveil appears therefore as some kind of reparation, or as a proof destined to awaken in Percival a strength, a conscience, and a vocation that he still lacked. In *Le Morte D'Arthur* (13.4) Galahad is induced to pursue the adventure of the Castle of the Maidens by a heavenly voice that he hears in a chapel on top of a mountain.

In Wolfram's text, in which this adventure is referred to Gawain, the events unfold as follows. Once inside the castle (in *Le Morte D'Arthur* this happens after the crossing of a river and the victory over seven knights), Gawain sees a moving bed that turns away as soon as one approaches it; it is said that "anyone lying on it will see his own hair turn white." Gawain, having caught up with it, feels as if he has been caught in a whirlwind. He hears thunder and horrible noises, which end only when the knight turns his mind to God. Then flying stones and arrows hit him, which do not kill him only thanks to the shield with which Gawain, lying on top of the bed, protects himself; nevertheless, he is wounded. What follows is the manifestation of a primordial power in the form of a wild lion, which Gawain, though wounded, manages to slay, losing consciousness immediately after. When he wakes up again, he finds himself healed by the women. Having passed this test, Gawain becomes the king of the castle and Klinschor loses all powers over it. This trial may be compared to the dangerous and deadly test of sleep. In the *Diu Crone* Gawain falls asleep in the bed, which begins to spin; the magical discharges leave him intact and he is found the following morning sound asleep. The test of dread, which is overcome with a reference to God, is followed by a "contact" and by a test that consists in enduring the discharges of a transcendent force that is awakened by this contact in the person who is to be initiated. Having mastered this force (symbolized by victory over the wild lion), the regal dignity is attained and the power of black magic is broken.

Another variation of the adventure is as follows. In the first stage, Gawain is supposed to conquer the sword. He gets it by proving capable of slaying a giant. In virtue of the conquered sword, he is admitted to the Grail's castle. When he sees the Grail he falls into ecstasy, and while in this state he has a vision of a seat occupied by a king who has been pierced by a lance. The question is not asked. Left alone, Gawain plays chess against an invisible opponent who has golden pieces, while his own are silver. Gawain is defeated three times in a row; then, enraged, he smashes the chessboard and falls asleep. The following morning, when he awakens, the castle has disappeared. In this episode, what visibly recurs is the theme of an incomplete force (the sword). The victory over the giant does not prevent Gawain from being associated with the "silver" element, which is destined to be defeated by the "golden" element. Traditionally, silver represents the lunar principle, while gold symbolizes the solar and regal principle, for which Gawain, who did not ask the question, is not yet sufficiently qualified.

In Gautier this test seems to correspond to the test of the woman, since it is said that it was Morgan le Fay who defeated Percival at chess; Morgan is a figuration of the supernatural woman of Avalon. In this version, Percival reaches his goal only after a new series of adventures, being conditioned by his ability to mend the broken sword (a new convergence of familiar themes). Moreover, the chess games he loses are followed by yet another adventure. A maiden appears to the knight, with whom he falls in love; but in order to have her he must get the head of a deer. With the help of a bloodhound Percival manages to procure this head. What ensues is an incident related to the theme of the "knight of the coffin." The knight of the Grail finds the tomb with a living knight locked inside who, once freed, attempts to lock Percival in. As Percival attempts to resist him, a knight who is the brother of the man closed in the coffin steals both the head of the deer and the bloodhound; later on, Percival catches up with him and kills him. The hero of the Grail is led by the bloodhound to the castle of chess, where he obtains the woman upon delivering the head of the deer. In *Le Morte D'Arthur* the bloodhound leads the hero (here, Lancelot) to an old castle, where he finds a dead knight and a maiden who beseeches him to heal her wounded brother; to do this he must first obtain a sword by completing the test of the Chapel Perilous.[9]

The meaning of the symbol of the deer is uncertain. In the *Grand Saint Graal*, Joseph of Arimathea and his knights, stopped by the waters, are magically led above them, without sinking, by a white deer carried by a group of four lions. The explanation given in this text, which has been strongly influenced by Christianity, according to which the four lions are the four evangelists and the white deer is Christ, seems to me not to rise above the allegorical level of a late religious overlay, considering that the deer had already played an often important role in ancient central European and Scandinavian symbolism. In

---

9. *Le Morte D'Arthur*, 17.22.

any event, in the text the reference to the power of walking over water, a universal symbol that has already been explained as the specific initiatory dignity, already suffices. In regard to the two episodes (i.e., the theft of the deer's head and the attempt to lock Percival in the coffin), considering that the two knights in both episodes are "brothers," they appear to be one of the many cases of duplication of the same motif, which are very frequent in this type of literature. The Percival who is about to be locked in the crypt is identical to the Percival who is temporarily deprived of the supernatural privilege symbolized by the deer; in function of this privilege, and once integrated by the possession of the woman, Percival will successfully and definitely conclude the adventure and bring about the effective restoration of the regality of the Grail.

The insufficiency of the mere heroic force, not in the special and technical sense that I have indicated, but in the ordinary sense of this term, is also expressed in the theme of the double sword. The first sword, which Percival naturally carries with him or which he has won in his preliminary adventures, corresponds to the purely warrior virtues that have been duly put to the test. The second sword, according to Wolfram, is gained by Percival only once inside the Grail castle, as the one who is expected to ask the question. Moreover, it is the sword that, in the *Diu Crone*, the king who is only apparently alive gives to Gawain before disappearing, in the sense of passing on to him his own function; in the *Grand St. Graal* Celidoine declares to hold the sword as dear as the Grail itself.

In Wolfram the first sword originally belonged to the Red Knight. The theme of the Red Knight is not very clear. In some respect, he can be identified with the type of knight who is determined to fight his way to the Grail, weapon at hand. But being such a type and having such a dignity is already the result of a preliminary and almost natural selection. Thus the Red Knight is sometimes the knight who finds the Grail and at other times a knight whom the latter has defeated, and whose red armor and sword he has appropriated.[10] The transmission of a function from one person to another through the test of arms is a theme that I have previously explained and that is closely related to the cycle. Moreover, it will be helpful to recall here a legend of the Celtic cycle that picks up the same theme, though the Grail does not directly appear in it.

Beneath a big tree is a fountain; while this tree recalls the Tree of the Center, the fountain in traditional symbolism alludes to the point at which the vivifying force gushes forth in its elemental state. He who pours water from this fountain causes a terrible thunder that causes heaven and earth to tremble;

---

10. An intermediate form is that of the Red Knight who comes to the aid of the Grail's knight just when the latter's enemies are about to overpower him.

then an icy wave mixed with hail rolls forward, which chills one to the bones,[11] a wave so powerful that one can scarcely endure it without dying (it is the equivalent of the discharges in the test of the Chastel Marveil). Then the tree becomes dry, without leaves. Wonderful birds come and sit in the tree, and when one is about to understand their language, a black knight arrives, issuing a challenge. Many lower-ranking knights at the court of King Arthur die at his hand, especially as a result of not having been able to endure the wave that they unleashed. The knight Owein, however, passes the test, wounds the black knight, and, as he chases him, reaches a "large, bright castle" in which he receives from a lady the ring of invulnerability and of invisibility, which are symbols of powers and of a dignity that I have already explained. The black knight, who was the lord of the castle, dies. The lady was his wife, the Lady of the Fountain, who now becomes the wife of the man who defeated her husband. Owein assumes the function of the knight whom he killed. The kings of the "large, bright castle" are the custodians and the defenders of the fountain; once they are defeated, their function passes on to the person who has won the match.[12] This is also the case of Percival, who after slaying the Red Knight becomes himself the Red Knight, which is suggested by the fact that he wears his armor and carries his sword.

In this legend, a part of the *Mabinogion*, the theme of the "test of arms" interacts with a test of a visibly initiatory character, which integrates the first. Ideally, it is to the successful completion of such an initiatory test, which is no longer "natural," that we may relate the possession of the second sword. Such a sword awaits Percival in the Grail's castle. "If you learn its secret virtues," Sigune tells him, "you will be able to engage in any fight without fear." The king of the Grail had used this sword prior to being wounded. The sword can break in half, but then, in order to mend it, one must use the water of the fountain called Lac. The hero, who through his unaided strength and bravery arrives at the inaccessible castle of the Grail, usually receives such a sword or is asked to mend it once it is broken. The last purpose of the quest, the "high glory," and the supreme dignity are achieved when the wielding of the sword or its mending immediately lead to asking the question. "To put the sword in his hand amounted to an invitation to ask the question," says Wolfram. Once the sword is obtained, or one has performed any of the many adventures that in their variety of symbolism correspond to the realization, one must feel the need to know the essence of the Grail and also the mystery of the lance and of the wounded king.

---

11. This reference to the bones is very interesting from an initiatory point of view.
12. In Wolfram the dangerous lady Orgeluse appears to Gawain near water gushing out of a rock.

Obtaining the sword or mending it means proving to be virtually quali-fied—or "invested"—to be admitted to the vision of the Grail, to assume the power of the Stone of Light or Foundation Stone, and thus to resurrect the king and to restore the ravaged or deserted kingdom. A first test may fail, and the sword may break; then it is necessary to mend it by the Fountain. In that event, it is necessary to go again through a cycle of adventures whose meaning is best expressed by the symbolism of the previously mentioned Celtic legend, the key to which is the "test of the fountain." This legend resembles the test of the Chastel Marveil indicated by Kundry to those who have been at the Grail's cas-tle without achieving the supreme goal.

The hero, to whom the sword has already been entrusted once, thereupon experiences an invincible nostalgia. Percival says: "Whether close at hand or far away the hour in which I will again behold the Grail, until then I will not know joy. All my thoughts go to the Grail. Nothing will distract me from it until I live." Little by little the hero will rise from the still passive and lunar quality, which is symbolized by the silver chess pieces, and will eventually attain the ac-tive and (in a transcendent sense) virile quality, proving worthy of it. It is a pro-gressive growth, simultaneously Promethean and Olympian, along the way on which Heracles and Jacob, the winner of angels, won, but on which Lucifer, Prometheus, and Adam were vanquished. It is the same transformation indi-cated by the Hermetic *ars regia* with this formula: "Our Work is the conversion and change of one being into another being, as from one thing into another thing, from debility to strength . . . from corporeality to spirituality."[13]

Having accomplished this much, the regal crown of the Grail is acquired once and for all and the true Lord of the Two Swords is now awake and alive. Here a fundamental point must be remembered: in the theological-political lit-erature, and especially the Ghibelline one dating from the time of the struggle for the investitures, the evangelical image of the two swords symbolized noth-ing else but the double power, namely, the political and the spiritual.

---

13. N. Flamel, *Le Désir désiré*, chapter 6, quoted in Evola, *The Hermetic Tradition* (p. 99).

23

The Grail as a
Ghibelline Mystery

Here we may briefly consider the meaning that the regality of the Grail and its order had in the system of both visible and secret forces that acted during the historical period in which these romances became popular.

The becoming invisible or inaccessible of all that with which the traditions of various people have dramatized and preserved the memory of the primordial seat and tradition symbolizes the passing from the visible to the occult of a power that should nonetheless be regarded as regal. The kingdom of the Grail, in terms of a center to which, as it is stated in Wolfram von Eschenbach, the elect from all over the world are called, from which knights leave to travel to faraway lands on secret missions, and which, finally, is the "seminary" that produces kings, is the seat whence many kings are sent to various lands. No one will ever know whence these kings came and what is their race and name.[1] The sign of the inaccessible and inviolable Grail remains a reality even in the form according to which it cannot be connected to any known kingdom on earth. It is a land that will never be invaded, to which one belongs for reasons other than mere physical birth, in virtue of a dignity that is different from all other dignities and that links in an unbreakable chain men who may appear to be scattered in the world, in space and time, among various nations. In my books I have often dwelled on this traditional teaching. In such an esoteric sense, the

---

1. The Grail has the same virtue of the "stone of kings" of the Celtic tradition of the Tuatha because it designates the one who must assume the regal function in a country without a king.

kingdom of the Grail, just like Arthur's, Prester John's, Thule, Avalon, and so forth, endure forever. The words "non vivit" found in the Sibylline formula "vivit non vivit" does not refer to it. In its polar character this kingdom is immobile. It does not get closer to various points in the flow of history; rather it *is* the flow of history, to which men and kingdoms get more or less close.

For a certain period of time it seemed that the Ghibelline Middle Ages approximated this kingdom to a great degree. This epoch appeared to offer sufficient conditions for the "kingdom of the Grail" to turn from occult into manifest, affirming itself as a reality that is simultaneously inner and outer, in a unity of the spiritual authority and of the temporal power, just as it was in the beginning. In this way it can be said that the regality of the Grail constituted the apex of the medieval imperial myth and the highest profession of faith of the great Ghibelline movement. The regality of the Grail lived more as a climate than at a particular point in time, being expressed more through legend and fantastic or "apocalyptic" representations than through the reflected consciousness and the unilaterally political ideology of that time. This was the case for the same reason that that which in the individual being is too deep and dangerous for the waking consciousness is often expressed less in the latter's clear forms than in symbols of dream and of subconscious spontaneity.

An in-depth understanding of the Middle Ages from this perspective would cause me to expound again the main features of that general metaphysics of Western history that I have already discussed elsewhere.[2] Thus, here I will only recall some points in an axiomatic form.

The inner decadence and finally the political collapse of the ancient Roman world represented the syncope of the attempt to shape the West according to the imperial symbol. The spread of Christianity, because of the particular type of dualism that it supported and because of its merely religious traditional character, rapidly led beyond the process of dissociation, up to the point at which, following the invasion of Nordic races, the medieval civilization developed and the symbol of the empire was resurrected. The Holy Roman Empire was both a *restauratio* and a *continuatio,* considering that its ultimate meaning—beyond any external appearance, compromise with contingent reality, and often limited awareness and various dignity of the individuals who represented its idea—was that of a renewal of the Roman movement toward an ecumenical "solar" synthesis. This renewal, which logically implied the overcoming of Christianity, was therefore destined to clash with the hegemonistic claims of the Church of Rome. In fact, the Church of Rome could not

---

2. *Revolt Against the Modern World,* part 2.

acknowledge the Empire as a superior principle to that which she herself embodied; at her height, and in flagrant contradiction to her evangelical premises, she attempted to usurp the Empire's rights; thus arose the theocratic vision of Guelphism.

Overall, according to the common perception (which, as a starting point, is correct), the medieval civilization was shaped by three elements: Northern-pagan, Christian, and Roman. The first played a decisive role in regard to ethics, lifestyle, and social structure. The feudal regime, the knightly morals, the civilization of the courts, the original substance that engendered the crusading spirit are inconceivable without a reference to Nordic-pagan blood and spirit. But while the races that descended upon Rome from the North should not be considered "barbarian" from this perspective (since it seems to me that they carried along values that were superior to those of a civilization that was already decayed in its principles and in its people), we can still talk of a certain barbarism, which does not mean primitivity but rather involution, in specific regard to their spiritual traditions. I have already mentioned the existence of a primordial Nordic-Hyperborean tradition. In the peoples living at the time of the invasions we can find only fragmentary echoes and obscure memories of such a tradition, which leave a wide margin to popular legends and to superstition. In any event, these memories were such that forms of a tough, warlike, and rough-hewn life prevailed over everything spiritual. The Nordic-Germanic traditions of the time, which were largely constituted by the Eddas, retained slight residues whose vital possibilities appear to have been exhausted and in which little was left of the wide scope and metaphysical tension that were proper to the great cycles of the primordial tradition.

Thus we may speak of a state of an involutive latency of the Nordic tradition. But as soon as contact with Christianity and with the symbol of Rome occurred, a different condition ensued; this contact had a galvanizing effect. In spite of everything, Christianity revived the generic sense of a supernatural transcendence. The Roman symbol offered the idea of a universal *regnum*, of an *aeternitas* carried by an imperial power. All this integrated the Nordic substance and provided superior reference points to its warrior ethos, so much as to gradually usher in one of those cycles of restoration that I have labeled "heroic" in a special sense. And so, from the type of the mere warrior the figure of the knight arose; the ancient Germanic traditions of war waged in function of Valhalla developed into the supranational epic of the "holy war" or crusade; a shift occurred from the type of the prince of a particular race to the type of the sacred and ecumenical emperor, who claimed that the principle of his power had a character and an origin no less supernatural and transcendent than that of the Church.

This true renaissance, however, this grandiose development and wonderful transformation of forces, required an ultimate reference point, a supreme center of crystallization higher than the Christian though Romanized ideal, and higher than the external and merely political idea of the Empire. This supreme point of integration was manifested precisely in the myth of the Grail's regality, according to the intimate relation it had with the several variations of the "imperial saga." The silent problem of the Ghibelline Middle Ages was expressed in the fundamental theme of that cycle of legends: the need for a hero of the two swords, who overcomes natural and supernatural tests, to really ask the question: the question that avenges and heals, the question that restores power to its regality.

The Middle Ages awaited the hero of the Grail, so that the head of the Holy Roman Empire could become an image or a manifestation of the Universal Ruler; so that all the forces could receive a new power; so that the Dry Tree could blossom again; so that an absolute driving force could arise to overcome any usurpation, antagonism, laceration; so that a real solar order could be formed; so that the invisible emperor could also be the manifest one; and finally, so that the "Middle Age" *(medium aeveum)* could also have the meaning of an "Age of the Center."

Anyone who follows the adventures of the heroes of the Grail up to the famous question is bound to have the clear and unmistakable feeling that something, all of a sudden, prevents the author from speaking freely, and that a trivial answer is given to conceal the real one. In fact, what really matters is not so much to know what are the objects according to the Christianized fable or to the ancient Celtic and Nordic legends, but rather to feel the tragedy of the paralyzed or wounded king; once one achieves that inner realization, the symbol of which is the vision of the Grail, what matters is to assume the initiative of the absolute action that brings about a restoration. The miraculously redeeming power that is attributed to the question can be perceived as extravagant only from this perspective. To ask is the equivalent of stating the problem. After all the conditions of the earthly and spiritual knighthood have been realized and the Grail has been known, the indifference that is considered a serious fault on the part of the hero is the indifference he displays when he witnesses without questioning the spectacle of the coffin and the surviving king, who is either maimed, killed, or retaining a merely artificial semblance of life. As I have already said, the dignity of the hero of the Grail is a dignity that obliges; such is its specific, prevalent and antimystical character. Historically speaking, the kingdom of the Grail, which was supposed to be restored to even higher heights, is the Empire itself; the hero of the Grail, who would have become the "lord of all creatures," the one who has received the "supreme power," is the same historical emperor, Federicus, in the event he would have realized the mystery of the Grail, or would have been the one who becomes the Grail itself. There are some texts in which such a theme is introduced in an even more immediate fashion.[3] Once the chosen knight arrives at the castle, he directly addresses the king and asks in an almost brutal fashion, skipping every ceremonial form, "Where is the Grail?" meaning: "Where is the power of which you should be the representative?" Once this question is asked, a miracle ensues.

At this point fragments of ancient Atlantic, Celtic, and Nordic traditions are mixed with confused images of the Judeo-Christian religion. Avalon; Seth; Solomon; Lucifer; the stone-thunderbolt; Joseph of Arimathea; the White Island; the fish; the Lord of the Center and the symbolism of his seat; the mystery of the revenge and the deliverance; the "signs" of the Tuatha dé Danaan, who in turn are confused with the race that brought the Grail to earth—they all form a whole in which the various elements, as I have endeavored to show, reveal a logical unity to those who are capable of penetrating its essence.

For about a century and a half, the entire knightly West lived intensely the myth of the court of King Arthur and his knights seeking the Grail. It was a progressive saturation of a historical climate that shortly after was followed by an abrupt break. This awakening of a heroic tradition connected to a universal imperial idea was destined to arouse inimical forces and lead to a clash with Catholicism.

The true reason why the Church became such a staunch antagonist of the Empire was the instinctive perception of the true nature of the force gaining momentum behind the external forms of the knightly spirit and the Ghibelline ideal. Even though on the other side, among the defenders of the Empire, an adequate awareness was present only in part, because of compromises, contradictions, and indecisions of which Dante himself was not exempt, the instinct of the Church was nevertheless absolutely correct. Hence the drama of medieval Ghibellinism, of the great knightly orders, and in particular, of the Order of the Knights Templar.

3. J. L. Weston, *From Ritual to Romance* (Cambridge, 1920).

PART FOUR

The Legacy of
the Grail

24

The Grail and the Knights Templar

It is hard to say through what representatives of the Holy Roman Empire the top of the hierarchy established an invisible connection with the center of the "Universal Ruler." Outside the Grail cycle, I have already mentioned legends foreshadowing the sensation of a mysterious mandate that the Hohenstaufens allegedly received, a mandate that they sometimes took on and sometimes failed to understand or even lost. In any event, it was not a coincidence that the popular imagination was led to relive through their persons the myth of the emperor who in the end will reawaken and triumph. The prophecy according to which the Dry Tree will blossom again at the encounter between Frederick and Prester John is yet another form of the hope in the contact that, during the peak years of the Ghibelline movement, could have produced the true restoration.

Generally speaking, up to Maximilian I (who was significantly called the "last knight," who was symbolically related to King Arthur, and who, it appears, intended to assume the pontifical function), in the representatives of the Holy Roman Empire was reflected something of the chrism of transcendent regality, of that superior "regal religion according to Melchizedek" to which the political ideology sometimes referred when claiming the superior right of kings, who, according to their ideology, were not merely lay people, but men anointed by God. When confronted by this, the Church was led to evoke confused apocalyptic images and the story of the coming of the Antichrist. Especially toward the end of the Middle Ages one can clearly discern the Church's attempt to attribute to kings of the French dynasty, which was friendly to the Roman Curia, the positive traits of the figure of the future victorious emperor and to associate the idea of the Antichrist to those elements of the legend that could be referred instead to the Ghibelline Teutonic princes. Thus some people were led to see the figuration of the Antichrist in the traits of Dante's Greyhound.

In any event, the Church was never able to overcome completely the imperial hierarchy. The mighty struggle between the two powers, which to a great degree degenerated into an antagonism between temporal interests and ambitions, was destined to end with the collapse of both, and eventually with the Lutheran deviation, which proved to be fatal both to the authority of the Church and to the sacred and integral idea of the Empire. Conversely, insofar as the militia of the Holy Roman Empire is concerned (i.e., knighthood), things went differently, sometimes even culminating in instances of repression and destruction.

Among the various knightly orders, the Order of the Knights Templar was the one that more than others overcame the double limitations constituted, on the one hand, by the mere warrior ideal of the secular knighthood and, on the other hand, by the merely ascetic ideal of Christianity and its monastic orders. The Order of the Knights Templar approached more than others the type of the "spiritual chivalry of the Grail"; moreover, its inner doctrine had an initiatory character. For this reason it was singled out and severely repressed by the alliance of the representatives of the two princes whom the order ideally transcended, namely, the pope and his ally, Philip the Fair, a secularized, profane, and despotic king who hated the aristocracy. These two princes may well correspond to Dante's symbols of the Giant and the Prostitute.

Whatever the "real" motives behind the destruction of the Templars were, they are of little or no account. In such cases, these motives are always occasional: they only help to set in motion the forces needed to implement a design, the directing intelligence of which is to be found on a much deeper plane. In virtue of the nature of the templar ideal, the order was bound to be destroyed. After all, the Church's sentiment against chivalry did not fail to manifest itself even against other orders, though through different excuses. In 1238 Pope Gregory IX targeted the Order of St. John for alleged abuses and betrayals, but also hinting at the presence of heretical elements in the Order. In 1307 the Teutonic Knights were likewise accused of heresy by the archbishop of Riga; their leader barely managed to save the order, though with great effort. But the main object of the Church's attack was the Knights Templar. The destruction of this order coincides with the interruption of the metaphysical tension of the

Ghibelline Middle Ages; when it was accomplished, the contacts were interrupted again. This marks the initial breaking point, the beginning of the decline of the West.

The struggle against the Templar Order may truly be regarded, more so than the one waged against the Cathars, as a crusade against the Grail. In Wolfram, the analogy between the Grail knights and the Templars is revealed by the name *Templeisen,* namely, Templars, which is given to the custodians of the Grail, even though no temple is mentioned. In *Perlesvax,* the guardians of the Grail in the "Island" are both ascetic and warriorlike and, like the Knights Templar, wear a red cross on a white garment. Joseph of Arimathea gives to Evelach (Galahad's ancestor, who was a hero of the Grail and of King Arthur) a white shield with a vermillion cross, which is the same emblem exclusively given by Pope Eugene III to the Templars, in 1147. A ship with this same Templar emblem, a red cross on a white sail, comes to take Percival to the unknown seat where the Grail had been taken to, and whence Percival will never return. The same themes are found in the romance *Som de Nansai,* since here too the Grail ends up being guarded by warrior monks who live on an island, whence from time to time those who are destined to become kings in other lands depart.

Templar chivalry was characteristically an order in which fighting and especially "holy war" were regarded as a path of asceticism and liberation. Externally, it embraced Christianity, but in its highest mystery, which was restricted to an inner circle, it went beyond the Christian religion, rejecting the worship of Christ and the main limitations of a devotional type. This chivalry also tended to shift the principle of supreme spiritual authority to a center other than Rome, a center more properly designated with the nobler and more universal term "Temple" rather than "Church."

This is clear enough in the acts and proceedings of the trial against the Knights Templar. Even though the evidence was distorted or painted with blasphemous tinges, either intentionally or because of a misunderstanding, the expert eye will easily recognize its true scope.

Of course one should not idealize the entire Templar Order in its historical concreteness, especially when the latter grew out of proportion (at one point it had nine thousand centers) and acquired a mighty temporal power and wealth. Among their members there certainly were men who did not live up to the ideal and who lacked all necessary skills, even in the case of Great Master Gerard of Ridfort (1184–1189). What I am going to say now does not apply to the great majority of the Templars in the last years of the order's life, but rather to a hierarchy that, as often happens in these cases, did not necessarily coincide with the visible and official hierarchy.

First of all, it has consistently been shown, not only through confessions extorted with torture but also through spontaneous declarations, that the Templars had a secret ritual of an authentically initiatory character. As a condition to be admitted to this rite, or as an introductory phase to it, one had to abjure the worship of Christ. The knight who aspired to the various levels of the order's inner hierarchy had to step over the crucifix and insult it. He was ordered "not to believe in the Crucified One, but in the Lord who is in heaven"; he was taught that Jesus had been a false prophet—not a divine figure who died to atone for men's sins, but a very ordinary man who died because of his own mistakes. The text of the indictment was formulated in this manner: *Et post crux portaretur et ibi dicetur sibi quod crucifixus non est Christus, sed quidam falsus propheta, depetatus per Iudaeos ad mortem propter delicta sua.* This should be regarded not as a true abjuration, much less as a blasphemy, but rather as a sort of test: the initiate had to demonstrate his capability to go beyond an exoteric cult of a merely religious-devotional type. The rite in question was apparently celebrated on Good Friday; however, Good Friday also happens to be the day that often corresponds to the celebration of the mystery of the Grail or to the arrival of the hero in the inaccessible castle of the Grail.

A further charge was that the Templars despised the sacraments, especially penance and confession—those practices most influenced by the pathos of sin and expiation. The Templars allegedly did not acknowledge the supreme authority of the pope and of the Church and followed Christian precepts only in appearance. All this could be the counterpart of the anti-Christolatric rite, namely, the overcoming of Christian exotericism and of the usurping claim to embody the supreme spiritual authority on the part of a merely dogmatic-religious institution, totally unaware of both the pragmatic justification of its own limitations and the traditional elements present at a latent state in its doctrines and symbols.[1]

Moreover, the Templars were charged with keeping secret liaisons with Muslims and being closer to the Islāmic faith than to the Christian one. This last charge is probably best understood by remembering that Islām too is characterized by the rejection of Christ worship. The "secret liaisons" allude to a perspective that is less sectarian, more universal, and thus more esoteric than that of militant Christianity. The Crusades, in which the Templars and in general the Ghibelline chivalry played a fundamental role, in many respects created a supratraditional bridge between West and East. The crusading knighthood ended up confronting a facsimile of itself, namely, warriors who abided by corresponding ethics, chivalrous customs, ideals of a "holy war," and initiatory

---

1. See my *Maschera e volto dello spiritualismo contemporaneo,* chapter 7.

currents. Thus the Templars were the Christian equivalent of the Arab Order of the Ishmaelites,[2] who likewise regarded themselves as the "guardians of the Holy Land" (in an esoteric and symbolic sense), and who had two hierarchies, one official and one secret. Such an order, which had a double character, both warrior and religious, almost met the same fate as that of the Templars, and for analogous reasons: its initiatory character and its upholding an esotericism that despised the literal meaning of sacred scriptures.[3] In Ishmaelite esotericism we find again the same theme of the Ghibelline imperial saga: the Islāmic dogma of the "resurrection" *(kiyama)* is here interpreted as the new manifestation of the Supreme Leader *(Mahdī)*, who became invisible during the so-called period of "absence" *(ghāyba)*. This is so because the Mahdī at one point disappeared, thus eluding death, leaving his followers under the obligation of swearing allegiance and obedience unto him as if he were Allah himself.[4]

In these terms it was possible to gradually establish an acknowledgment *inter pares* beyond any partisan spirit and historical contingency, or a sort of supratraditional understanding like the symbol of the "Temple." Moreover, exclusivism and sectarianism being features of exotericism, that is, of a tradition's external and profane aspects, we find again here the "overcoming" attitude that already characterized the Templars. In reference to the Crusades we learn from history that this "secret understanding" never amounted to a military betrayal, considering that the Templars were among the bravest, most faithful and warriorlike soldiers during all the Crusades. That which rather corresponded to it was probably the expunging from the notion of "holy war" of its materialistic and external aspect of war waged against the "infidel" and of death for the "true" faith, and its restoration to its purest, most metaphysical meaning. According to this meaning, what really mattered was no longer a particular profession of faith, but the simple capacity to turn war into an ascetic preparation

---

2. The Nizārī Ismā'īlīyah, whose members were called *hashīshīyah*, or "hashish smokers," whence their English name, Assassins, is derived. [Trans.]

3. Templars and Ishmaelites carried the same colors (red and white): cross and cloak the former, belt and garment the latter. The supreme leader of the Ishmaelites, the "lord of the mountain," shaykh al-jabal, was thought of as an invisible dominator "who had in his hands the life and death of kings." To his person and to his inaccessible dwelling, identified with Paradise, was applied a symbolism that corresponds to that of the King of the Grail and of the Universal Ruler. One of the charges against the Templars was of having allied with the Lord of the Mountain.

4. These views, with minor variations, are common to the branch of the Shi'a that still is the official religion in modern Iran. The Ishmaelites had an initiation with seven degrees, starting from the fourth of which the transmission of the suprareligious esoteric teaching *(ta'wil)* began; the adept was then believed to be above any law. Antinomianism replaced blind and unconditional obedience to the leader, which was the rule of the first three degrees.

for the attainment of immortality. On the Muslim side, too, the ultimate meaning of the "holy war" (jihad) was not any different.[5]

In the cycle of the Grail we have something similar to the "secret liaisons" considered in the supratraditional sense of the term: that is, in the mixture of Arab, pagan, and Christian elements. Wolfram eventually attributed to a "pagan" source the story of the Grail found by Kyot. Likewise, we have seen that Percival's father, though a Christian, felt no repugnance to fight under Saracen princes; that Joseph of Arimathea himself is described as benefiting from the Grail even before being baptized; that not only Christian but also pagan knights fought for the Grail; and that the pagan knight Firefiz, through the test of arms, almost proved to be better than his Christian brother, and before being baptized became a member of Arthur's knights. Conversely, Baruch is presented as a caliph, that is, as a non-Christian. The dynasty of Prester John, which is connected to the dynasty of the Grail, includes pagans and Christians, and even, according to some, a majority of pagan princes. In conclusion, apart from some later texts that reflect a heavy Christian influence, in many of its parts the Grail literature displays the same antisectarian and supratraditional spirit that inspired the charge leveled against the Templars, of developing "secret liaisons." These liaisons probably consisted in the capability of acknowledging the same tradition even in forms other than the Christian one.

The central ritual of Templar initiation was kept very secret. From one of the proceedings of the trial we learn that a knight who underwent it returned as pale as a corpse and with a lost expression on his face, claiming that from then on he could never be happy again. Shortly after, the same knight fell into a state of invincible depression and died. Such effects recall those produced in some of the tests of the Grails, tests that "turn one's hair as white as snow" and induce, in those who fail, a deep disgust with all earthly things as well as a deep and incurable unhappiness. What produces an extreme terror in some knights and causes them to flee, according to another testimony of the Templars, is the vision of an "idol," which is described in various forms. These forms, as they are described in the proceedings of the trial, are difficult to interpret: a majestic golden figure, a virgin, the apparition of an animal's head such as a ram's, a crowned older man, an androgynous or two-faced figure. Most likely these are dramatizations of the initiatory consciousness, in which a given content of an

---

5. See my *Revolt Against the Modern World*, chapters 18 and 19. This too was the true meaning of fighting according to the knights of the Grail: to them it did not matter whether their opponent was a Christian or a Saracen, just as it did not matter whether their fight ended in victory or death, since fighting for them was an ascesis and a purification, with the exception of their "superordained" task of defending the "seat of the Grail" and of blocking access to it.

individual's imagination can play a determining role. We may also get some orientation through testimonies such as the one claiming that the idol is a "demon" who (allegorically) "bestows wisdom and riches," that are virtues which we have already seen referred to the Grail. The name frequently given to the mysterious idol, Baphomet, in all likelihood comes from the Greek βαρη μητομς, meaning "baptism of wisdom," or a gnosis in a higher sense; this may have been the name of a ritual that most likely passed on to the idol.

The vision of the idol allegedly occurred at a given point during Mass, as a mystery to which Mass itself was subordinated. This recalls the ceremonies described in the more Christianized Grail texts: a sort of Mass having the Grail as its main reference point, with the sense of a mystery too dangerous to explore, least one is stricken by a sword or loses his sight.

In Wolfram, however, wisdom is what Percival, a "soul of steel," eventually achieves. According to others, "wisdom" (Philosophine) is Percival's own mother, who is conceived as the original bearer of the Grail. In gnostic literature, wisdom is often symbolized by a woman (the virgin Sophia); while this, on the one hand, points to that explanation according to which Baphomet, as the center of the Templar baptism of wisdom, is a "virgin," on the other hand it recalls how the symbolism of the woman played such a great role in knightly adventures and in the heroic cycle. Bernard of Clairvaux, who was regarded as a sort of spiritual father of the Templars, was also called the Knight of the Virgin. In another testimony, of Nordic or English origins, the Templar mystery, like the Grail's, seems to have a relation with a sacred stone: the Templars, in their most difficult times, allegedly turned for help to a stone contained in their altar. In Medieval Hermeticism, *Rebis,* the "double thing," designated the "stone." This may also establish a relation with the symbol of Baphomet in its "androgyne" form. He who has rejoined the "woman" and has reabsorbed her in himself during the work of initiatory reintegration was often conceived, even in the East, as the lord of two natures, or as an androgyne.

In this regard, typical is the distortion behind the charge that the Templars used to burn before their idol the children that they begat in sin. All this probably amounted to a "baptism of fire," namely, to a heroic-solar initiation that was administered to the neophytes who, according to a terminology common to all traditions, were regarded as the children of the masters, or as newborns, according to their second, spiritual birth. In the coded language of Greek mythology, we find the symbol of a goddess, Demeter, who places a baby in the fire in order to grant him immortality. This rebirth was symbolized by a belt that had to be worn day and night, which every knight received and which had to be put on the idol, so that it may become impregnated with a special influence. The belt or cord, called ταινία in the classical Mysteries, was the mark of the initiates, just as in the Indo-Aryan Orient it used to characterize the higher castes of the "twice born" and especially the *brāhmaṇa* caste. The cord is also the symbol of the immaterial chain, the connection that invisibly joins together all those who have received the same initiation, thus becoming the carriers of the same invisible influence.

The "double fire" is an image that to a certain degree corresponds to that of the "double sword" (see the end of the previous chapter): in the East the doctrine of the double birth of Agni and, in the classical world, the doctrine of the double fire (telluric and Uranian), referred to it. One of the main symbols of the Templars, the "double torch," leads back to the same idea and comes together with a chalice that plays the role of some sort of Grail. The two torches already appeared in the Mithraic symbolism in relation to an initiation that was especially open to the warrior element.[6]

I have already mentioned that Innocent III accused the Templars of cultivating the "doctrine of demons," meaning supernatural sciences. Concerning the Templars, they were suspected of practicing black magic and necromancy. According to some, they practiced alchemy; even though this probably was not the case, the fact remains that some sculptures of the monuments and of the tombs of the Templars had astrological-alchemical signs, such as the pentagram and various symbols of planets and metals. In the cycle of the Grail we have already encountered elements of this kind. Astrological references abound in Wolfram von Eschenbach. Kyot, in order to decipher the texts containing the mysteries of the Grail, which can be "read in the stars," first had to learn magical characters. The Fisher King sometimes is described as a magician who can take many forms at will. The counterpart of Arthur is Merlin the sorcerer; in *Le Morte D'Arthur* he helps Sir Balin pass the test of weapons through the aid of a magical force. Finally, we may recall the tradition according to which the Grail itself was brought down to earth and guarded by fallen angels, who are the equivalent of those demons to whom Innocent III attributed the doctrine of Templars, or of the demons to whom some Christianized Celtic texts assimilated the Tuatha dé Danaan (the race "from above," or from Avalon, which was the holder of divine sciences). The pentagram, which is found on a Templar tomb, is a traditional sign of supernatural sovereignty; in an English Grail text, *Sir Gawain and the Green Knight,* the hero of the Grail receives it as a mark, while in other texts of the same cycle he consecrates the Sword of the Grail so it will not break and thus may retain its virtue.

---

6. See my *The Path of Enlightenment in the Mithraic Mysteries,* trans. Guido Stucco (Edmonds, Wash.: The Alexandrian Press, 1994).

While, on the one hand, the enemies of the Templars tendentiously emphasized the latter's misogyny, on the other hand they accused the initiates of
breaking the order's vow of chastity and of engaging in homosexual practices.
Purity and chastity sometimes, though not always, appear also in the cycle of
the Grail as characteristics required in the predestined hero. I have already indicated the possibility of bestowing on these concepts a meaning higher than a
merely sexual and moralistic one. The renunciation of the earthly woman essentially alludes to the overcoming of desire: Amfortas is doomed by mating
not with the woman of the Grail but with Orgeluse. In any event, just as the
kings of the Grail were given a woman, according to Wolfram, while the simple knights had to be without one, likewise one may think that while the simple Templars practiced ascetic material chastity, the initiates of the Order
practiced a transcendent chastity. If it is legitimate to refer, in regard to initiatory Templarism, to the views of sexual magic that I have mentioned when
talking about Amfortas, it would not be difficult to understand what was really
the case in the charge of "unnatural intercourse."[7]

From all these elements we can easily discern an analogical tie between the
ideal model of the Grail's chivalry and the inner dimension of historical
Templarism. On the other hand, the mysterious exhaustion of the source of inspiration of the Grail romances on the eve of the Templars' tragic end and of
the massive persecutions unleashed by the Inquisition indicates a sort of occult
syntony even on a more concrete plane. With the destruction of the Order of
the Knights Templar and with the collapse of the tension that had led to great-
ness the Ghibelline Middle Ages at the time of Frederick I and Otto the Great,
what was about to be manifested became invisible again; history departed
again from what is higher than history. What remained was the myth of the
Emperor who has not died but whose life is lethargic, and whose seat is an inaccessible mountain. In other words, we have a renewal in a new, pessimistic
sense, of the ancient theme of the awaiting; the cycle of the Grail, which had
previously assumed this supratraditional theme in positive terms by introducing the avenging and restoring hero, ended up reflecting such pessimism.

Thus, while on the one hand the themes of the *Diu Crone* still echo the affirming spirit of the period of high tension—since the disappearance of the old
king and of his court with the Grail marks the fulfilled task and the advent of
the hero who has succeeded in his mission, who now becomes the new ruler,

---

7. See my *Eros and the Mysteries of Love: The Metaphysics of Sex,* chapter 6. There is a novel by G.
Meyrink, *Der Engle vom westlichen Fenster,* which I translated in 1949 into Italian, in which the
Templar symbol of Baphomet is the central motif; this novel may be helpful to my reader in
putting into perspective what I have said so far.

having at his side the invincible sword—on the other hand, other texts witness a very different spirit: that of the redactions of the imperial saga, in which the outcome of the "last battle" is negative for the king who has awoken from his sleep. This king does not know how to cope with the unleashed forces against which he goes to battle; his hanging the shield on the Dry Tree no longer has (as in the previously mentioned story) the meaning of a participation in the power of the universal empire, but that of an abdication of the *regnum* and of going to heaven. Thus, in the epilogue of Manessier's text, Percival achieves his revenge, but then renounces the regal dignity and, taking with him the Grail, the sword, and the lance, withdraws to ascetic life. This is the same life that, in Wolfram, the brother of the wounded king of the Grail had espoused in order to attempt, through a different way from the heroic one, to remedy the decay and the pain of his brother, during the period of interregnum and the long wait. After Percival dies no one knows whatever happened to the three objects: sword, cup, and lance.

Likewise, in *Perceval li Gallois*, Percival and his companions withdraw to an ascetic life in a seat in which the Grail does not manifest itself anymore. In order to lead them to it, the Templars' ship appears, with a red cross on a white sail; from then on, no one ever hears again about Percival or the Grail. The same theme appears again in the *Queste du Graal*: a heavenly hand takes the Grail and the lance, which are no longer seen after that, while Percival withdraws to solitude and dies. In the *Titurel*, the Grail travels to India, to the symbolical kingdom of Prester John. The people around Salvaterre and Montsalvatsche practiced a sinful life, and Montsalvatsche's knights, despite all their efforts, cannot change that. Thus the Grail cannot remain in it and must be taken where the light arises: a ship, after a fantastic symbolic voyage, carries it to India, to the kingdom of Prester John, which is located in "proximity of heaven." The Templars travel there, and all of a sudden, the castle of Montsalvatsche too is magically transferred here, since nothing sacred must be left behind, among the sinful populations. The same Percival assumes the function of Prester John, who is the image of the invisible Universal Ruler. Finally, in *Le Morte D'Arthur*, in the sense of some new version of the theme of the mortally wounded Arthur who withdraws to Avalon, we find Galahad, who, during a period of incarceration, is fed by the Grail and who, having had the full view of it, does not attempt to affirm himself and to become its king, but rather asks to leave earth; then the angels come to take his soul to heaven. A heavenly hand takes the vessel and the lance, and "since then no one can be so bold as to say he saw the Sangreal."[8]

---

8. *Le Morte D'Arthur*, 17.21, 22.

After the climax represented by the Middle Ages, tradition goes underground everywhere. A cycle ends. The current of becoming leads further and further away from the "Immobile Lands," or from the "Island." Men and entire nations at this time precipitate into the most critical phase of that which was traditionally referred to as the Dark Age, or *Kali Yuga*.[9]

9. In Wolfram von Eschenbach, Percival appears to have been conceived as the last of those who succeeded to become Lords of the Grail through the heroic path and not through the divine right. After the advent of Percival notice is sent to every land that the only person who can achieve the Grail is the one called by God and that the Grail cannot be obtained by fighting. By attempting to achieve the Grail many people died: this is why the Grail has been hidden ever since. It seems the equivalent of traditional prophecy concerning Hesiod's Iron Age, the last or Dark Age, in which the heroic path is no longer available.

25

The Grail, the Cathars, and the Love's Lieges

The legend of the Grail has historical relationships with troubadour literature, and more in particular with the Love's Lieges. Some have considered it a part of the medieval genre of chivalric romance. However, it seems that troubadour literature had, to a certain extent, an esoteric dimension and secret tendencies; this fact has been acknowledged by many Italian scholars, following Luigi Valli's studies on Rossetti and Aroux. After hinting at this esotericism, I will then indicate how such currents reflected analogous influences to those that shaped the Grail cycle.

First of all, there is no doubt that the current of the Love's Lieges often had a marked Ghibelline, anti-Catholic, and even heretical character. Aroux had already shown how the "gay science" developed mainly in those cities and castles of Provence that were also centers of heresy and especially of Catharism. Starting from these premises, Aroux tried to identify the secret and sectarian content of troubadour literature. Rahn tended to see in Wolfram von Eschenbach's narrative a sort of transcription of a Provençal story, strictly connected with the vicissitudes of the Cathars and especially with their castle, Montsegur. Personally, I believe that a distinction should be made between the Love's Lieges and the Cathars; I also think that the spirit of Catharism in particular had indeed very little in common with the spirit of the Grail's Templarism.

The Cathars also claimed to be the keepers of a superior knowledge and a spirituality purer than the Catholic one. They did not acknowledge the supreme authority of the Church and regarded the adoration of the cross to be an insult to the divine nature of Christ, even to the point of saying, "May I never be saved under this sign." They had Mysteries, which were included in the rituals of the *manisola* and of the *consolamentum spiritus sancti*, which were destined to elevate the members of the community to the rank of the so-called Perfect Ones. Overall, their tradition appears to be a dubious mixture of primitive Christianity, Manicheism, and second-rate Buddhism.[1] Catharism is characterized by an emphasis on Christian escapism. Its main features (such as dualism; the pessimistic denial of the world; the accentuation of the pathos of love and renunciation; the impulse to an undetermined liberation; an asceticism wavering between a "lunar" type and a spiritual exaltation that was carried to such extremes that some Cathars starved themselves to death, hoping to become free from the world, which they conceived as an evil creation of the anti-God and as a place of exile) show how distant this tradition was from what may be ascribed to a heroic spirituality characterized by strict initiation. This does not mean, however, that Catharism was unable to make a contribution to the Ghibelline movement, though only indirectly, owing to contingent historical reasons, and not because of a true affinity with the soul of the imperial myth.

Provence, the center of Catharism, may be considered one of the main places in which, through the Crusades, the transmission of various themes and traditional symbols from the Arab-Persian East to the Christian West took place. But while in the Grail cycle the positive and virile aspect of an ancient, pre-Christian Nordic-Celtic legacy was resurrected, in Catharism what apparently reemerged was the negative, feminine, gynecocratic aspect, belonging to a different pre-Christian legacy, which I have characterized elsewhere as "Atlantic-Southern"[2] and which should be considered as an alteration of the primordial tradition in the sense of the "cycle of the Mother."[3] While it seems that the Cathars borrowed from Manicheism and Buddhism the symbol of

---

1. This translator has come across a very interesting study on dualism by Yuri Stoyanov, *The Hidden Tradition in Europe: The Secret History of Medieval Christian Heresy* (London: Penguin, 1994).

2. See my *Revolt Against the Modern World*, chapters 26 and 27.

3. N. Peyrat, in his *Histoire des Albigeois* (Paris, 1880), noticed that in the Provençal cycle the theme of the divinization of the woman allegedly had two roots, an Iberian and a Christian one. The Iberians, like the German, saw in their women some prophetic and divine element. The Iberian woman had her own name, which characterized her family; thus one said: "Belissena's children," or "Imperia's son," or "Oliviera's daughter." The husband took second place, like Joseph did to Mary, who was almost deified. According to Peyrat, the mariolatric myth was embodied in the type of the Cathar woman, the queen of the "empire" of the troubadours' love.

mani, a bright stone that brightens the world and eradicates every worldly desire, this is only a superficial correspondence with the Grail, since the Cathar symbol merely had the lunar and religious character of a "jewel of compassion" and of "divine love." Catharism's opposition to the Church was based on its perception of Catholicism as a sort of continuation of the Mosaic religion (according to the Cathars, as also for some Gnostic sects and for Marcion, the God of Moses was a god of this earth, opposed to the God of "love"): in other words, the Catholic Church was too "Roman" to be the Cathar Church of Love.

Thus the Crusade against the Cathars had a deeply different meaning from the one waged against the Templars.[4] I have to agree with Peyrat, who, in spite of his personal preference, saw in this crusade the struggle of the Roman authoritarian theocracy allied to the feudal and monarchical northern-Gallic France against the democratic, federal, and municipal Hiberic Aquitaine, which was the cradle of a knighthood yearning to become emancipated from Rome and from northern France. Still, the attack of the Church (in league with the Dantean "Giant") against the Cathars, unlike the attack against the Templars, targeted an element that was inseparable from the original pathos of true Christianity, namely, something that could be characterized as more authentically Christian than Roman Catholicism.

As I was saying, we must be careful not to put the movement of the Love's Lieges in a unilateral relation with the Cathars. This movement often presents a mainly initiatory and Ghibelline character, although, in comparison with the spirit of the Grail cycle, it had an already dissociated form.

According to tradition, the troubadoric *leys d'amors* were allegedly found by a Briton knight, on the golden branch of an oak on which Arthur's falcon had come to rest. This symbolism is notorious, just like that of the golden ring that the troubadour received from his lady when he swore her eternal faithfulness. In Provence, as a way to consecrate this ritual, the Virgin was invoked; in Germany the minnesingers invoked that Frau Saelde whom we have previously known to be the guardian of Arthur's kingdom and the one who favors and supports the conquest of the Grail.

In this type of literature, "woman" and "love" have a symbolic character that is even more evident than that found in the various women and queens described in the Grail texts and in chivalric literature, becoming the center of every event. In this case, the symbolism did not have to exclude a concrete aspect, connected to a special, divergent way of spiritual realization, in which the exhilaration and desire aroused by a real woman (who would be conceived and

---

4. Interestingly enough, Bernard of Clairvaux, who notoriously sympathized with the Templars, deplored the spread of Catharism.

experienced through a sort of evocative process, as the incarnation of a vivifying and transfiguring force transcending her person) could play a role or act as a starting point.

In regard to this I will refer my reader to another work of mine, *Eros and the Mysteries of Love: The Metaphysics of Sex.* Here I will only emphasize that the goal of this path was, generally speaking, the same of every initiation. Jaques de Baisieux, a Provençal Love's Liege, said this expressedly when he identified love as the destruction of death, by saying, "A senefie en sa patie sans, et mor senefie mort;—or l'asemblons, s'aurons sans mort"; for him, lovers, or those who have obtained love, are "those who do not die" or "those who will live in another era of glory and joy." That the "literature of love" often had a secret content can be clearly seen in more than one hint dropped by the authors themselves. Francesco da Barberino, for instance, cautioned against "coarse people," and wrote: "I hereby state and declare that all of my works dealing with love have a spiritual sense and that not all of them can be understood by everybody." His "Documents of Love" are marked by the eloquent figure of a warrior with a sword in his hands, from whose mouth comes this significant sentence: "I am vigor and I am watching out for somebody to come and open any of these books; and if one is not qualified to read them, I will strike him in the chest with this sword." This was a caveat to the profane reader: it represented a defense of a secret doctrine that recalls an aspect of the defense of the Grail.

Valli has shown that the women of the Love's Lieges, no matter whether their names were Rose or Beatrice, Johanna or Selvaggia, beginning with Dante, Cavalcanti, Dino Compagni, and the poets of Sicily's courts, including Frederick II, must be regarded as the same woman. According to this scholar, this woman represents secret doctrine, which is protected by a group of people joined together in an invisible bond and by a militant attitude that was, for the most part, opposed to the Church. This is undoubtedly an aspect of this symbolism. Here are some examples: Dante's love, at one point, is revealed as love for "Holy Wisdom." His woman, Beatrice, confers upon him initiatory freedom—not only is Dante's soul "separated from his body" through her, but once in Paradise, "her sun" obscures "Christ's sun." Dino Compagni wrote: "The loving Lady Intelligence, who dwells in the human soul, caused me to fall in love with her beauty." And also: "You who have subtle knowledge, love the queen Intelligence, who dwells in the presence of God. She is a woman of great value, who nourishes the soul and pacifies the heart; those who serve her will never go astray."

Cavalcanti related "such a beautiful woman, whom the mind cannot understand" with the statement "Your salvation has appeared." The love of Guido

Guinizelli was for a woman who should "bestow truth, as the Intelligence from heaven." In the *Jugement d'Amour*, in which we find Blancheflor, who appeared as one of Percival's women, mention is made of the "mysteries of love," which should not be revealed to "cowardly, indiscreet, and vulgar people" and should be reserved for "clerics and knights." Finally, Arnaldo Daniello, whom Petrarch called "Great Master of Love," claims that if he could have his woman, he would love her "ten thousand times more than a hermit or a monk loves God." From all this we sense the theme that secretly informed this literature and to which one should refer even where it is less visible and more hidden behind poetic and pathetic expressions. Likewise, as I have said, we must also consider another, more concrete aspect, typical of a special "way of sex," in which the rapture and exaltation of Eros played a technical role, as the support of initiatory realization. Hence a difference in regard to the realizations not only of an intellectual and ascetic nature but also of a heroic, action-oriented nature (as in chivalry and the "path of the warrior").

As in the cycle of the Grail, in the Love's Lieges too we find the theme of the woman as widow. Francesco da Barberino spoke of a mysterious widow ("I am telling you, very openly, that there was and is a certain widow who was not widowed"), whom he allegedly met and thanks to whom he found again his strength. She is the Veve Dame, who was also Percival's mother and who, in a version of the legend, is the carrier of the Grail (her name, Philosophine, may correspond, in one of her aspects, to Lady Intelligence). She is also the widow or solitary queen who was often freed and married by some knights in the Grail sagas. Thus even a Love's Liege seeks that wisdom or tradition that does not have, or no longer has, a husband (i.e., the widow) and that alone gives strength.[5]

Again, in regard to the initiatory aspect, the Love's Lieges knew many degrees. Nicolò de Rossi arranged the "degrees and the virtue of true love" according to a hierarchical ladder that goes from *liquefatio* [melting] to *languor* [feebleness], to *studium* [zeal], and finally to *extasim* [ecstasy], which *dicitur excessus mentis* [is referred to an excess of the mind], namely, to a suprarational experience. In Francesco da Barberino we find a figure of Love with roses, arrows, and a white horse, next to twelve sleeping figures, who represent twelve virtues or degrees in a hierarchy that *introducit in Amoris curiam* (penultimate degree) and that finally culminates in "eternity."[6] Here we find again the

---

5. In the *Diu Crone* we find the following variation on the theme of the widow: in the Grail's court the king and his knights are all dead, though they retain a semblance of life; on the contrary, the Grail carrier and her maidens are really alive; God has left the Grail in their care during the interregnum until the hero comes.

6. L. Valli, in his *Il linguaggio segreto di Dante e dei Fedeli d'Amore* (Rome, 1928), wrote: "These figures are: first Meekness, who *data novitiis notitia vitiorum, docet illos ab illorum vilitate*

symbolism of the horse, in reference to the principle of "non-death" *(a-mor):* concerning the four arrows and the roses, they obviously correspond to the double power to kill or pierce and to resuscitate ("to blossom again"), which is among those attributed to the Grail or its lance. Moreover, it is as a "perennial rose" that Dante clearly symbolizes the vision of the superworld, thus teaching us what one must think of women who ostensibly are named Rose, who were celebrated, almost to the point of monotony, especially in the literature pro-duced in Ghibelline milieus, such as that of Frederick II's court, beginning with the Emperor himself.

In regard to the other, opposite aspect of the "love" principle, that it may act in a destructive fashion, here we find again the Grail theme of being wounded, not only by darts, but also by a lance. In Jacques de Baisieux we read: "Love, who is not slow in recognizing his lieges, flies to him with whom a lady is in love, wounds him with his lance, strikes him in such a way as to tear his heart out of his chest, and then carries it to his lady." According to the same author, who does not hesitate to declare that the first and most noble of Love's Lieges were the knights of Arthur and of the Grail, Love wants his lieges to "be armed for a fight, because he wants to break and bring down the arrogance of the proud, of those who are hostile to him." These "proud" people will be pierced by him with a lance, just as Amfortas was pierced for having become Orgeluse's lover. Cavalcanti says of Love that it arouses "the mind that was asleep," (i.e.,that it causes an initiatory awakening), but also that it slays the heart and makes the soul tremble, just as Dante says, before the vision of the woman, that he "made an effort not to fall" and that his "heart died though I was still alive."[7] All these expressions, together with many other analogies, which are often re-ferred to the effect of an enigmatic "greeting" from the woman, makes us think of the effects of transcendent experiences, similar to that of the already men-tioned Templar witness, instead of appearing as heroic transpositions of emo-tions of love.

---

abstinere; this *docilitas* that is bestowed upon the novices is clearly the initiatory virtue. Others fol-low: Industriousness, who makes some strange purses in which one hides precious things. The third virtue is Perseverance, the fourth Discretion, the fifth Patience, the sixth Hope, the seventh Prudence, *quae te docet custodire quaesita;* the eighth is Glory, the ninth Justice, *quae male custodi-entem quaesita punit,* which is sent by Love to punish those who do not keep the secret and are found unworthy of such great honor; the tenth is Innocence, which signifies the condition of those who serve Love in a worthy and honorable manner; the eleventh is Gratitude, who *introducit in Amoris curiam;* the last is Eternity, which promises eternal life.
7. *Vita Nova* I, 2.

26

Dante and the Love's Lieges as a Ghibelline Militia

The Templars' battle cry was "Long Live God Holy Love!" In Jacques de Baisieux, the lord of the "land of love" was called Holy Love, who was one and the same with God himself, since the land of love was identified with the inalienable "heavenly region," which was opposed to all contingent earthly lands. Moreover, the Love's Lieges displayed the traits of a fighting militia, as they were endowed with weapons and secret accords of their own. Ricolfi, after saying that "they must not reveal the secrets of Love, but conceal them as best as they can," added that "they must cooperate in their wills, words, and deeds." In Francesco da Barberino, the Court of Love was represented as a heavenly curia of the elect, arranged in a hierarchical fashion, with angels in correspondence to each degree; considering what I have already mentioned about the bird as a symbol, this figuration (which recalls the castle of the Grail as a "spiritual palace" and "castle of souls") does not have a different meaning from that of the Court of Love that is composed entirely of birds, which from time to time speak there. Moreover, da Barberino was a soldier and an ardent supporter of the Ghibelline cause, who joined the army of Henry VII (1308–13). The most characteristic Italian love poets were either moderate or radical Ghibellines, some with the scent of heresy, others undoubtedly heretics; and although they exalted women and spoke of love, they were men of action, of struggle, of war and faction.

Troubadours such as Guillaume Figueira and Guillaume Anelier, who survived the Crusade against the Cathars, sided enthusiastically with the Emperor, launching bitter attacks against the Church. Even Andrea Cappellano's treatise was solemnly condemned by the Church in 1277, despite a visible lack of good reasons.[1] Dante, who in his *Divine Comedy* used as a central symbol the seal of the Templars' Grand Master (i.e., the eagle and cross), traveled to Paris just when the great tragedy of the Templars unfolded, without telling anyone and without anyone ever learning the reasons for this trip.

From these elements, and from many other similar ones, one can suppose that the Love's Lieges, besides constituting an initiatory chain, also had their own organization, which supported the cause of the Empire and opposed the Church. Not only were they the custodians of a secret doctrine, which was not compatible with the more exoteric Catholic teachings, but they were also people who militated against the hegemonistic claims of Rome's Curia.

This was the thesis endorsed by Rossetti and Aroux, taken up by Valli and to a degree by Ricolfi and, more recently, by Alessandrini, though with a heavy emphasis on the merely political dimension. On this basis, the above-mentioned symbolism could allow a further interpretation. The symbol of the woman as the safekeeper of the doctrine must be applied to the same organization. Laws of love, such as the one stating that "the woman who has received and accepted from the perfect lover the gifts of Massenia, namely, gloves and mystical cordon,[2] must give herself to him, least she be regarded a prostitute" are supposed to be formulas of faithfulness or militant solidarity, and so forth. The woman who according to Dante usurps Beatrice's (that is, Holy Wisdom's) role, forcing her to go in exile, is the Catholic Church's exotericism, which has forcibly replaced the "true doctrine"; this is the meaning of the "petrifying stone" that encloses the woman Petra alive.

In this regard, there are some significant figurations by da Barberino. In that figuration with the fourteen figures who, arranged in couples, form seven hierarchical degrees, we can see that the lower degrees are constituted by the "religious" element, corresponding to a "cadaver," which reproduces Dante's view of the stone as synonymous with death. The representatives of the ecclesiastical hierarchy, compared to the Love's Lieges, are secular and far from possessing a vivifying knowledge, or the true woman, or the Widow, who corresponds to the higher degrees, or to the "deserving knight" who has the "rose" and "life"

---

1. In this treatise we find again the image of the center; moreover, maxims such as "Love hardly lasts when it is divulgated" and "He who does not know how to conceal does not know how to love" also reflect the conduct that was expected from a member of a secret organization.

2. The cordon recalls the one worn by the Templars; concerning the gloves, we may recall here the adventure found in the *Diu Crone* in which they were related to the help provided by Saelde to the Grail seekers who have successfully completed a preliminary test. The glove also plays an important role in Masonic ritual.

while the former know only "death."[3] We may suppose that these higher degrees constituted the same suprareligious mystery to which the Templars were admitted only after rejecting the cross, and which in the cycle of the Round Table was represented by the Grail as a super and extraeucharistic mystery.

In the same literature are some reliable references to historical events about the Love's Lieges as a militia and as a Ghibelline organization. One of the most significant documents is another illustration by da Barberino, in which we find the representation of the tragic victory of Death over Love. Death shoots an arrow at a woman, who is portrayed in the act of falling down, pierced. Next to her is Love, divided in two parts, the left one whole, the right one fragmented. Here I subscribe to Valli's interpretation according to which Death is the Church and the pierced woman is the organization of the Love's Lieges.[4] As far as the bipartite figure of Love is concerned, its broken part corresponds to the wounded woman, that is, to the external and persecuted part of the organization, while its left side represents the invisible part of the organization, which, despite all, continued to exist. Moreover, in traditional symbolism, the left side was often related to what is occult and unmanifested.

At this point I will briefly consider the ultimate and general meaning of the movement of the Love's Lieges in relation to the spirit of the Grail cycle and of the other traditions connected with it.

We may allow for a certain continuity or interference between the plane of an organization's secret, initiatory doctrine and the plane of its militant Ghibelline orientation. However, as I have already said about the Love's Lieges, this may well be an already dissociated form, mainly for two reasons. First, the action they promoted was militant and political, and not an action assumed as the basis for a spiritual or initiatory realization, as in the knightly and heroic path in general and as in the ideal orientation of the Templar movement. I have noted that, in regard to the initiatory dimension, the members of that tradition and organization were supposed to follow the "path of love."

Second, as we analyze the background of the Love's Lieges' initiation, we notice that the woman, in her appearance in the form of Holy Wisdom, Lady Intelligence, or gnosis (as Valli and others have noted), suggests an essentially sapiential and contemplative plane, which is not disjoined from an ecstatic el-

---

3. The fact that da Barberino indicates somewhere else that members of religious orders are those who deserve "celestem curiam introire" [to enter into the heavenly curia] does not represent a recantation, as Ricolfi suggests; rather, we may think that this is a reference to those members of religious orders who were able to go beyond the more external and exoteric dimension of their faith. 4. Dante talks about Beatrice's scattered limbs, meaning the various surviving groups of the organization.

ement; Dante's intellectual horizon confirms this. Thus we may think that if in these groups the religious attitude of those who merely "believe" was overcome, one nevertheless remained in the sphere of a sort of Platonizing initiation and did not orient himself in the sense of a "regal" initiation that included the warrior and the sacral elements in a unity, as in the symbols of the Lord of the Two Swords, of the resurrection of the *imperator* and the king of the Grail. This is to say that the Ghibellinism of the Love's Lieges lacked a spiritual counterpart that was truly congenial; this I why I have referred to it as a "dissociated form," even though in some regards it perpetuated, as a secret organization, the previous or parallel tradition.

This consideration leads us to the historical plane; we may wonder if the antiecclesiastical character of this organization was merely contingent and not really connected to a true overcoming of Catholicism. In fact, within orthodox Catholicism there was room for a realization of a contemplative and more or less Platonic type; moreover, many dogmas and symbols of the apostolic tradition were susceptible to be vivified on its basis.[5] Moreover, there are reasons to believe that the Love's Lieges were quite open, at least in principle, to a purified and dignified Catholicism and that Dante's stone had nothing to do with the Grail, but that it merely alluded to the Catholic Church of which Peter was the cornerstone. When he said that this stone, which was previously white, had turned black, apparently he alluded to its corruption, owing to which the Church had become some kind of tomb of Christ's live doctrine, of which she was supposed to be the pure repository. Thus the Love's Lieges opposed the Church not because they represented an essentially different tradition but because, according to them, the Church was no longer worthy of the pure Christian doctrine.[6]

If this is true, then Dante and the Love's Lieges should not be put on the same level as the Grail's knights. The Widow whom they talked about would not have been the solar tradition of the Empire, but an already weakened and lunar tradition, which therefore would not have been totally irreconcilable with the premises of a renewed Catholicism. An indirect proof of this is Dante's view of the relationship between the Church and the Empire.

---

5. There is a good book by R. L. John, *Dante* (Vienna, 1947), in which the author tries to adduce many proofs of Dante's membership in the Templar organization, which he did not consider to be incompatible with Catholic doctrine. Interesting enough, this book was published with an ecclesiastical imprimatur.

6. In this regard, we also should not exclude the influence of Joachimism, centered on the idea of a new ecclesia spiritualis, which corresponds to a new era of Christianity, with the prophecy of the advent of an "angelic pope," who was the mystical-ecclesiastical counterpart of the prophecy concerning the "new Frederick."

As I have said before, Dante's view is centered on a limiting dualism and on a polarity between contemplative life and active life. Now, if starting from this dualism Dante bitterly attacked the Church for those aspects in which it did not confine itself to the pure contemplative life, becoming greedy for earthly powers and goods, denying in the process the Empire's supreme right in the dimension of active life, and worse yet, attempting to usurp the Empire's prerogatives, then it logically follows that on the basis of the same premises, Dante should have cultivated an equal aversion for the opposite tendency, namely, for any attempt on the part of the Empire to totally affirm its own dignity in the same spiritual domain to which the Church laid exclusive claims; a right, we should recall, that Dante granted it. In other words, Dante should have opposed radical Ghibellinism and the transcendent view of the *imperium* in the same way he opposed Guelphism, and this because of an initial theory that is "heterodox," not so much from the point of view of a purified Catholicism but from the point of view of the primordial tradition of "regal" spirituality.

Therefore, against the tendency of some people to overvalue Dante's "esotericism," and despite the effective presence of this esotericism in many of his views, on the plane that I am discussing, Dante emerges much more as a poet and a fighter than as a man upholding an uncompromising doctrine. He displays too much passion and too much factionalism in his militant temporal views, while he tends to be much too Christian and contemplative in the spiritual domain. Hence, many of his confusions and oscillations, such as his confining Frederick II in hell, while at the same time defending the Templars against Philip the Fair. Generally speaking, everything seems to suggest that, in spite of everything, Dante used the Catholic tradition as his starting point, which he endeavored to elevate to a relatively initiatory (i.e., suprareligious) plane instead of being directly connected to the representatives of traditions that were superior to and predated both Christianity and Catholicism. Some of these traditions, for instance, would include the main sources of inspiration in the cycle of the Grail and of the Hermetic tradition.

Thus, when we consider the Love's Lieges, we should see in it a Ghibelline group with an initiatory character, and as such endowed with a higher knowledge than the Church's orthodox doctrine, yet upholding an already weakened and compromised view of the Imperial idea. Thus the most positive aspect of the current is that the Court of Love assumes the character of an immaterial kingdom and that the Lieges are individual personalities committed to a suprarational and ecstatic realization. In a certain way, this ideally corresponds to a pessimistic conclusion of the Grail legend, namely, to the Grail that becomes invisible again and to the Percival who abdicates to become an ascetic. It is especially in this form that tradition was preserved in the following period, increasingly divesting itself of the militant aspect and sometimes revivifying deeper and more original currents.

As far as the movement of the Love's Lieges is concerned, in Italy it lasted up to the time of Boccaccio and Petrarch, though it assumed increasingly humanistic traits, until the artistic aspect eventually prevailed over the esoteric one. Then the symbols were transformed into mere allegories, their meaning no longer understood even by those who continued to employ them in their poems. During the early seventeenth century the vital principle of tradition appears to have been totally extinguished, not only overall, but also in individual authors. For a relative continuation one must refer to other groups and to other currents.

27
The Grail and the Hermetic Tradition

I have devoted an entire book to the Hermetic tradition, aimed at showing the essentially symbolic character of what in a very complex and abstruse literature was superficially known as alchemy and as alchemical procedures, aimed at producing Gold and the Philosopher's Stone.[1] I refer my readers to that work, in case they wish to gain a deeper understanding of Hermetic-alchemical doctrines: here, I will limit myself to indicating some of their themes that reproduce those of the mystery of the Grail and of initiatory regality, though in other forms.

In regard to the historical dimension, the Hermetic-alchemical tradition appeared in the West at the time of the Crusades: it reached its peak between the thirteenth and the sixteenth centuries, and it lasted up to the eighteenth century, interfering, in these last developments, with Rosicrucianism. And yet the origins of the Hermetic tradition can be traced to an even more distant past. Between the seventh and twelfth centuries it was known among the Arabs, who became the instruments of the revival, in the medieval West, of the older legacy of the pre-Christian wisdom tradition. In effect, the Arab and Syriac Hermetic-alchemical texts were inspired by texts of the Alexandrian and Byzantine period (third to fifth centuries); these texts, while representing the oldest testimonies from a historical and scientific point of view, must have gathered and transmitted older traditions that had been previously preserved in oral forms of a strict initiatory transmission.

---

1. Julius Evola, *The Hermetic Tradition*, trans. E. E. Rhemus (Rochester, Vt.: Inner Traditions, 1994).

The Hellenistic texts refer to all kinds of authors, both real and imaginary, of pre-Christian antiquity. Though they have a scant scientific basis, they have the meaning of a symptom or of the confused perception of a truth.

First of all, the tradition claims to be the repository of a secret, regal, and priestly knowledge, or of a mystery that according to Olympiodorus was reserved for the higher castes, kings, wise men, and priests. The prevailing term became *ars regia*, or Royal Art.

Through imaginary and sometimes extravagant references, the tradition of the Royal Art was traced to the Egyptian tradition (under classical-pagan disguises it was traced to Hermes, who was regarded as the forefather or teacher of Egyptian kings) and to the Iranian tradition. According to Synesius and to the *Democritean Texts*, it was the science already known to Egyptian kings and Persian seers. Mention was made not only of Zarathustra but also of Mithras, who together with Osiris characterized certain phases of the "divine opus." We may recall here that it was in ancient Egypt and Iran that the tradition of "solar regality" was established in typical forms.

The Hellenistic alchemical texts talk about an ancient and immaterial stock that enjoyed total freedom and was without kings. A medieval text claimed that alchemy was known in antediluvian times. Another ancient author attributed it to the "first of the angels," who mated with Isis. Thus Isis came to learn the science, which was revealed to Horus. Here the theme of the divine woman and the restoring hero (Horus, who avenges the dead and dismembered Osiris) is confusedly but also significantly associated with biblical reminiscences concerning the angels who descended on earth and with their stock, which according to tradition had been (before the flood) a stock of "glorious" or "famous beings." This suggests the presence of elements of the primordial tradition that were preserved during the ascending, solar, or heroic cycle of civilizations, such as the Egyptian or the Iranian ones. These forms later assumed a mysteric form, mixing with other elements and assuming the Hermetic-alchemical disguise, along with the employment of a symbolism derived from classic mythology and astrology.

The Hermetic doctrine, per se much older than Christianity and alien to the latter's spirit, thanks to its clever and impenetrable metallurgic disguise, was able to perpetuate itself during historical periods dominated by Islām and Catholicism, without being forced to borrow from those religions any external elements and without undergoing significant deviations. The references to Christianity found in Western medieval texts prove to be superficial and extrinsic, much more so than those found in the Grail cycle; the classical-pagan element remains very visible, even in the external forms. It was only in a later period that the interference with Rosicrucianism led to a mixture of the

Hermetic symbols with those derived from some sort of Christian esotericism sharing some common traits with the Love's Lieges tradition. From these considerations we learn that the Hermetic tradition, in its Western positive documentation, historically encompassed a period much wider than the initiatory and knightly cycle that I previously discussed. In this context I wish to consider the phase that historically emerged as a current. This current, after emerging in the West in the same period as the Grail cycle and the Love's Lieges, outlived these cycles, thus establishing a continuity characterized by the correspondence of some fundamental symbols. I will now briefly discuss some of these symbols:

1. The mystery of the Royal Art is strictly related to that of the heroic reintegration. This is explicitly stated, for instance, in a text of Cesare della Riviera (1605), in which the central theme consists in the identification of the "Heroes" with those who succeed in conquering the "second Tree of Life" and in introducing a second "earthly paradise," an image of the primordial center. This center, like the Grail's castle, "does not appear to base and impure souls, but remains hidden in the celestial spheres of the inaccessible light of the heavenly Sun. It shows itself only to the 'happy' magical hero, who alone gloriously possesses it, enjoying the salvific Tree of Life, located in the middle of this universe."[2]

In Basil Valentine we find the same theme, namely, the quest for the center of the Tree, which is located in the middle of the "earthly paradise." This quest begins with the quest for the material of the Opus Magnum, which implies a brutal fight. We have previously learned that access to the Grail's castle, where according to the *Titurel* the Golden Tree is located, can be attained with weapons in hand. The "material" pursued in the Hermetic tradition is often identified with the "stone" (in Wolfram and in other authors, the "stone" is the Grail); the second operation described by Basil Valentine is destined to find in this material the blood of the lion as well as the ashes of the eagle. The meaning of these two symbols, which are also characteristic of the Ghibelline-knightly cycle, should be rather clear after what I have discussed.[3]

2. The regal symbolism played a fundamental role in medieval and postmedieval Hermetic texts, and was closely associated with the symbolism of gold. This association can be traced back to the ancient Egyptian tradition. One

---

2. Cesare della Riviera, *Il mondo magico degli heroi*, 14. Compare this hero with the symbolism of Saelde, who protects the Grail's heroes; this symbolism personifies the quality of "being happy," namely, of succeeding in an adventure.

3. Della Riviera, among the effects of the heroic realization, mentions invincibility, or becoming similar to a "terrible lion" and to a god who is honored on earth "among the regal disciples of the most high Jupiter."

of the old titles bestowed on the pharaoh was "Golden Horus"; As the god Horus, the king was seen as an incarnation of the restoring solar deity. Being made of gold signified his immortality and incorruptibility, and, at the same time, alluded to a primordial state, namely to the age which among many people was characterized by this metal. Thus, in Hermeticism too the terms Gold, Sun, and King were regarded as synonymous and used interchangeably. Aside from this, the development of the *Opus Hermeticum* was often portrayed in the form of a sick king who eventually heals; or of a king or a knight laying in a coffin or a tomb who is finally resurrected; or of an old and decrepit man who gains back vigor and youth; or of a king who is stricken, sacrificed, or killed, but who later acquires a higher life and a stronger power than any man who preceded him. These are analogous themes to those of the mystery of the Grail.

3. The medieval Hermetic texts contain plenty of references to Saturn, who, like Osiris, is the king of the Golden Age, an age that is notoriously related to the primordial tradition. See for instance the very significant title of a small work by Gino of Barma: *Saturn's Kingdom Transformed into the Golden Age.* In Hermeticism the theme of a primordial state that needs to be reawakened takes the form of the production of gold through the transformation of Saturn's metal, lead, in which it is hidden. In a hieroglyphic drawn by Basil Valentine we can see crowned Saturn atop a complex symbol that represents the overall Hermetic Work. Beneath Saturn is the symbol of sulfur, which in turn contains the symbol of resurrection, the Phoenix.[4] According to Philalethes, the wise find the missing element in Saturn's race, after adding the needed sulfur: here the key is provided by the double meaning of the Greek term θεῖον which means both "sulfur" and "divine." Moreover, sulfur is often the equivalent of fire, the active and vivifying principle of the Hermetic tradition. In the Hellenistic texts we find the theme of the sacred black stone, the power of which is stronger than any spell. This stone, in order to be truly regarded as "our Gold," "namely Mithras," and to produce the "great Mithraic mystery," must possess the right power or the "medicine of the right action"; this is just another way to express the mystery of awakening and of reintegration. What we have here is a further parallelism with the themes of the Grail: symbols of a primordial regality and of a stone that await a virile and divine power (sulfur = divine) in order to be manifested as "gold" and as the "philosopher's stone" endowed with the medicinal power to destroy every "illness."

4. On this basis it would be possible to interpret the mysterious term *lapsit exillis,* employed by Wolfram in reference to the Grail, as the *lapis elixir,* thus acknowledging a correspondence between the Grail and the divine or heavenly

---

4. See J. Evola, *The Hermetic Tradition,* 79–83.

stone described in Hermetic texts: the latter has also been perceived as an elixir or as a principle that renews itself and bestows eternal life, health, and victory. When we read in a text by Kitab-el-Focul, "The stone speaks but you heed it not: it calls to you and you answer not! O you sleepers! What deafness stops your ears? What vise grips your hearts and minds?" we cannot help but think about the question associated with the Grail that the hero at first does not ponder, but that later on he poses, thus fulfilling his task. The Hermetic philosophers seek their "stone" just like the knights seek the Grail, or the heavenly stone. When Zacharias wrote "Our body, which is our occult stone, cannot be known nor seen without inspiration . . . without this body our science is vain,"[5] he reproduced, like many other authors, the theme of the invisibility and of the mysterious location of the Grail, which is reserved for those who are either called or led to it, following an inspiration or a fortuitous coincidence.

The theme that the stone is not a stone and that this knowledge should be understood in a mystical rather than in a physical sense goes back to the Hellenistic age; it appears in several Hermetic texts and it recalls the immaterial nature of the Grail which, according to previously mentioned authors, is not made of gold, stone, horn, or any other known material. In Arabic Hermetic texts, the quest for the stone is significantly connected to the themes of the mountain (i.e., Monsalvatsche), of the Woman, and of virility. "The stone that is not made of stone, and which does not have the nature of a stone" could be found on top of the highest mountain: from it, it is possible to obtain arsenic, that is, virility. (Due to the double meaning of the Greek word ἀρσενικὸν, in the Hermetic tradition "arsenic" has often been employed as the symbol of the virile principle which is synonymous to that active sulfur that needs to be added to Saturn as Philalethes suggests.) Beneath arsenic we find its "bride," mercury, to which it is joined. I will expand on this matter further on. For now, I wish to recall that according to one of its most recurrent themes, the Royal Art of the Hermetists is focused on a "stone" that is often identified with Saturn; this stone contains the phoenix, the elixir, the gold, or "Our King" at the latent state. Moreover, I also wish to recall that the "strange and terrible mystery that was transmitted to the disciples of king Hermes" and to the "Heroes" who try to find their way to the "earthly paradise" through "fierce fighting," consists in destroying that state of latency often referred to as "death" or "disease" or "impurity" or "imperfection," through operations of an initiatory character.

5. Finally, I wish to mention the *mysterium coniunctionis*. The union of the "male" with the "female," as per the teachings of the Hellenistic texts, is an essential part of the Hermetic Work. The "male" is the Sun, Sulfur, Fire, Arsenic. This principle must be turned from a passive into a "living and active" one. For

5. *De la philosophie naturelle des metaux,* 502.

this to happen it must be joined with the feminine principle, which is called the "Woman of the Hermetic philosophers," their "Fountain" or "Divine Water," or, in the metallurgical symbolism, "mercury." Here we find in a very explicit way the hidden role that the Woman played in several parts of the chivalrous literature and of the literature of the Love's Lieges. In the words of Della Riviera she is "our Hebes," connected with the "second Tree of Life," who bestows to the Heroes the "natural [i.e., Olympian] beatitude of the soul and bodily immortality." She often corresponds to the "Water of Life." Moreover, Hermeticism points out her dangerous side, which—like the Grail, like the spear or the second sword—may destroy those who join her without being able to take their own "gold" or "fire" (namely the principle of personality and of the heroic force) beyond their natural limit. The wedding, the union with the Woman, may turn out to be harmful unless it is preceded by a radical purification. Mercury, or the Philosophers' Woman, while being Water of Life, has also the character of a "thunderbolt," of a "fiery poison that dissolves everything" and that "burns and kills everything"; thus, the "Fire of the philosophers" that it generates, is applied to a symbolism that is also used in the Grail cycle: the sword, the lance, the axe, or everything that breaks and wounds.

In this context, we should recall the interesting allegories found in a Hermetic-Rosicrucian work by J. V. Andreae, namely *The Chemical Wedding of Christian Rosenkreuz*. Here we need to note two things. First, the presence of some trials (of which it is said: "It is better to run away than to face that which is beyond one's strength") that are overcome only by warriors and by those who, not trusting their might, have proven to be free of pride. Secondly, mention is made of a fountain, next to which lies a lion, which suddenly grabs a sword and breaks it in half, and which calms down only when a dove gives it an olive branch, which it devours. The lion, the sword, and the dove too are found in the symbolism of the Grail cycle. The sword, the symbol of pure warrior strength, is broken by the unleashed power connected to the fountain. The crisis ends only thanks to the dove, which is a bird sacred to Diana (Diana is one of the Hermetic names designating the Philosophers' Woman) and sometimes associated, in the Grail tales, with the mystery of the renewal of the strength of the Grail itself. Once again we have the allusion to a realization beyond ordinary virility and the "crisis of contact."

I will not discuss at length here the various phases of the Hermetic Work. What matters at this point is only to indicate two essential symbols that characterize the fulfillment of this work, the period of initiation. The first symbol is the Rebis, or the Androgynous, based on erotic symbolism and on the symbolism of the "occult wedding." We have previously encountered this symbolism among the Templars and the Love's Lieges. The second symbol is the color red, the regal color (e.g., the "purple tiara" of the *Imperator*), which is super-ordained to the color white, the latter being used to characterize a preliminary ecstatic and even "lunar" phase of the Work (in this phase the Woman plays a dominating role) that eventually needs to be overcome. Red corresponds to the initiatory regality. A parallel symbol for the overall Work used by Philalethes is that of the "access to the closed palace of the King"; this is almost the counter-part to the access to Montsalvatsche's castle, just as the healing virtue of the stone and of the Hermetic-alchemical elixir is almost a parallel to the healing or awakening of the Grail's fallen king and of other corresponding symbols.

Having said that, we may wonder what was the meaning of the Hermetic tradition in the West. I have to repeat what I have said before. The *Ars Regia*, or Royal Art, witnesses a secret current of initiation, the virile, "heroic," and solar character of which is beyond question. But unlike everything that in the cycle of the Grail and in the imperial saga reflects the same spirit (besides having connections with the primordial tradition), it lacks a committed character. What I mean is that we should not suppose any precise connection between the Hermetic initiates and militant organizations such as the Ghibelline knight-hood and Love's Lieges. Thus, what is missing is any attempt of direct inter-vention in the interplay of historical forces in order (a) to reestablish contact between a given political power and the invisible "center"; (b) to actualize through the Mystery that transcendent dignity which the Ghibelline move-ment claimed for a particular sovereign; and (c) to establish again the union of the "two powers." Therefore, the witness proper to the abovementioned tradi-tion was merely the special inner dignity which a number of individuals con-tinued to aspire to; these people in this way preserved an ancient legacy even after the decline of medieval civilization and of the Sacrum Imperium, beyond the humanistic collapse of the traditions of the Love's Lieges, beyond the devi-ations represented by naturalism, humanism, and secularism which character-ize later ages. Thus, "our Gold," the corpse that has to be resuscitated, the solar Lord of the two powers, appeared in Hermeticism essentially as symbols of the inner work which is as invisible as were the "center" and the "second paradise" which the "Heroes" of Della Riviera intended to reach by fighting.

Moreover, following the Renaissance and the Reformation, the visible dom-inators appeared more and more as merely temporal leaders lacking any higher chrism, transcendent authority, or the ability to represent that which in the Ghibelline movement was called the "regal religion of Melchizedek." Not only did monarchies decay and the "spiritual knighthood" cease to exist, but knight-hood itself began to decline, since the knights turned into soldiers and officers fighting as mercenaries for various nations and for their political ambitions. During this period the best way to pass on the tradition seemed to be the "hermetic" form in the ordinary sense of the term that alludes to everything that is impenetrable and sibylline. This form essentially employed the metallurgical and chemical jargon, as well as its extravagant and disheartening combinations of symbols, signs, operations, and mythological references.[6] This "covering" worked perfectly, and since Hermeticism was inspired mostly by autonomous, pre-Christian traditions it did not clash with orthodox Catholicism, even though it had less in common with it than with Dante's or the Love's Lieges' esotericism. In the later forms of a prevalently Rosicrucian Hermeticism things went otherwise. What occurred then was a sort of temporary reemergence of the secret tradition in history, though this reappearance eventually marked its final disappearance.

---

6. In *The Hermetic Tradition* I have suggested that alchemy, understood as the art of transforming metals into gold and of producing the elixir through physical procedures, was only the result of the misunderstanding of some outsiders who interpreted in a material sense the metallurgical symbolism of the Royal Art. It was only to these outsiders that we should attribute that type of alchemy which historians of science regard as a superstitious chemistry at the infantile state. However, this does not mean that some individuals, on the basis of the powers inherent in the Hermetic realization, have not applied themselves to produce a certain kind of abnormal physical phenomena, even in the field of experiments with real metals; this was indeed possible, though it had nothing to do with the misunderstandings of those misled alchemists, nor with any realization of modern science.

28

The Grail and
the Rosicrucians

It is difficult to separate Rosicrucianism from Hermeticism; while Hermeticism in its essential features may be studied independently from Rosicrucianism, the opposite is not true, because what we know about Rosicrucianism appears to be heavily influenced by Hermetic symbols and elements.

Historically speaking, Rosicrucianism should be regarded as one of the secret currents that emerged following the destruction of the Templar Order; some of these currents existed in embryonic form before this tragic event but became defined and organized especially after it, as an underground continuation of the same tendency. This marks a strong difference from Hermeticism, which, as I have said, seems to have existed in unchanged forms before and after the events surrounding the medieval attempt to bring about a traditional reconstruction. A second peculiar character is that Rosicrucianism incorporated many Christian elements, even though as a starting point in the direction of an esoteric interpretation, as well as elements from the literature of the Love's Lieges and of the romance and troubadour traditions, where the rose had become a symbol of particular importance. The terms that designate the movement, "Rose" and "Cross," already hint at this connection. Thus this movement presents a character that is less original than the Grail's, with its Nordic pre-Christian nucleus, and than Hermeticism's, with its pagan and Mediterranean nucleus.

From a spiritual point of view, "Rosicrucian" (just like "Buddha," "Prester John," or "Knight of the Two Swords") is essentially a title that characterizes a specific degree of inner realization. The term should be explained on the basis of a universal symbolism, rather than on the basis of Christian symbolism. The cross, in this symbolism, represents the encounter of the direction from above, expressed by the vertical line, with the earthly level, expressed by a horizontal line. This encounter in most people occurs in the sense of a suspension, neutralization, or fall (the "crucifixion of transcendent man in matter," as the ancient Gnostics and Manicheans used to say). In the initiate, instead, this encounter results in a full possession of the human condition, which is thereby transformed; therefore such a development, conceived as an opening up, as an expanding and as a blossoming, is indicated by the rose, which in the Rosicrucian symbol blossoms at the center of the cross, that is, at the intersecting point of the vertical and horizontal lines.[1] The people united through the identity of such a realization must be regarded as true Rosicrucians. The organization to which they belonged must be regarded as a derivative and contingent thing.

It seems that the Rosicrucians' activity began in the second half of the fourteenth century and that the birth of the founder or legendary reorganizer of the order, Christian Rosenkreuz, in 1378, was only a symbol of the first period of organization. Various traits of Rosenkreuz's life also appear to have an equally symbolic character: he allegedly spent twelve years in a monastery; later on, he traveled to the East, where he was initiated to true wisdom. We have already seen that Frederick II had claimed a mysterious Eastern origin for his "Rose." This could be the reintegration of the Christian ascetic teaching (e.g., Rosenkreuz in the monastery) through a higher kind of knowledge, of which some secret Eastern organizations of Arabic-Persian origins were the depositories. Once Christian Rosenkreuz returned to the West, he was expelled from ultra-Catholic Spain for carrying the scent of heresy and finally settled down in Germany, his original homeland. His native town, Rosenkreuz, is in Germany, "and yet it is not found on any map." He imparted his knowledge only to a very restricted group of people. Having withdrawn to a cave, which became his tomb, he wanted his tomb to be left alone until the right time came, namely, 120 years after his death. Since Rosenkreuz allegedly died in 1484, the discovery of the cave and of his tomb occurred in 1604; this is more or less the time in which the Rosicrucian movement begins to be known and emerges in history, as if it literally sprang from beneath the

---

1. See my *Hermetic Tradition*, chapter 10. Since the vertical line symbolizes the masculine and the horizontal line the feminine, the overall symbol of the cross as an active integration of the two principles has a meaning not very far from that of the so-called magical wedding and of the androgyne.

ground.[2] The intermediate period, in this symbolic tale, may allude to a period of underground reorganization; the period between 1604 and 1648, the date around which, according to tradition, the Rosicrucians permanently left Europe, could be seen as that of an attempt to exercise a given influence on the historical climate of the West by arousing the feeling of certain "presences" and by evoking again the symbol of the invisible kingdom. The number of writings about the Rosicrucians published in this period is astonishing; owing to some kind of collective suggestion, even though not much was known about them, the Rosicrucians became a myth and produced a varied literature, pro and contra, until the interest vanished with the same rapidity with which it first arose, more or less as it had happened with the Grail literature.

The most important documents, besides the *Allgemeine Reformation,* with its complement *Confessio fraternitatis Rosae Crucis, ad eruditos Europe* (Cassel, 1615), are the so-called Manifestos of the Rosicrucians, which were published in Frankfurt and in Paris in the period between 1613 and 1623. The most important points we may gather from these writings, once the spurious and most external parts are removed, are more or less the following:

1. There is a "confraternity" of beings who "dwell in a both invisible and visible manner" in the cities of men. "God has covered them with a cloud to protect them from their evil enemies." The former were called *alumbrados* and the Invisible Ones in Spain and France. This must refer to the transcendent nature of these enigmatic personalities, properly called Rosicrucians. Anyone animated by mere curiosity cannot communicate with them; but a contact is established automatically and one is truly enrolled in the "roster of our confraternity" through the "intention and the real will of the reader." According to the Rosicrucians Manifestos, this is the only way "to make our acquaintance." It is thanks to revelation (as in the Grail's order) that the Rosicrucians know those who are worthy to become members of their order and who, being part of it, can be Rosicrucians without knowing it.

2. "Rosicrucian," as I have said, represents essentially an initiatory level and a function, not a person as such. Thus it is said that the Rosicrucian is not subject to the contingencies of nature and to its needs, to illnesses and old age: he lives in every age as he lived from the beginning of the world. The order

---

2. The legend of Christian Rosenkreutz is contained in an anonymous writing first published in 1614 and then again one year later, entitled *Allgemeine und generale Reformation der gantzen weiten Welt,* especially in the part known by the name "Fama fraternitatis, oder Bruderschaft des hochloblichen Ordens des R + C."

predated its founders or organizers, namely, Rosenkreutz and, some say, King Solomon. Practically speaking, when the Rosicrucian is ready to die, that is, to leave the human condition, he chooses a person capable of succeeding him and of assuming his function, which therefore continues unchanged. This person assumes the name of his predecessor. The order is led by a mysterious *imperator*, whose real identity and seat remain unknown. A writing published in 1618, *Clipeum veritatis*, presents the sequence of the Rosicrucians *imperatores*: among them were the names of Seth (whose symbolic role in the Grail cycle is well known), Enoch, and Elijah, prophets "who never died," sometimes even presented as mysterious initiators.

3. The Rosicrucians are supposed to adopt the clothes of the countries to which they travel or where they take residence: in other words, they must choose an external way of appearance proper to the place and the environment in which they are supposed to act. Without books or signs they can speak and teach the language of all the lands where they choose to be present in order to free human beings from error and death. Allegorically speaking, I am referring to the so-called gift of languages, the ability to translate and speak in the terms of each of the individual traditions of the one primordial tradition. The knowledge possessed by the Rosicrucians is not considered new: it is the knowledge of the origins, "the light that Adam received before the Fall." Thus this knowledge cannot be compared and contrasted to any human opinion *(Confessio fraternitatis)*. The Rosicrucians continuously help the world, but in invisible and unfathomable ways.

4. The restoration of the king, which is a main motif of the Grail cycle and of Hermeticism, is also the main theme of the *Chymische Hochzeit Christiani Rosencreutz: Anno 1459* (Strasburg, 1616), where various adventures, taking place over a period of seven days, allegorize the seven degrees or stages of initiation. In the last day the elect are consecrated "Knights of the Golden Stone" *(eques aurei lapidis).* In this book we find the description of a journey to the king's residence. This is followed by the mystery of the resurrection of the king, a mystery that is significantly transformed in the realization that the king is already alive and awake: "Many find it strange that he is already risen, being under the impression that it was their task to awaken him." This is an allusion to the idea that the principle of regality in its metaphysical essence has always existed and should not be confused with a mere human creation, nor with the action of those who can precipitate a new manifestation of it in history. Besides the risen king, Rosenkreutz, who in him shall recognize "his father," wears the same insignia of the Templars and of Percival's ship: a white flag with a red cross. Here we also find the Grail's bird, the dove. The knights

of the Golden Stone swear allegiance to the risen or newly manifested king.[3] The formula, found in another text, with which the participation in the Rosicrucian mystery is requested, corresponds in an exact way to the Templars' saying: "Not to ours, but to your name only, O God, Supreme One, we give glory forever and ever."[4]

5. The images of the seat of the Rosicrucians and of their emperor correspond to those of the center: this seat is the "solar citadel," the "mountain in the middle of the earth," simultaneously "close and far away," the "Palace of the Spirit at the further end of the earth, on top of a mountain, surrounded by clouds," almost a facsimile of Montsalvatsche. Here I will provide some references contained in Rosicrucians texts: the correspondence between the two traditions is sufficiently visible, just as the search for that mysterious center is connected (as in the Grail's legend) to initiatory tests and experiences having heroic traits.

According to the *Lettre de F. G. Menapius 15 Juillet 1617*, the Rosicrucians live in a castle built on a rock, encompassed by the clouds above and by the waters below; in the middle of it are a golden scepter and a spring from which the Water of Life flows. In order to reach this castle it is necessary to first go through a tower, dubbed the "uncertain tower," and then through a second one, named the "dangerous tower"; finally one must climb the rock and touch the scepter. Then a Virgin will appear and lead the knight. The clouds disappear, the castle becomes visible, and the elect can now share in the "heavenly and earthly lordship."

We can also refer to a text called *Grundlicher Bericht von dem Vorhaben, Gelegenheit und Inhalt der lobl. Bruderschaft des R + C* (Frankfurt, 1617), in which we read:

> In the middle of the world there is a mountain, both close and far away, endowed with the greatest treasures guarded by the devil's malice. The path leading to it can be found only through one's effort. Pray and inquire

---

3. Here we may detect a variation on the Grail's theme, in the form of a person "who sinned by seeing Venus without veils" and who, because of it, has been sentenced to guard a door until the arrival of another man guilty of the same sin, who in turn will assume that function. This is what happened to Rosenkreutz, who wanted to free the guardian and who will himself not be freed "until the wedding feast of the next king's son."

4. The secret stone plays an important role in the Rosicrucian text by Sincerus Renatus, *Die wahrafte und volkommene Bereitung des philosophischen Steins der Bruderschaft aus dem Orden des Golden und Rosenkreuzes* (Breslau, 1710). In this text we also find the list of the order's rules; the order is characterized both by the stone, (like the Grail's knights in Wolfram) and by the rose (the Love's Lieges). Every member of this order uses the stone, which he still must not show anyone; the stone has the power of renewing the knight, and this transformation occurs every time a Rosicrucian travels to another country.

about the way, follow the guide, who is not an earthly being and who lives among you, though you do not know her. She will lead you to your destination at midnight [i.e., the "Midnight Sun" of the classical Mysteries]. You will have to show the courage of a lion. . . . Just about the time you are ready to see the castle, a raging wind will shake the rocks. Tigers and dragons will assail you. An earthquake will knock down everything the wind has spared, and a mighty fire will destroy all earthly matter [see the tests taking place in Orgeluse's castle]. At dawn calm will return and you will see the treasure.

This treasure, like the Hermeticists' Stone, has the power of transforming matter into "gold," that is, of reawakening in man the original "solar" condition. It restores health: "No one must know that you have it." After discovering the treasure, "you must turn around and you will find someone who will introduce you to the Confraternity and who will be your guide in every circumstance."

6. The Rosicrucians did not hesitate to condemn the "Middle Eastern and Western blasphemers," this expression visibly alluding to Muslims and Catholics respectively. They added that they wanted to "pulverize the triple diadem of the pope," claiming for themselves a higher "orthodoxy" and spiritual authority. The reference to the triple papal diadem has a special meaning, since this diadem is among the symbols that properly refer to the Universal Ruler and to his function,[5] which according to the Rosicrucians was usurped by the head of the Catholic Church, and whose real representative was their *imperator*. These enigmatic personalities declared that Europe was pregnant and destined to give birth to a powerful child: they also spoke of a "Roman" *imperator*, "Lord of the Fourth Empire," whom they vowed to supply with inexhaustible treasures. The fundamental idea of the *Allgemeine Reformation der gantzen weiten Welt* and *Fama fraternitatis* is that the Rosicrucians' mission is to bring out a general restoration in the name of their mysterious *imperator*, before the end of the world.

After the last two Rosicrucian manifestos appeared in Paris, and after the Thirty Years War ended with the Treaty of Wesphalia, which imparted the final blow to what was left of the authority of the Holy Roman Empire, the last true Rosicrucians allegedly left Europe to go to an "India," which should probably be understood as that symbolic country, assimilated to Prester John's kingdom, to which Montsalvatsche, the Grail, and its knights had previously gone. The "end of the world" that the Rosicrucians talked about probably alluded only to

---

5. R. Guénon, *Le Roi du monde,* chapter 4.

the end of one of the many worlds, namely, to a cycle of civilizations, like the vision of the hordes of Gog and Magog, which in the imperial saga was the prefiguration of that "daimony of the masses" that in modern times, following the French Revolution and the downfall of the major European dynastic traditions, was bound to assume increasingly apocalyptic overtones.

Concerning the mission of the real Rosicrucians during the eighteenth century, it must have been limited to producing a certain rumor and restlessness in the environment, not without a specific "experimental" intention, by "inspiring" various authors, yet without a true militant intention. Everything seems to suggest that the Rosicrucians never constituted a material organization involved in the political arena, thus susceptible of being individuated and dealt with, and that they remained invisible, beyond the myth that grew about them (one of the designations of their group was "The Congress of the Invisible People.") It seems that the Rosicrucians' experiment elicited a negative response, which eventually induced them "to leave." We cannot exclude that one of the factors that contributed to this decision was the deformation that certain ideas, owing to the environment, were immediately destined to undergo, thus producing opposite effects from the ones desired. In the mixture represented by the works of Johann Valentin Andreae, and of other authors inspired by the Rosy Cross, we can clearly see a marked tendency to employ, in a manner typical of Protestantism and the Enlightenment, the Rosicrucian aversion for the Catholic Church, thus generating one of the worst misunderstandings and one of the most dangerous deviations: I am referring to that misunderstanding that led the Teutonic princes to betray the sacred idea of the Empire at the very time they followed the Lutheran emancipation from Rome. This was an involution that, instead of overcoming the imperfect, lunar spirituality represented by the Church with a higher form, closer in spirit to the transcendent regality of the Grail, people failed to unmask and reject. And so it happened that people became emancipated from this involution only by siding with the rationalism of the Enlightenment, with liberalism and with secular culture: this indeed almost represents a quasi-demonic overturning of Ghibellinism.

In the modern age it is possible to find several instances of an inverted use of the Mystery. The Mystery, which in its proper context and in previous times had always been an aristocratic privilege as well as the basis for an absolute and legitimate authority "from above," has been transformed in a weapon of heretics, of those degenerated forces that rise up from below against the last hierarchies, against the authority of the Church and finally against the authority of the representatives of traditional political organizations. I will discuss this in greater detail in the epilogue.

In more recent times Hermeticism and Rosicrucianism have inspired various sects and authors who have illegitimately claimed to be the representatives of these traditions, but who militate in the ranks of Theosophy of occultism, of Anthroposophy, and in analogous by-products of the contemporary pseudo-spiritual deviation. Thus the majority of people, who ignore even the principles behind these matters, are led to think of these sects as soon as they hear mention of Hermeticism and Rosicrucianism. The truth is quite the opposite, however: these sects have nothing to do with the traditions the names and the symbols of which they have usurped. Moreover, the authentic representatives of these traditional organizations have not resided in the Western world for quite some time. The relationship between these organizations, on the one hand, and the Theosophical Society, Anthroposophy, and the like, on the other hand, is the same as that between Wagner's mystical-Christian and romantic-musical portrayal of the Grail in *Parzifal* and the authentic tradition of the Lords of the Temple.

The Inversion of Ghibellinism

Since my investigation has also uncovered the connections between initiatory organizations and historical currents, I think it is necessary, in conclusion, to say something about the existing relationship between what I have called the legacy of the Grail, namely, high Ghibellinism, and the modern secret societies, particularly those that since the Enlightenment have been labeled as Masonic. Obviously, the following is only a brief overview.

In the so-called sect of Bavaria's Illuminati we find a typical example of the overturning of tendencies that I have previously described. This can be seen in the change of meaning undergone by the term *Enlightenment*. Originally the term referred to a suprarational, spiritual illumination; slowly but inexorably, it became synonymous with rationalism, with the theory of "natural light," and with antitradition. We may speak, in regard to it, of a counterfeited and subversive use of the right belonging to the initiate alone. The initiate, if truly such, may regard himself to be above the contingent historical forms of a particular tradition; denounce its limitations (if he received the mandate to do so) and place himself above their authority; reject dogmas, because he possesses something higher, namely, a transcendent knowledge that he regards as the ultimate authority; and finally, claim for himself the dignity of a free being, because he has freed himself from the bonds of the merely human, inferior nature. To this effect the "free ones" constitute a community of equals, which may be regarded as a true confraternity.

Therefore, if we materialize, secularize, and democratize these aspects of the initiatory right and translate them into individualistic terms, what we have are the fundamental principles of the modern subversive and revolutionary ideologies. The light of mere human reason replaces the illumination, giving rise to the havoc brought about by "free inquiry" and secular criticism. The supernatural is banned or confused with nature. Freedom and equality are illegitimately claimed by the individual who is "conscious of his dignity" (though he is not conscious of being enslaved to his empirical self) and who now arises against any form of established authority, vainly setting himself up as his own ultimate reason for being. I say "vainly" because in the inexorable unfolding of the various phases of modern decadence, individualism has been only a short-lived mirage and a misleading intoxication; the collective and irrational element in the age of the masses and of technology has rapidly overcome the emancipated "individual" who is without roots and without traditions.

Beginning in the eighteenth century, new groups arise, alongside the so-called *sociétés de pensée*, flaunting an initiatory character while at the same time engaging in a revolutionary and "reform-minded" activity of "enlightenment" and rationalism.[1] Some of these groups were truly the continuation of previous organizations of a regular and traditional type. Thus, in their case, we must think of a process of involution reaching a point at which, owing to the withdrawal of the principle that originally animated these organizations, a real inversion of polarity occurred. Influences of another order and kind infiltrated and began to act in organisms that represented more or less the cadaver or the automatic survival of what they once used to be, utilizing and turning their energies toward the opposite direction of what had previously been their normal and traditional one.[2] The prologue of A. Dumas's *Joseph Balsam* is a symptom of the climate proper to the lodges and meetings of the Illuminati and of similar groups responsible for promoting that "intellectual revolution" that eventually unleashed the political revolutions of 1789 and 1848. In this prologue, which is something more than mere fancy because it uses data produced at the trial of this character, we learn about a leader who introduces himself as a Rosicrucian Great Master; this leader, at a secret meeting of initiates who have gathered from every nation, gives out as the general password "L.P.D." (the initials of *lilia destrue pedibus*, i.e., "destroy and step over the House of France").[3]

The contradictory duplicity of the two motifs—on the hand, residues of

---

1. It was owing to sheer chance that positive proofs were adduced, documenting also a revolutionary activity promoted by the sect of the Illuminati; documents were found on the body of a courier killed by lightning.

2. On the mechanism of this process, in its analogy with a necromantic action, see R. Guénon's *Le Regne de la quantité et les signes des temps* (Paris, 1945), chapters 26–27.

3. The initials L.P.D. appear in the first of the so-called knightly degrees of Freemasonry (the

symbolic and initiatory hierarchical ritualism; on the other hand, the profession of ideologies totally opposed to those that may deduced from any authentic initiatory doctrine—is apparent especially in modern Freemasonry. It seems that this Freemasonry was organized at the time of the Rosicrucian developments and of the departure of true Rosicrucians from Europe. Elias Ashmole, who is believed to have played a fundamental role in the organization of early English Freemasonry, lived between 1617 and 1692. Moreover, according to the prevalent opinion, Freemasonry in its actual form as a semi-secret, militant association, does not predate 1700.[4] It was precisely in 1717 that the Great Lodge of London was founded. The positive rather than fanciful antecedents of Freemasonry were the traditions of some medieval guilds, in which the main elements of the art of construction and building were simultaneously considered in their allegorical and initiatory meaning. Thus the "construction of the Temple" became synonymous with the initiatory Great Work, the molding of the coarse stone into a square block alluded to the preliminary task of inner formation, and so forth. We may assume that up to the beginning of the eighteenth century, Freemasonry retained this initiatory and traditional character, thus being named "operative," in reference to the task of an inner action.[5] It was in 1717 that an inversion of polarity and a radical upheaval occurred, with the foundation of London's Great Lodge and with the diffusion of the so-called continental speculative Freemasonry. The "speculation" adopted was that proper to the ideology of the Enlightenment, the Encyclopédie, and Rationalism, which was connected with a corresponding, misguided interpretation of symbols. The activity of the organization focused entirely on the sociopolitical plane, though it prevalently employed the tactics

---

fifteenth in the overall hierarchy of the Scottish rite). Allegedly, the legend of this degree alludes obscurely to the shift of the function of the initiate; mention is made of marks of princely dignities that the person to be initiated is supposed to receive, together with freedom, from "Cyrus," though he eventually loses them; once he reaches the master who took refuge among the ruins of Solomon's Temple with a small group of surviving followers, he is told about the dubious value of those titles and receives a new title and sword.

4. See A. Pike, *Morals and Dogmas of the Ancient and Accepted Scottish Rite* (Richmond, 1927).

5. However, we must note that in Freemasonry's operative and initiatory period it is already possible to detect a certain usurpation, in that this organization attributes to itself the Royal Art. The initiation connected to the arts is that which corresponds to the ancient Third Estate (the Hindu caste of the *vaiśya*), that is, to social strata that are hierarchically inferior to the caste of the warriors, to whom the Royal Art legitimately belongs. Moreover, we must also note that the revolutionary action of modern, speculative Freemasonry is that which undermined the civilizations of the Second Estate and prepared, through democracies, the advent of the Third Estate. Concerning the first point, even on the most external level one cannot help laughing at the sight of pictures of English kings who, as Masonic dignitaries, wear the apron and other signs of artisan corporations.

of indirect action, maneuvering with influences and suggestions the origins of which is difficult to trace.

It is claimed that this transformation occurred only in some lodges and that others retained their initiatory and operative character even after 1717. True enough, this character can be found in the Masonic milieus to which Martinez de Pasqually, Claude de Saint-Martin, and Joseph de Maistre belonged. We must also think, however, that this same kind of Freemasonry must have undergone a phase of degeneration if it could not stem the growth of the other kind and avoid being overcome by it. Nor can we see any action on the part of that Freemasonry that allegedly had retained the initiatory dimension to disavow the other, condemning its sociopolitical activity and trying to prevent it from asserting itself as the authentic and official Freemasonry.

"Speculative" Freemasonry's initiatory vestiges remained confined to a ritual superstructure, which had an inorganic and syncretistic character, especially in the Scottish Rite. In fact, for many of its degrees following the first three (the only ones that have some effective connection with the previous guild traditions), symbols of the most various initiatory traditions were gathered, obviously with the intention of giving the impression of having inherited their legacy. Thus in this Freemasonry we also find elements of chivalry, Hermeticism, and Rosicrucianism. In it we find "dignities" such as that of "Knight of the West" or "of the Sword"; "Knight of the Sun"; "Knight of the Two Eagles"; "Initiate Prince"; "Dignitary of the Sacred Empire"; and "Knight Kadosh" (in Hebrew "Holy Knight"), which corresponds to "Knight Templar" and "Rosicrucian Prince."

Generally speaking—and this is what is particularly significant to my book—there is a particular ambition, on the part of the Freemasonry of the Scottish Rite, to evoke the Templar tradition. Thus the claim was made that at least seven of its degrees after the thirtieth, which in several lodges explicitly carries the designation of "Templar Knight," have a Templar origin. One of the jewels of the highest degree in the entire hierarchy (the thirty-third) is a Teutonic cross that carries the initials J.B.M. These initials are usually explained to stand for Jacopus Burgundus Molay, who was the last Great Master of the Order of the Temple; "de Molay" also appears as the password of this degree, almost to suggest that those who are initiated in it could reclaim the dignity and the function of the leader of the destroyed Ghibelline Order. After all, Scottish Freemasonry claims to have received many of its elements from an even older organization called The Rite of Heredom. This expression is translated by various Masonic authors as "rite of the heirs," meaning the heirs of the Knights Templar. The corresponding legend is that a few surviving Templars withdrew to Scotland, where they put themselves under the protection of

Robert the Bruce; from him they were aggregated to a preexisting initiatory organization of guild origins, which then assumed the name Great Royal Lodge of Heredom.

One can easily see the consequence of these references in regard to what I have called the "legacy of the Grail" if they had a real foundation: they would supply Freemasonry with the character of traditional orthodoxy. Things are otherwise, however. This is a real usurpation: what we have here is not a continuation but rather an inversion of the previous tradition. This can be clearly seen when we consider the abovementioned thirtieth degree of the Scottish rite, which in some Masonic lodges has the password "The Templars' Revenge." The "legend" referred to it develops the abovementioned motif: the Templars allegedly found refuge in some secret English organizations and established in them this degree with the intention of reorganizing their order and perpetrating their revenge. The inversion of Ghibellinism I talked about could not be formulated more clearly than in this elucidation from their manual: "The Templar revenge reached Clement V, not on the day when his bones were burned on a pyre by Provence's Calvinists, but when Luther aroused half of Europe against the papacy in the name of the rights of one's conscience. The revenge also reached Philip the Fair, not on the day when his remains were thrown into the garbage by a rioting mob and not even when the last descendant of absolute power left the Temple, which had become the state's prison, to mount the scaffold, but rather when the French Constitutional Assembly proclaimed to the surviving monarchies the 'rights of the individual and of the citizen.'"[6]

That the level eventually descended from the plane of the individual (i.e., "Man" and "Citizen") to that of the anonymous masses and of their representatives can be established by a story related to the ritual of various degrees; in the Scottish Rite of the Supreme Counsel of Germany it was in the fourth degree, that of "The Secret Master." It is the story of Hiram, the builder of Jerusalem's Temple, who before the sacred king Solomon proved to have such prodigious power over the masses that "the king, who was renowned as one of the world's wisest men, discovered that beyond his own, there is a much greater

---

6. *The Ritual of the XXXth Degree of the Supreme Belgian Counsel of the Ancient and Accepted Scottish Rite* (Brussels), 49–50. In a dramatic ritual action, Squin de Florian, the alleged accuser of the Templars, is made to say as his justification: "The Church is above freedom!" This is countered by the Master of the Great Lodge, who says: "Freedom is above the Church!" Obviously, the first statement is correct if we are dealing with the claim to freedom on the part of any individual; the second statement is true if we are dealing with a person who has the required qualification to put himself beyond the inevitable limitations proper of a particular historical form of spiritual authority.

power, a power that in the future will assert itself and exercise a sovereignty greater than Solomon's: this power is the people *(das Volk)*." It is also stated: "We, Freemasons of the Scottish Rite, see in Hiram a personification of mankind." The rite, in making them "Secret Masters," should convey to the Masonic initiates the nature of Hiram: in other words, it should make them partakers of this mysterious power to lead mankind in the form of people, and masses, a power that should eclipse that of the sacred symbolic king.

Concerning the specifically Templar degree (the thirtieth), we should also note, in its rite, the confirmation of the association between the initiatory element and the subversive, antitraditional element, which necessarily bestows on the former the character of an effective counterinitiation wherever the rite is not reduced to an empty ceremony but instead activates subtle forces. In this degree, the initiate who knocks down the Temple's columns and steps over the cross, being admitted, after this, to the Mystery of the ascending and descending stairs with seven steps, must swear revenge and ritually actualize this oath by striking with a dagger the Crown and the Tiara, which are the symbols of the traditional double power, namely, of the regal and pontifical authority. All this properly conveys the meaning of what Freemasonry, as an occult force of global subversion, has precipitated in the modern world, from the preparation for the French Revolution and the establishment of the American democracy to the revolutions of 1848, World War I, the Turkish revolution, the Spanish revolution, and other analogous events. While in the cycle of the Grail the initiatory realization was conceived in such a way as to be connected with the goal of resurrecting the king, in the abovementioned ritual we have exactly the opposite, namely, the counterfeit of an initiation that is tied to the oath (sometimes expressed with the formula "Victory or Death!") of striking or overturning any authority from above.

In any event, the reason behind these considerations is to indicate the point where the "legacy of the Grail" and of analogous initiatory traditions stops and where, with the exception of the survival of a few surviving names and symbols, we can no longer detect any legitimate filiation from them. In the specific case of modern Freemasonry the following factors would make it appear as a typical example of a pseudoinitiatory organization: its confused syncretism; the artificiality of most of its hierarchy's degrees (something that even a layman would notice); and the banality of the moralistic, social, rationalistic, and modern exegesis applied to various borrowed elements that have an authentic esoteric character.[7] And yet, considering the "efficient direction" of that organization in

---

7. It is surprising to find in a very qualified expert in traditional studies, such as Guénon, the claim that together with Compagnionaggio, Freemasonry is almost the only organization in the West

reference to the previously mentioned elements and to its revolutionary activity, one cannot help feeling that he is confronting a force that, on the spiritual plane, acts against the spirit itself: a dark force of antitradition and counterinitiation. In that case it is possible that its rites are more harmful than one may think, and that those who partake of it, without realizing it, establish contact with this force, which cannot be grasped by ordinary consciousness.

A final note. In the legend of the thirty-second degree of the Scottish rite ("Sublime Prince of the Regal Secret"), mention is often made of the organization and of the inspection of forces (conceived as having been gathered from many "camps") that, after conquering "Jerusalem," will erect the "Third Temple." This Temple should be identified as the "Sacred Empire" or "Empire of the World" was mentioned often in the so-called *Protocols of the Elders of Zion,* which contain the myth of a detailed conspiracy against the traditional European world. I said "myth" on purpose, thus leaving open the issue of the authenticity or falsehood of this document, which is often exploited by a vulgar anti-Semitism.[8] The fact remains that this document, like many other

---

that currently may claim, despite its degeneration, "an authentic traditional origin and a regular initiatory transmission" (*Apercus sur l'initiation* [Paris, 1946], 40, 103.) Guénon apparently rejects the correct diagnosis of Freemasonry as a pseudoinitiatory syncretism promoted by underground forces of counterinitiation, a diagnosis that could be established even on the basis of his own views. How Guénon's view of Freemasonry as a traditional organization could possibly be reconciled with his positive assessment of Catholicism, a sworn enemy of modern Freemasonry, still needs to be clarified. Such a misunderstanding is also dangerous under another aspect, since it offers valuble weapons to Catholic apologetics. The mystification and the subversive use of the Mystery, which took place by inversion in the previously mentioned currents and especially in contemporary Freemasonry, has been comforting to a bizarre thesis of militant Catholicism, according to which the entire initiatory tradition, everywhere, in every time, has had a dark, diabolical, anti-Christian, and subversive aspect. This is obviously a preposterous interpretation. And yet isn't it possible that such a thesis is comforted by those who thoughtlessly attribute a character of orthodoxy and of regular initiatory filiation to Freemasonry?

At this point I fear that my readers will think that I nurture some preconceived bias and hostility toward Freemasonry. Personally, I have had friendly relationships with high-level representatives of this organization, who have endeavored to emphasize its initiatory and traditional vestiges. I am thinking here of people such as A. Reghini, Ragon, and O. Wirth. I also know about lodges such as the Johannis Loge and others, which have refrained from engaging in sociopolitical activity and have essentially acted as centers of study. But out of love for the truth I cannot possibly modify in any part my evaluation of modern Freemasonry because of the predominant direction of its actions. [For an exchange of views between Evola and Guénon on Freemasonry, see J. Evola's *René Guénon: A Teacher for Modern Times* (Edmonds, Wash.: Sure Fire Press, 1994)—Trans.]

8. In the *Protocols of the Elders of Zion* the plot is allegedly orchestrated by the Jewish community, though mention is made of Freemasonry. Another point that must be emphasized is that the elements that Freemasonry borrows from Western traditions are almost secondary to the Jewish ones, since the greater part of the legends and passwords have a Jewish origin. This too is rather

similar ones, has a symptomatic value, since the main upheavals of contemporary history that have taken place after its publication have displayed an uncanny resemblance to the plan described in it. Generally speaking, writings such as these reflect the obscure sensation of the existence of a scheming "intelligence" behind the most characteristic events of modern subversion. Therefore, regardless of their authenticity, of whether they are totally conjured up, they have caught some vibrations in the air that history itself has confirmed. It is exactly in the *Protocols* that we see the reemergence of the idea of a universal future empire and of organizations that work underground for its advent,[9] though in a counterfeit that I do not hesitate to call "satanic," because what is effectively happening is the destruction and the uprooting of all that is traditional, of the values of personality and true spirituality. The alleged empire is nothing but the supreme concretization of the religion of earthly man, who has become the ultimate reason unto himself and who views God as an enemy. It is the theme with which Spengler's *Decline of the West* and the ancient Hindu tradition of the Kali Yuga, or Dark Age, seem to end.

In conclusion, it is opportune to mention the reason why this book was written. My goal is obviously not to add yet another contribution to the numerous critical-literary essays that have been written on the subject. In this area my book will be valuable insofar as it demonstrates the fecundity of the method that I have labeled "traditional," vis-à-vis that employed by current academic research.

Another goal of mine was to establish the nature of the spiritual content of the subject matter. In this regard, the present book relates to other books I have written with the intent of denouncing the distortions that traditional symbols and doctrines have undergone because of modern authors and trends. In the course of my exposition I have pointed out, in reference to the cycle of the Grail,

suspicious. In fact, in the whole Judaic tradition it is possible to detect a process of degeneration and inversion that has likewise aroused counterinitiatory forces or forces of antitraditional subversion. These forces have probably played a not negligible role in the secret history of Freemasonry.

9. In passing, we must note that the revolutionary work of Freemasonry is essentially limited to the preparation and consolidation of the Age of the Third Estate (which has given rise to the world of capitalism, democracy, and bourgeois civilization and society). The last phase of world subversion, since it corresponds to the advent of the Fourth Estate, is also connected to other forces that necessarily go beyond Freemasonry and Judaism, even though they have often used the destruction promoted by both of these movements. It is significant that the actual avant-garde of the Age of the Fourth Estate have elected the symbol of the pentagram, the five-pointed star, as the red star of the Soviets. The ancient magical symbol of the power of man as initiate and master of the supernatural (a symbol that also consecrated the sword of the Grail) becomes, by inversion, the symbol of the omnipotence and the rule of materialized and collectivized man in the reign of the Fourth Estate.

the falsification of its spirit and themes by Richard Wagner. Unfortunately, most people know about the Grail, Percival, and related things only because of the arbitrary, pseudomystical, and decadent way in which Wagner portrayed them on the basis of a fundamental misunderstanding: this misunderstanding was further compounded by the employment of several themes of ancient Nordic-Germanic mythology in his *Ring of the Nibelungs*.

The same applies to the interpretations of some spiritualism that, often under the influence of Wagner, and lacking any serious and direct knowledge of the primary sources, has interpreted in a rather amateurish way the cycle of the Grail as some kind of "Christian esotericism," building upon it all kind of fancies, small groups and gatherings. On the contrary, I have shown that the main themes of the Grail are non-Christian and even pre-Christian and to what traditional order of ideas (i.e., those shaped by the regal and heroic spirituality) they are properly connected. In this cycle, the Christian elements are only secondary and serve as a cover-up. They derive from an attempt at adaptation that has never succesfully unraveled what shows a substantial heterogeneity of inspiration. As in other cases, this effort at fabricating a nonexistent "Christian esotericism" should be regarded as lacking any serious foundation.

If the Grail is presented as an allegedly Christian mystery, it still lacks the special, essential relation with a task and an ideal that, as we have seen, go beyond the mere initiatory plane and that presented themselves even in the West within a given historical cycle.

Having said that, this study of mine has one further goal, which the reader may have already detected thanks to the last remarks I made concerning the inversion of Ghibellinism. Today we have reached such low levels that the word *Ghibellinism* has been employed, in the course of political controversies, to designate the defense of the rights of a "secular," "modern," and non-confessional state against the interferences of the Catholic Church and of clerical-minded parties in the political, social, and cultural arenas. I hope the whole of my presentation has established very clearly that this is one of the most deprecable instances of the loss of the original meaning of a term. In its essence, Ghibellinism has been nothing less than a form of the reapperance of the sacred and spiritual (in the currents that I have discussed, even initiatory) ideal of the authority befitting a leader of a traditional political organization. Thus it is exactly the opposite of everything that is "secular," and of everything that is political and governmental in the modern, degenerate sense of the word.[10]

One may wonder what is the point of shedding light on this essence of Ghibellinism, the Grail's kingdom, and Templarism, other than to reestablish

---

10. Concerning the Ghibelline movement in relation to the contemporary political situation, see my *Gli uomini e le rovine* (Rome, 3rd edition, 1971).

the truth before the previously mentioned misunderstandings and counterfeits. The answer to this question must remain undetermined. Already in the mere arena of ideas, the character of the dominating culture is such that most people could not even imagine what the issue at stake is. After all, only a small minority could understand that just as the ascetic-monastic orders played a fundamental role during the material and moral chaos that brought about the collapse of the Roman Empire, likewise an order following in the footsteps of Templarism would have a decisive role in a world such as the modern one, which displays forms of greater dissolution and inner collapse than the previous period. The Grail retains the meaning of a symbol in which the antithesis between "priest" and "warrior" is overcome, but also retains the modern equivalent of this antithesis, that is to say, materialized, telluric, and titanic, or better yet, Luciferian forms of the will to power on the one hand, and the lunar forms of the surviving devotional religion and of confused mystical and neospiritualist impulses toward the supernatural and what is not ordinary.

If we just consider the individual and some people, the symbol always retains an intrinsic value, which is indicative for a given type of inner formation. But to go from this to the notion of an order, of a modern Templarism, and to believe that even if it were to come to be, it would be able to exercise an influence directly and sensibly on the general historical forces that are dominant today—that is hasty. Even the Rosicrucians (the real Rosicrucians), back in the eighteenth century, regarded this attempt as vain. Moreover, even those who have received the "sword" must wait for the right time to wield it, the right moment being only that in which forces, the power of which is still unknown owing to an intrinsic determinism, will encounter a real limit and the cycle will end. The right moment will be that in which, even before the most extreme existential situations, a desperate defense instinct rising from the deepest recesses (I almost said, from the *memoire de sangc*) will eventually regalvanize and give strength to myths and ideas connected to the legacy of better times. I believe that before this happens, a possible Templarism may play only an inner defensive role, in relation to the task of protecting the symbolic, yet not merely symbolic, "solar stronghold."

This will clarify the ultimate meaning of a serious and committed study of the witnesses and of the motifs of the Templar saga and of higher Ghibellinism. To understand and to live by these motifs means to enter into a dimension of suprahistorical realities and, in this way, to gradually reach the certainty that the invisible and inviolable center, the king who must awake, and the avenging and restorating hero are not mere fancies of a dead and romantic past, but rather the truth of those who, today, alone may legitimately be said to be alive.

Index

OTHER WORKS BY JULIUS EVOLA

REVOLT AGAINST THE MODERN WORLD

In what is considered to be his masterwork, Julius Evola here turns his keen powers of analysis to the modern world as he traces the remote causes and processes that have exercised a corrosive influence on what he considers to be higher values, ideals, beliefs, and codes of conduct. He agrees with Hindu philosophers who argue that history moves in huge cycles, and that we are now in the Kali Yuga, an age of dissolution and decadence. Evola challenges our assumptions about the most fundamental aspects of spiritual and social life, and concludes that revolt is the only logical attitude to be adopted by those who oppose the materialism of everyday life.

ISBN 0-89281-506-X
cloth

THE HERMETIC TRADITION
Symbols and Teachings of the Royal Art

Originally published in Italian in 1931, now available for the first time in English, this important survey of alchemical symbols and doctrines draws from a wide variety of writings in the Western esoteric tradition—works on theurgy, magic, and gnosticism from neoplatonic, Arab, and medieval sources. Evola demonstrates the singularity of subject matter that lies behind the words of all adepts in all ages, showing how alchemy—often misunderstood as primitive chemistry or a mere template for the Jungian process of individuation—is nothing less than a universal secret science of human and natural transformation.

"An erudite, superbly knowledgeable collection of hermetic lore...A vast accessible panorama of occult wisdom written with elegance." The Book Reader

ISBN 0-89281-451-9
paperback

THE YOGA OF POWER
Tantra, Shakti, and the Secret Way

Evola introduces two Hindu movements—Tantrism and Shaktism—both of which emphasize a path of action as well as mastery over secret energies latent in the body. He draws from original texts to describe methods of self-mastery, including awakening of the serpent power, initiatic sexual magic, and evoking the names of power. While the movements of Tantrism and Shaktism have had a major influence on the Hindu tradition from the fourth century onward, Evola focuses on the appropriateness of their practices (known as the Way of the Left Hand) in our present age of dissolution and decadence.

ISBN 0-89281-368-7
paperback

THE DOCTRINE OF AWAKENING
The Attainment of Self-Mastery
According to the Early Buddhist Texts

In a probing analysis of the oldest Buddhist texts, Evola places the doctrine of liberation in its original context. The early teachings suggest an active spirituality that is opposed to the more passive, modern forms of theistic religions. This sophisticated text, first published in Italian in 1943, sets forth the central truths of the eight-fold path. Evola presents actual practices of concentration and visualization and places them in the larger metaphysical context of the Buddhist model of mind and universe.

ISBN 0-89281-553-1
paperback

EROS AND THE MYSTERIES OF LOVE
The Metaphysics of Sex

"Evola's study of the spirituality of sex focuses on what both science and popular culture have overlooked, invoking the rich symbolism of religious myths and mysteries throughout history, from the I Ching to the Kabbalah, to illustrate the redemptive power of the sexual act. He treats his subject with respect and circumspection."

The Los Angeles Times

ISBN 0-89281-315-6
paperback

OTHER TITLES IN THE CELTIC TRADITION

THE CELTS
Uncovering the Historic and Mythic Origins of Western Culture

Jean Markale

"Markale has created a vivid picture—poetic and philosophical—of this deeply spiritual people. Here are the prophecies of Merlin and the druids, Celtic mythology, the Britons and Bretons, the Celtic Christian church, the history of the Gaels. This is a well-researched, erudite study of Celticism and its core beliefs." The Book Reader

One of the most comprehensive treatments of Celtic civilization ever written, this history positions the Celts as the primary European civilization, who occupied the whole of Western Europe for more than a thousand years before the Greco-Roman hegemony.

While historians generally accord the Celts a place of minor significance in comparison to the Romans, Markale restores the Celtic civilization to its true importance in the development of European social, political, and literary values. Regarding myth as a branch of history, he examines mythological material to reveal the culture from which it springs, offering an approach to Celtic studies that is both original and convincing.

ISBN 0-89281-413-6
paperback

MERLIN
Priest of Nature
Jean Markale

Once again drawing on his extensive knowledge of Celtic and Druidic cultures, Jean Markale offers a radical new interpretation of the literary and historical texts that speak of Merlin. The result is a revealing portrait of the archetypal Wild Man and shaman known as Merlin, who lived in the lowlands of Scotland late in the sixth century. A "divine madman," Merlin found refuge in a sacred clearing in the forest, and with his companion Vivian sought enlightenment and union with nature. When the Merlin legend resurfaced in the 12th century, his message of the universal brotherhood of all beings called out to a rapidly urbanizing society that was losing touch with nature, and as such, it is still relevant to us today.

ISBN 0-89281-517-5
paperback

KING OF THE CELTS
Arthurian Legend and Celtic Tradition

Jean Markale

In this absorbing book, Jean Markale places King Arthur at the center of a brilliant revisioning of Celtic culture and history. Through close examination of the legends, the mythic elements of ancient histories, and the names of people and places, Markale provides new insights into the identity of Arthur and the society in which he flourished.

Sorting through the many variants of the Arthurian romances, Markale strips away the religious and political embellishments added to the tales by medieval monks and court storytellers to reveal a different kind of king—a Celtic warrior-hero who resisted the Saxon invasions in fifth-century England. From this vestigial core of genuine Celtic myth, the author reconstructs a new version of the life of Arthur.

Finally, bringing the reader into the present, the author uses Celtic Britain as a lens to examine the pretenses and ills of our contemporary society and offers the Celtic model as a way to integrate the often competing values of unity and diversity.

ISBN 0-89281-452-7
paperback

THE PROPHET OF COMPOSTELA
A Novel of Apprenticeship and Initiation
Henri Vincenot

In *The Prophet of Compostela,* award-winning French author Henri Vincenot addresses the themes of journey, initiation, and spiritual growth in 12th-century Burgundy. Seen through the eyes of a young builder's apprentice, it is a tale of youthful adventure, an exploration of Gothic architecture and Freemasonry, a meditation on the relationship between Celtic wisdom and Christianity, and a spiritual allegory of self-knowledge.

ISBN 0-89281-524-8
pb

These and other Inner Traditions titles are available at many fine bookstores or, to order directly from the publisher, send a check or money order for the total amount, payable to Inner Traditions, plus $3.00 shipping and handling for the first book and $1.00 for each additional book to:

Inner Traditions, One Park Street, P.O. Box 388, Rochester, VT 05767